NELSON
MATHEMATICS

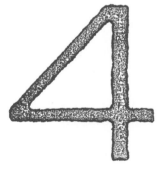

Task MATHS 4

BARBARA BALL & DEREK BALL

Nelson

Thomas Nelson and Sons Ltd
Nelson House   Mayfield Road
Walton-on-Thames   Surrey
KT12 5PL   UK

51 York Place
Edinburgh
EH1 3JD   UK

Thomas Nelson (Hong Kong) Ltd
Toppan Building 10/F
22A Westlands Road
Quarry Bay   Hong Kong

Thomas Nelson Australia
102 Dodds Street
South Melbourne
Victoria 3205
Australia

Nelson Canada
1120 Birchmount Road
Scarborough   Ontario
M1K 5G4   Canada

© Barbara Ball, Derek Ball 1991

First published by Thomas Nelson and Sons Ltd 1991

ISBN 0-17-431144-3
NPN 9 8 7 6 5 4 3 2 1

ACKNOWLEDGEMENTS

The authors are grateful to the following authorities for permission to use questions from some of their examination
papers in the Review Exercises.

London and East Anglian Group, Syllabus A	LEAG
Midland and Examining Group	MEG
	Nuffield* MEG (Nuffield)
Northern Examining Association, Syllabus A	NEA[A]
Syllabus B*	NEA[B]
	Joint GCE & CSE syllabus Joint 16+
Associated Lancashire Schools Examining Board	
Joint Matriculation Board	
North Regional Examinations Board	
North West Regional Examinations Board	
Yorkshire and Humberside Regional Examinations Board	
Southern Examining Group	SEG
	Alternative syllabus* SEG[ALT]

The authors are grateful to all those who helped by trialling the material in this book. They value, in particular, the
frequent and most helpful advice they received from Wendy Fisher, Linda Lord, Chris Miles, Sue Pope and Dave
Short.

The publishers would like to thank the following for permission to reproduce photographs: Ace Photo Agency
p.187; Bike Events/John Bartholomew & Sons p.186; Bleinham Palace p.50; Bridgeman Art Library pp.73, 201; John
Clark p.203; Simon Collier p.49; Deutsch Museum p.72; Fastline Promotions pp.172, 202; Leicester Mercury p.70;
Magnet pp.50, 59; Rex Features p.173; Chris Ridgers pp.2, 3, 11, 13, 15, 34, 36, 39, 42, 44, 47, 55, 57, 58, 62, 74, 75,
82, 87, 101, 104, 108, 113, 114, 139, 140, 141, 142, 143, 144, 145, 147, 148, 155, 166, 168, 185, 205, 213; Sealand
Aerial Photography p.169.

Thanks are also due to the following for permission to reproduce copyright material: BBC Enterprises for the
information from the Radio Times on p.114; British Rail for the train time tables on pp.170, 171, 172 and the map of
railway routes on p.176; Hodder and Stoughton for the extract from New Fables, *Thus Spoke the Marabou* by Kurt
Kauter on p.193; *Independent* for the world weather table on p.178; London Regional Transport for the underground
map on p.177; Ordnance Survey for the map reproduced from the 1976 Ordnance Survey 1:50000 Landranger map
with the permission of the Controller of Her Majesty's Stationery Office © Crown copyright.

A NOTE TO STUDENTS

This book is organised into tasks, not into mathematical topics as most mathematics books are. Each chapter of this book sets a different task. While working on this task you might meet a number of different mathematical topics.

Each chapter begins with an activity which introduces the task. This introduction is followed by some questions, arranged in sections. These questions give you suggestions for developing the task. They also help to develop your knowledge, skills and understanding of mathematics, and your ability to use and apply your mathematics to the task. Sometimes there are information boxes to explain mathematical words, ideas or techniques.

Some of the questions are marked with ▬ . These are somewhat harder than the unmarked questions. Some are marked with ▬ . These are difficult questions.

At the end of each chapter there are some Further Coursework Tasks. Each of these extends the task in some way. You are unlikely to want to tackle more than one of the Further Coursework Tasks in any chapter.

Throughout this book it is assumed that you have a calculator available whenever you need it. On many pages there is also a red picture of a computer. This indicates that a computer, or sometimes a graphical or programmable calculator, would be very useful for working on a particular question or coursework task.

There are two sections of Review Exercises in the book. These exercises contain questions of the type set in GCSE examination papers, and enable you to consolidate particular mathematical topics.

At the end of the book there is an Information section. You might need to refer to this when you are answering some of the questions or when you are tackling some of the Further Coursework Tasks.

CONTENTS

CUBE MODELS

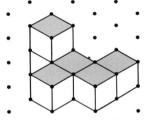

Figure 1

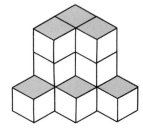

Figure 1 shows a drawing on isometric paper of a model made from 6 interlocking cubes.

● Use six cubes to make the model shown.

● What is the surface area of the model? (Use the face of one cube as the unit of area.)

● Now make a different model using six interlocking cubes.

   Draw your model on isometric paper and record the surface area of your model.

● Make several models using six cubes, draw them and record their surface areas.

   What is the largest possible surface area for a model made of six cubes?

   Is there more than one model which has this largest surface area?

   What is the smallest possible surface area for a model made of six cubes?

   Is there more than one model which has this smallest surface area?

● Find the largest and smallest possible surface areas for models made of 1, 2, 3, 4 . . . cubes.

● Find the largest and smallest possible surface areas for a model made with 12 cubes.

1

SECTION A

Almost certainly, some of the models you have made had mirror symmetry. The model shown below has mirror symmetry.

If you looked at half the model in the mirror shown you would see the other half of the model. The plane where the mirror goes is called the plane of symmetry of the model.

1 Each of the models in figure 2 has mirror symmetry. Draw the model and show its plane of symmetry by shading. (You need not draw the mirror.)

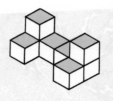 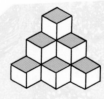

Figure 2

2 Make a model which does **not** have mirror symmetry. Use as few cubes as possible. Draw it.

3 Make a model which has two planes of symmetry. Draw it and mark its planes of symmetry by shading.

4 Add one extra cube to each of the models in figure 3 to make a model which has mirror symmetry. Draw your new models and mark their planes of symmetry. In each drawing shade in the extra cube.

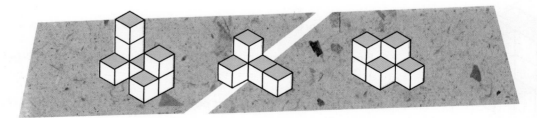

Figure 3

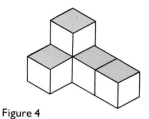

Figure 4

5 (a) Add two extra cubes to the model in figure 4 to make a model that has two planes of symmetry. Draw your model, shade the extra cubes and mark its planes of symmetry.

(b) This time start again and add two extra cubes to the model (figure 4) to make a model that has three planes of symmetry. Draw your model, shade the extra cubes and mark the planes of symmetry.

 The first two models shown both have rotational symmetry. Either of them can be rotated about the axis shown. The first model has rotational symmetry of order 4, because if you rotate it about its axis through $\frac{1}{4}$ of a turn it still looks the same. The second has rotational symmetry of order 2, because it still looks the same if you rotate it about its axis through $\frac{1}{2}$ a turn. It may be harder to spot the axis of symmetry of the third model (there are no cubes along it). This model has rotational symmetry of order 3.

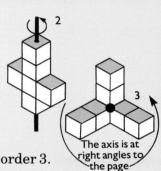

The axis is at right angles to the page

6 Draw each of the models shown in figure 5 and mark their axes of symmetry. State the order of rotational symmetry of each model.

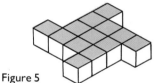 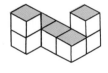

Figure 5

7 Add a cube to each of the models in figure 6 so that it has rotational symmetry. Draw the model, mark its axis, shade the extra cube and state the order of rotational symmetry.

Figure 6

8 Make a model which has rotational symmetry of order 2. Use as few cubes as possible. Draw it and mark its axis.

9 Draw each of the models in figure 7 and mark their planes of symmetry.

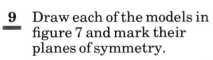 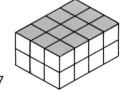 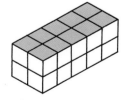

Figure 7

10 Mark all the axes of rotational symmetry on the second model you drew for question 9. There are 5 axes to find. State the order of rotational symmetry about each axis.

11 Describe the symmetries of a cube.

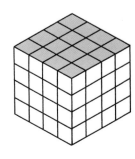

SECTION B

Models of interlocking cubes which have only 6 faces are called **cuboids**. A cuboid has 12 edges. If you know the length of 3 edges in 3 different directions you know the shape and size of the cuboid.

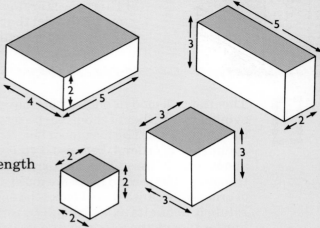

If all these three edges are the same length the cuboid is called a **cube**.

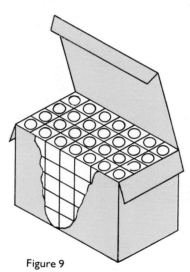

Figure 9

1 Use interlocking cubes to make a cuboid with edges of length 2, 3 and 4. Find its volume and surface area.

2 Find the volume and surface area of the cuboid shown in figure 8.

3 Find the volume and surface area of a cube with edges of length 5.

4 Figure 9 shows a pack of interlocking cubes. How many cubes are there in the pack?

5 A cuboid like that seen in figure 10(a) is broken up. The cubes are used to make several cuboids like the smaller cuboid (figure 10(b)). How many can be made?

Figure 8

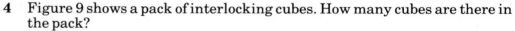

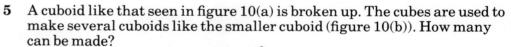

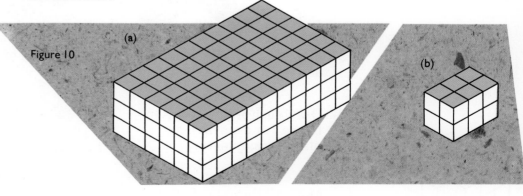

Figure 10

(a)

(b)

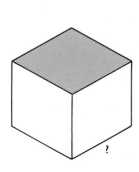

?

6 If 512 interlocking cubes are used to make a large cube how long is one edge of the cube? What is its surface area?

7 What is the volume of a cube if its surface area is 150?

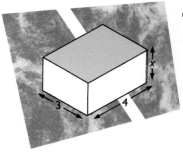

8 A cuboid model is 4 cubes long, 3 cubes wide and x cubes high.

(a) What, in terms of x, is its volume?

(b) What, in terms of x, is its surface area?

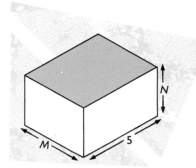

9 A cuboid model is 5 cubes long, M cubes wide and N cubes high.

(a) What, in terms of M and N, is its volume?

(b) What, in terms of M and N, is its surface area?

10 A cuboid is c cubes long, 7 cubes wide and 4 cubes high.

(a) What, in terms of c, is its surface area?

(b) If its surface area is 342, find c.

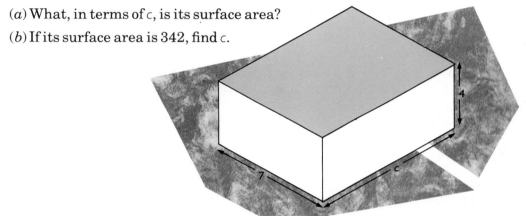

11 Find three cuboid models, each of which has a volume of 36.

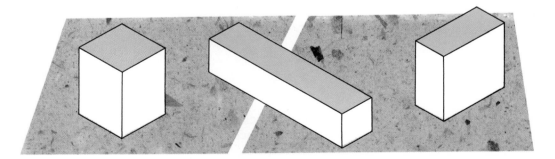

12 Find three cuboid models, each of which has a volume of 1728.

13 Find three cuboid models whose volumes are between 100 and 120.

14 Find three cuboid models whose volumes are between 200 and 250 and whose surface areas are between 250 and 300.

15 Find three cuboid models, each of which has a surface area of 128.

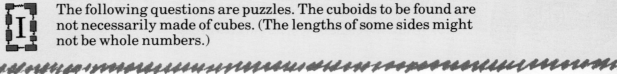

The following questions are puzzles. The cuboids to be found are not necessarily made of cubes. (The lengths of some sides might not be whole numbers.)

16 Find three cuboids, each of which has a surface area of 100.

17 Find three cuboids, each of which has a volume which is an even number and a surface area which is an even number.

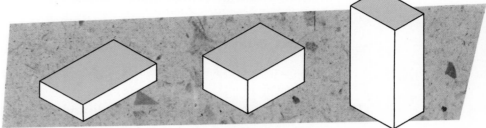

18 Find three cuboids, each of which has a volume which is an odd number and a surface area which is an even number.

19 Find three cuboids, each of which has a volume which is an odd number and a surface area which is an odd number.

20 Find three cuboids, each of which has a volume which is an even number and a surface area which is an odd number.

21 What is the surface area of a cube whose volume is 100?

22 A cube can be built from four black and four white cubes, in such a way that each face of the cube is half black and half white.

Build a cube from nine black, nine white and nine red cubes, in such a way that each face is one third black, one third white and one third red.

And finally, puzzles about interlocking cubes.

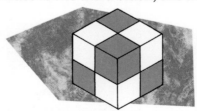

23 Using 27 interlocking cubes, 3 cubes of each of 9 colours, build a cube so that each of the faces of the cube is coloured by all 9 colours. Record your solution in some suitable way.

FURTHER COURSEWORK TASKS

1) Take another look at the problem posed at the beginning of this chapter.

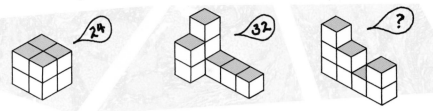

What surface areas are possible for models made of 8 cubes?

What is the greatest possible surface area for a model with 8 cubes? How many different models with 8 cubes have this greatest possible surface area?

Can you give rules for constructing models with the least or greatest surface area?

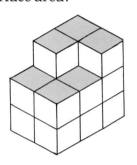
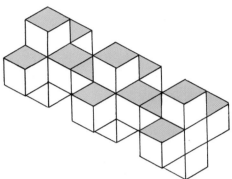

2) Collect together some cubes of two different colours. Make a 'tower' from 3 of the cubes. By choosing different colour combinations, how many different towers can you make?

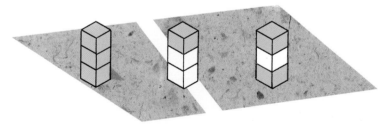

How many different towers can you make if you use 4 cubes for a tower? What if you use cubes of three different colours? Try the same problem with towers of different heights and different numbers of colours.

How many different 'squares' can be made using cubes of 2 different colours? Try this same problem with a different number of colours.

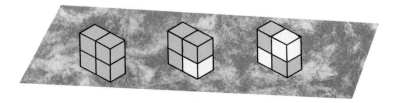

3) A cuboid has 6 faces, 12 edges and 8 vertices.

The model shown in figure 11 has 8 faces, 18 edges and 12 vertices.

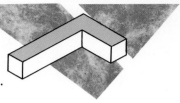

Figure 11

Make some other models and find
the number of vertices, edges and faces.

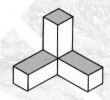

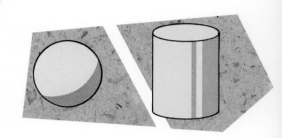

Look for patterns in your results.

4) Think of a solid. A sphere has 1 face
and a cylinder has 3 faces.

Can you think of a solid with 2 faces? 4 faces? 5, 6, 7 . . . faces?

Can you think of a solid with no edges? 1 edge? 2, 3, 4 . . . edges?

Can you think of a solid with no vertices, 1 vertex, 2, 3, 4 . . . vertices?

What about solids with 2 faces and 1 edge? 2 vertices and 1 edge? 2 faces,
1 edge and 1 vertex?

Are there any combinations which are not possible?

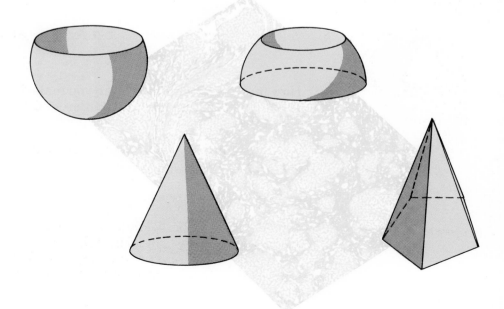

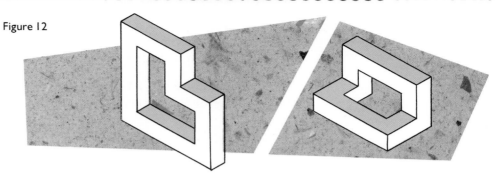

Figure 12

5〉 Figure 12 shows two different rings made from interlocking cubes. Both rings have six corners.

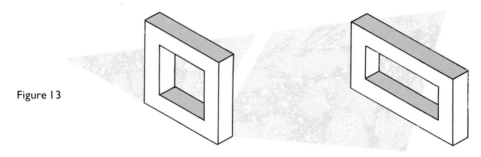

Figure 13

Figure 13 shows two rings with four corners. Although the rings are different sizes they are the same in other respects. They are both flat and they both have four corners.

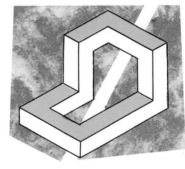

How many **different** cube rings (different in some way other than size) are there with 4 corners? 5 corners? 6 corners? 7, 8, 9 . . . corners? You will need to decide exactly what you mean by different.

Find some way of recording the rings you make and of showing how they are different.

6〉 Each of the models shown in figure 14 has a surface area of 22.

Figure 14

These are the only two cuboid models with this surface area.

Look at the statement made in figure 15. Is this statement true? Give reasons for your answer.

There are no cuboid models with a surface area of 20.

Figure 15

Which positive whole numbers are possible surface areas for cuboid models? How many cuboid models can have the same surface area? You might find it useful to write a **Logo** or a **BASIC** program, or to use a programmable calculator, or to use a spreadsheet to help you explore this problem.

7〉 Investigate the ways in which cube models can be symmetrical. If you have some Multilink prisms you might want to use these as well as Multilink cubes.

Each of the models below has mirror symmetry. One of them has two planes of mirror symmetry.

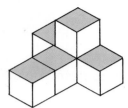 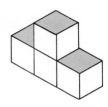 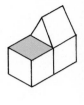

Is it possible to make models with 3 planes of mirror symmetry? 4 planes? 5 planes? . . . What is the smallest model of each type? Is it possible to give rules for making models of different sizes, but with the same type of mirror symmetry?

Each of the models below has rotational symmetry.

 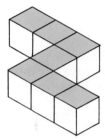 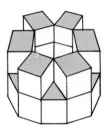

Is it possible to make models with rotational symmetry of order 2? 3? 4? 5? . . . What is the smallest model of each type? Is it possible to give rules for making models of different sizes, but with the same type of rotational symmetry?

Each of the models below has point symmetry.

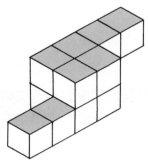 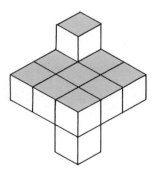 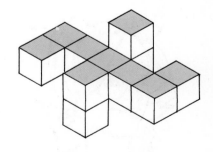

Describe what point symmetry means. Can you give rules for making models with point symmetry?

Investigate which combinations of symmetries are possible within the same model. For example, can you have a model with 1 plane of mirror symmetry *and* rotational symmetry of order 2? Or a model with two planes of mirror symmetry *and* rotational symmetry of order 3? Or a model with 3 planes of mirror symmetry *and* point symmetry?

2 CIRCLE PATTERNS

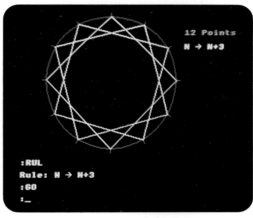

```
                    12 Points
                    N → N+3

:RUL
Rule: N → N+3
:60
:_
```

Figure 1 shows 3 squares drawn inside a circle.

The picture was produced as follows. Each marked point on the circumference of the circle is numbered. The points are then joined by straight lines. The rule for joining them is this:

Join a point with number N to the point with number N+3

This can be written N → N+3 for short.

Using this rule, 2 is joined to 5, 4 is joined to 7 and 7 is joined to 10.

11 should be joined to 14. It is joined to 2, because 2 is where 14 comes if you continue the numbers beyond 12.

Figure 2 shows 4 equilateral triangles in a circle.

- What is the rule for joining the points this time?

  Is there more than one possible answer?

- Get the sheet called '12-point circles'.

  Join the points using the rule N → N+2.

  What shapes are produced?

- Investigate what happens with other rules (e.g. N → N+5, N → N+9).

  Describe geometrically the patterns produced.

- What do you notice about different rules which produce the same pattern?

- Get the sheet called '9-point circles'.

  Look at the patterns produced by different rules using a circle with 9 points.

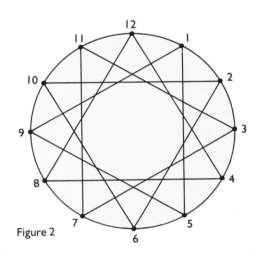

Figure 2

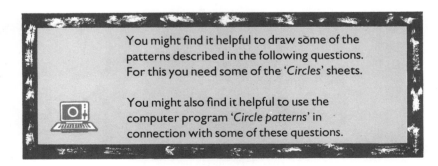

SECTION A

You might find it helpful to draw some of the patterns described in the following questions. For this you need some of the 'Circles' sheets.

You might also find it helpful to use the computer program 'Circle patterns' in connection with some of these questions.

1   With 6 points, the rule N → N + ☐ can be used to get a regular hexagon. Give 6 different numbers which could go into the box to make this statement true.

2 (*a*) What rule do you need to use with 8 points to get a pattern made up of squares? How many squares are there?

(*b*) What rule do you need to use with 16 points to get a pattern of squares?

(*c*) Can you get a pattern of squares with 10 points? Explain.

3 (*a*) If there are 15 points what rule would you use to get a pattern of equilateral triangles?

(*b*) If there are 51 points what rule would you use to get equilateral triangles?

(*c*) Explain how, when you know how many points there are, you can find a rule that gives equilateral triangles.

4 If there are 8 points the rule N → N+4 produces diameters of the circle.

What rule produces diameters if there are

(*a*) 10 points?

(*b*) 36 points?

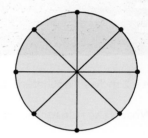

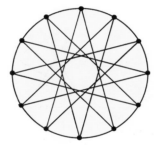

Figure 3

5 Figure 3 shows the pattern produced with 12 points using the rule N→N+5.

There is only one polygon drawn in the circle. The polygon has 12 sides and is called a star polygon, for obvious reasons.

Find another rule which produces a star polygon with 12 points and 12 sides.

6 If 7 points are used several rules produce star polygons with 7 sides, but only 2 **different** star polygons can be produced. These are shown in figure 4.

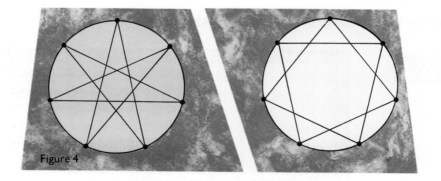

Figure 4

How many **different** star polygons are there with

(*a*) 5 points and 5 sides?   (*b*) 8 points and 8 sides?

(*c*) 11 points and 11 sides?   (*d*) 6 points and 6 sides?

Here is a picture of the computer's screen when the rule $N \rightarrow N+3$ is used with 12 points.

A rule like this is sometimes called a **function**.

Sometimes a letter is used to describe the function. You can write

$f: x \longrightarrow x+3$

to describe the function used for the pattern above.

When this notation is used $f(2) = 5$, because the rule tells you to join 2 to 5. Similarly $f(6) = 9$.

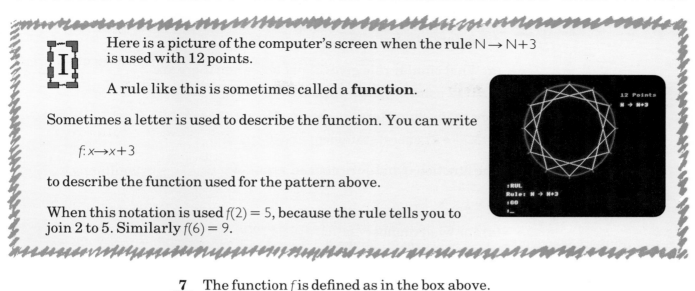

7   The function f is defined as in the box above.

What is   (a) $f(3)$?   (b) $f(8)$?   (c) $f(10)$?

8 g is the function defined as follows

$g: x \longrightarrow x-5$

What is   (a) $g(6)$?   (b) $g(8)$?   (c) $g(10)$?

9   The functions f and g are defined as follows.

$f: x \longrightarrow 2x+4, \quad g: x \longrightarrow 2x-2$

(a) Draw circle patterns for the rules f and g, using 6 points.

(b) What do you notice about these two circle patterns?

Give a reason for what you noticed.

10   The functions f, g and h are defined as follows.

$f: x \longrightarrow 5x, \quad g: x \longrightarrow 5x+1, \quad h: x \longrightarrow 5x-9$

(a) What is   (i) $f(2)$?   (ii) $g(3)$?   (iii) $h(2)$?   (iv) $g(0)$?

(b) Using 12-point circles, draw circle patterns for the rules f, g and h.

(c) Describe any similarities and differences between patterns.

11   The pattern shown in figure 5 is made up of 3 lines.
It is produced with 8 points using the rule $N \rightarrow -N$.

(a) How many lines are there in the patterns using the same rule when there are

(i) 9 points?   (ii) 10 points?   (iii) 12 points?
(iv) 100 points?   (v) 101 points?

(b) How many different lengths of line are there in each of the patterns in (a)?

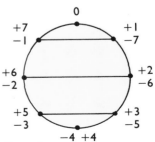

Figure 5

13

12 With 8 points the rule $N \rightarrow 5N$ produces a pattern consisting of 2 diameters.

(a) What similar rule gives diameters when there are

   (i) 12 points?   (ii) 10 points?

How many diameters are obtained in each case?

(b) Make a general statement about p points.

13 The functions f and g are defined as follows:

   $f: x \rightarrow x+3 \quad g: x \rightarrow 3x-5$

(a) For what number c is $f(c) = g(c)$?

(b) Draw circle patterns for the rules f and g when there are 12 points.

(c) Why does your answer to (a) explain the fact that the line joining 4 to 7 is part of both patterns?

(d) Explain why there is another line which is part of both patterns.

14 Find rules which will produce the patterns shown on the worksheet 'Circle patterns.'

SECTION B

1 Get the sheet 'Circle patterns.'

(a) On each circle pattern mark the lines of symmetry.

(b) State the order of rotational symmetry of each pattern.

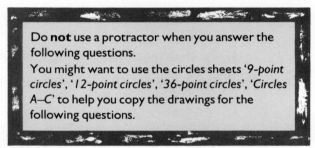

Do **not** use a protractor when you answer the following questions.

You might want to use the circles sheets '9-point circles', '12-point circles', '36-point circles', 'Circles A–C' to help you copy the drawings for the following questions.

2 (a) The circle pattern in figure 6 consists of 3 lines. Find the angles between the lines.

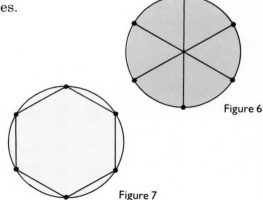

Figure 6

(b) The circle pattern in figure 7 shows a regular hexagon.

Figure 7

Find the angle at the corner of the hexagon. (Putting in the three lines from the previous pattern might help you to do this.)

3 How many times will the small shaded triangle in the circle pattern in figure 8 fit into one of the large triangles?

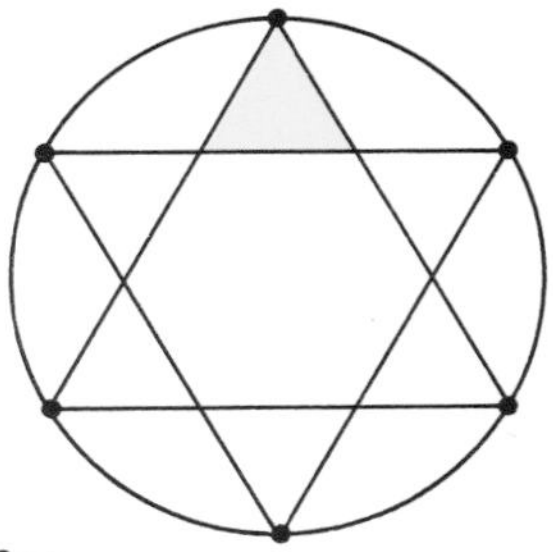

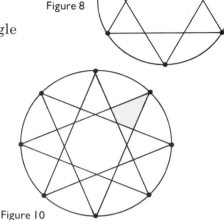

Figure 8

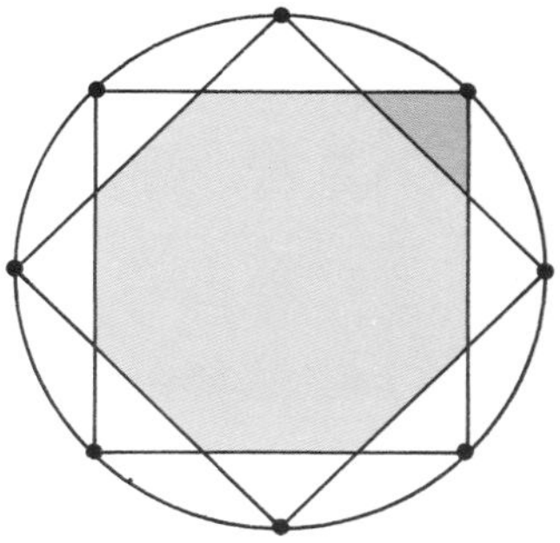

4 (*a*) Find the angles of the shaded triangle in the circle pattern in figure 9.

(*b*) Find the angles at the corners of the shaded octagon.

(*c*) Explain why the octagon is a regular octagon.

5 Find the angles of the shaded kite in the circle pattern seen in figure 10.

Figure 9

Figure 10

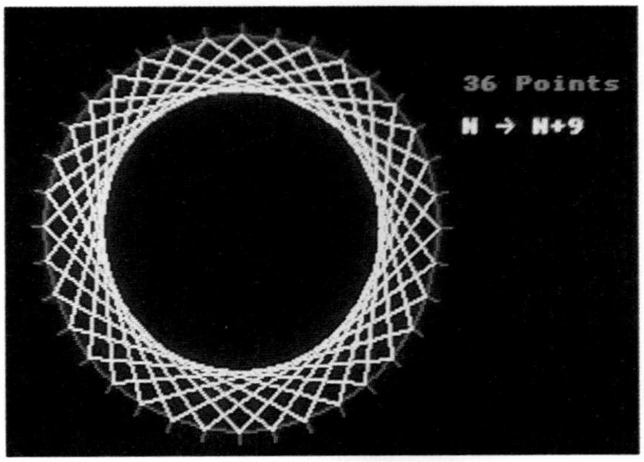

6 The pattern in figure 11 is produced with 36 points using the rule N → N+9.

If you look very carefully you can perhaps see that this pattern consists of 9 squares. But what you probably see first when you look at the pattern is the circle inside the squares, even though this circle has not been drawn.

This circle is called the **envelope** of the pattern.

(*a*) Find a rule which produces a larger envelope circle when using 36 points.

(*b*) Find a rule which produces a smaller envelope circle when using 36 points.

(*c*) What rule will make the largest possible envelope circle when using 36 points?

(*d*) What rule will make the smallest possible envelope circle when using 36 points?

Figure 11

7 The pattern seen in figure 12 is produced with 8 points using the rule N → 2N.

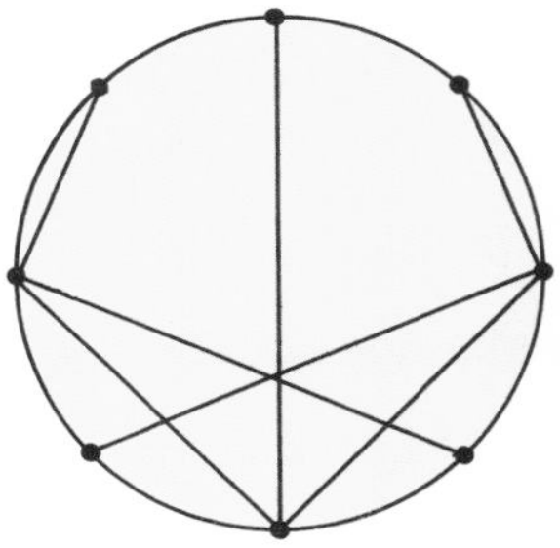

(*a*) Using the rule N → 2N draw the pattern you get when you use 12 points instead of 8 points.

(*b*) Using the rule N → 2N draw the pattern you get when you use 36 points. Describe the shape of the envelope. (It is called a **cardioid**.) How many lines of symmetry does the envelope have?

(*c*) Draw the pattern with 36 points using the rule N → 3N. Describe the shape of the envelope. (It is called a **nephroid**.) How many lines of symmetry does it have?

Figure 12

8 (*a*) Find a rule which produces the cardioid of question 7, but turned upside down.

(*b*) Find a rule which produces the nephroid of question 7, but rotated through 90°.

9 With 36 points, what rule will give an envelope circle which has a radius exactly half the radius of the starting circle? Justify your answer.

SECTION C

Drawings are often made on the screen of a computer by using coordinates.

Suppose a computer screen has coordinates as shown in the diagram

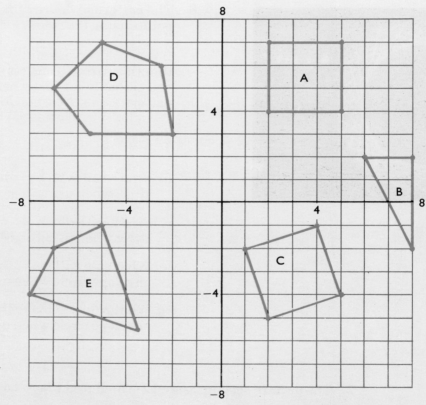

You could get it to draw the square labelled A by telling it the coordinates of the corners. These are (2,4), (5,4) (5,7) and 2,7).

1 What coordinates would you tell the computer to get it to draw the triangle B, the square C, the pentagon D and the kite E?

By giving coordinates you can get the computer to draw any shape made up of straight lines.

To get it to draw a circle you have to cheat. You tell the computer to draw a shape made up of a large number of straight lines.

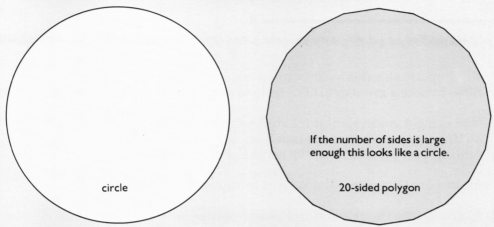

circle

If the number of sides is large enough this looks like a circle.

20-sided polygon

You need to tell the computer the coordinates of a large number of points on the circle. You are now going to find out how to calculate the coordinates of points on a circle.

Get the worksheet called '*Computer circle*'.

The radius of the circle drawn on this sheet is 10 cm.

It is easy to see that the points with coordinates (10,0), (0,10), (−10, 0) and (0, −10) lie on the circle.

It is not so easy to find the coordinates of most of the points on the circle. Before finding the coordinates of a particular point the first task is to make it clear which point you are talking about. One way of doing this is to use angles.

In the type of work you are about to do people always measure angles **anticlockwise** from the **positive x-axis**.

2 The sheet shows an angle of 40°, measured from the positive x-axis. P is the point on the circle corresponding to this angle.

What are the coordinates of this point? Find them as accurately as possible by measuring with a ruler.

3 (*a*) Using a protractor, mark on the worksheet the point corresponding to an angle of 60°. What are the coordinates of this point?

(*b*) Do the same for the points corresponding to angles of 70° and 20°.

(*c*) Find the coordinates of the point corresponding to an angle of 120°. (Remember that one of the coordinates of this point is negative).

In the following questions you are asked to give your answers to 3 significant figures. If you do not know what this means look at Review Exercise 3, *'Rounding off '*, on page 103.

Finding coordinates by drawing is a slow process, and also you have to take a great deal of trouble to get the answers fairly accurate.

You can get your calculator to tell you coordinates on a circle. To do this you use the buttons labelled $\boxed{\text{sin}}$ and $\boxed{\text{cos}}$. Start by finding the coordinates of the point P. Follow these instructions.

Make sure that your calculator is in 'degrees' mode.

Enter 40 into the calculator. Press the $\boxed{\text{cos}}$ button. Record your answer correct to 3 significant figures. The answer should be 0.766.

Now enter 40 into the calculator again. Press the $\boxed{\text{sin}}$ button. Record your answer correct to 3 significant figures. This should be 0.643.

To get the coordinates of the point P multiply your calculator answers by 10. **This is because the radius of the circle is 10**. Do this and check the results against your answer to question 2.

4 Use the calculator to check your answers to question 3.

5 Use the calculator to find the coordinates of points on the circle corresponding to angles of

(*a*) 75°   (*b*) 35°   (*c*) 140°   (*d*) 240°

Give all your answers correct to 3 significant figures. Explain the signs of the numbers in the last answer.

6 On squared paper draw a circle of radius 8cm.

Now draw axes with the origin at the centre of the circle.

Using the calculator, find the coordinates of the point on the circle corresponding to an angle of

(*a*) 80°   (*b*) 45°   (*c*) 25°

(*d*) 150°   (*e*) 180°   (*f*) 300°

Use your drawing of the circle to check that your answers are sensible.

Look at the point marked Q on the 'Computer circle' worksheet.

The first coordinate of Q is 2. You can find the angle corresponding to Q by using a calculator. Do the following.

Divide the first coordinate of Q by 10 and record your answer. **Do this because the radius of the circle is 10**.

Enter the adjusted first coordinate 0.2 into the calculator. Press [inv] [cos] or [cos⁻¹]. This tells you the angle corresponding to Q. You should find that this angle is 78°, correct to the nearest degree.

You can use a protractor to check that the answer is sensible.

Look at the point marked R on the worksheet. The second coordinate of R is 3. You can use a calculator to find the angle corresponding to R. To do this follow the same instructions as above, but use [inv] [sin] (or [sin⁻¹]) instead of [inv] [cos] (or [cos⁻¹]).

This tells you the angle corresponding to R. You should find that this angle is 17°, correct to the nearest degree.

7 Now find, correct to the nearest degree, the angles corresponding to the points S, T, U and V on the worksheet. Use a protractor to check that all your answers are sensible.

8 The points described below are all on an 8 cm circle with centre at the origin. Find the angle corresponding to each of the points.

(a) The first coordinate is 4 and the second coordinate is positive.

(b) The second coordinate is 5.3 and the first coordinate is positive.

(c) The first coordinate is −3 and the second coordinate is positive.

(d) The first coordinate is 7 and the second coordinate is negative.

(e) The second coordinate is −2 and the first coordinate is negative.

Use your drawing of the circle of radius 8 cm to check that your answers are sensible.

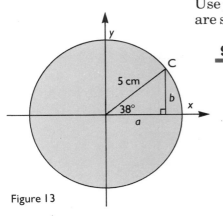

Figure 13

9 Figure 13 shows a right-angled triangle drawn inside a circle of radius 5 cm. The lengths of the sides marked a and b are the same as the coordinates of the point C. So a and b can be found using the method described in the box that comes before question 4.

(a) Use this method to check that a is 3.94 cm.

(b) Use this method to find b, correct to 3 significant figures.

Check that your answer is a sensible one.

19

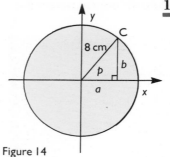

Figure 14

10 Figure 14 shows a right-angled triangle drawn inside a circle of radius 8 cm. The lengths of the sides marked a and b are the same as the coordinates of the point C.

If you know either a or b you can use the method described in the box that comes after question 6 to find the angle marked p.

(a) Use this method to check that, if $a = 5$ cm, p is 51°

(b) Find p to the nearest degree if $b = 2$ cm.

(c) Find p to the nearest degree if $a = 3.7$ cm.

1〉 If you join all the points marked on the circle you get a shape called a **mystic rose**.

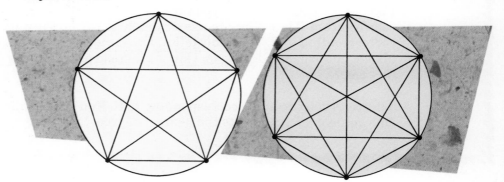

Draw some mystic roses. Answer some of the following questions about them and ask and answer some questions of your own.

What happens in the middle of a mystic rose?

How many lines are there in a mystic rose?

In how many points do the lines intersect?

How many regions are there?

What differences does it make if the points on the circle are not evenly spaced?

2〉 Choose a fixed rule, such as $N \to 5N$, $N \to N^2$ or $N \to N^3$. Look at the symmetries, and other properties, of the patterns produced when different numbers of points are used.

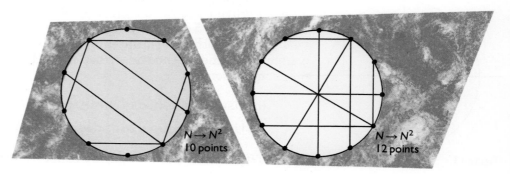

$N \to N^2$
10 points

$N \to N^2$
12 points

3〉 Investigate patterns on a circle with 36 points. You can use various rules.

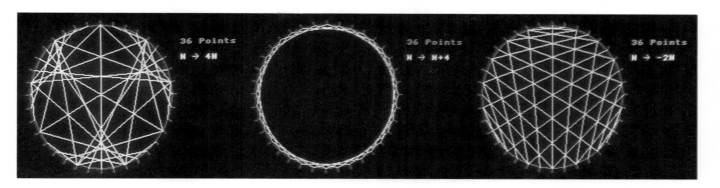

4〉 Investigate the effect of adding different numbers to the end of a rule.

One possibility is to take a fixed number of points, say 12, and the rule $N \rightarrow 2N$. Find what the rules $N \rightarrow 2N+1$, $N \rightarrow 2N+2$, $N \rightarrow 2N+3$, . . . produce. Then do the same with $N \rightarrow 3N$, etc.

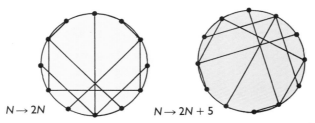

5〉 Choose a particular shape (such as a square) and find as many ways as possible of obtaining patterns which contain that shape.

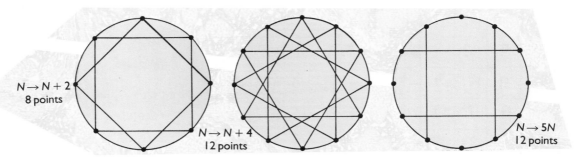

Try to explain what you find.

6〉 Investigate ways of obtaining the same pattern from two different rules.

7〉 Investigate how to produce patterns with a small number of lines compared with the number of points marked on the circle.

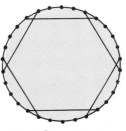

$N \rightarrow N^3$ 30 points

8〉 Investigate ideas of your own about circle patterns.

21

3 INVESTIGATING NUMBERS

Now that calculators are readily available it is much easier to produce number patterns and to explore their properties.

Find out how the constant facility on your calculator works, so that you can get the calculator to produce the sequence of multiples of 9 (9, 18, 27, 36 . . .). You may need to press

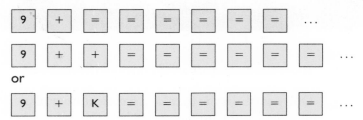

Figure 1 shows the notes of someone looking for patterns in the list of multiples of 9.

Multiple	sum of digits								
9	9	108	9	207	9	306	9	405	9
18	9	117	9	216	9	315	9	414	9
27	9	126	9	225	9	324	9	423	9
36	9	135	9	234	9	333	9	432	9
45	9	144	9	243	9	342	9	441	9
54	9	153	9	252	9	351	9	450	9
63	9	162	9	261	9	360	9	459	18
72	9	171	9	270	9	369	18	468	18
81	9	180	9	279	18	378	18	477	18
90	9	189	18	288	18	387	18	486	18
99	18	198	18	297	18	396	18	495	18

Figure 1

the units go down in ones

the tens go up in ones

if you add the digits up you get either 9 or 18

it starts off with 10, 9's then 1, 18, then 9, 9's + 2, 18 and so on.

the first ten numbers are reversed, 09 + 90, 18 + 81, 27, 72 and so on.

There are similar patterns in the multiples of other numbers.

● Choose a number.

● Use the constant facility on your calculator to make a list of multiples of this number.

● Find several patterns in your list and explain them clearly.

● Choose a different number and do the same task for this new number.

SECTION A

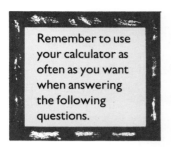

Remember to use your calculator as often as you want when answering the following questions.

1 Here are the beginnings of lists of multiples of 4 and 8.

4	8
8	16
12	24
16	32
20	40
24	48
28	56
...	...

(a) What is the 8th number in the list of multiples of 4?

(b) What is the 9th number in the list of multiples of 8?

(c) What is the 13th multiple of 4?

(d) What is the 37th multiple of 8?

The 3rd multiple of 8 is the same as the 6th multiple of 4.

(e) Which multiple of 4 is the same as the 5th multiple of 8?

(f) Which multiple of 8 is the same as the 14th multiple of 4?

(g) Which multiple of 4 is the same as the 42nd multiple of 8?

(h) What is the sum of the digits of each of the first 12 multiples of 8? Describe the pattern these sums form.

2 (a) Write down the first 12 multiples of 6.

(b) What is the 23rd multiple of 6?

(c) Which multiple of 6 is the same as the 4th multiple of 9?

(d) Which multiple of 9 is the same as the 12th multiple of 6?

(e) Which multiple of 6 is the same as the 20th multiple of 9?

(f) Which is larger, the 30th multiple of 9 or the 40th multiple of 6?

(g) If you wrote out the first 100 multiples of 6 how many of them would also be multiples of 9?

3 Each of the lists below is part of a list of the multiples of a number. Some of the digits have been replaced by stars.

(a)...	(b)...	(c)...	(d)...
...	...	...	...
18	345	238	425
**	***	***	***
30	351	***	***
**	***	***	***
42	357	***	***
**	***	273	55*
54	363	...	...
...	...	...	...

Copy each of the lists, putting back the digits which are missing. Remember that each of your lists should be multiples of a number. For each list write down what this number is.

Look at the following calculations.

$$17 \times 2 = 34 \qquad 87 \times 2 = 174 \qquad 337 \times 2 = 674 \qquad 997 \times 2 = 1994$$

Notice that, if any number ending in 7 is multiplied by 2 the result ends in 4.

4 (*a*) What can you say about the result when a number ending in 8 is multiplied by 2?

(*b*) A number is multiplied by 2 and the answer ends in 2. What digit did the number you started with end in? There are **two** possibilities.

In the following calculations some digits have been replaced by stars.

$$17 \times 3 = ** \qquad 24 \times ** = 312 \qquad *3 \times 4 = **$$

With the help of your calculator you should be able to discover what **some** of the missing digits are.

The calculations below are the same as the ones above. The missing digits have been filled in *only* if we can be *sure* what they are.

$$17 \times 3 = 51 \qquad 24 \times 13 = 312 \qquad *3 \times 4 = *2$$

In the last calculation only **one** star has been replaced with a number. There is no way of telling what the other stars stand for, so these are left as stars.

5 Copy each of the following calculations. Instead of stars fill in missing digits *only* if you can be *certain* what they are. Leave stars if there is no way of telling what a digit should be.

(*a*) $34 \times 2 = **$ (*b*) $** \times 7 = 119$ (*c*) $*9 \times 2 = **$

(*d*) $*6 \times 3 = **$ (*e*) $*6 \times 2 = ***$ (*f*) $*5 \times 7 = ***$

(*g*) $*2 \times 8 = ***$ (*h*) $*2 \times 8 = **$ (*i*) $*25 \times 5 = ****$

6 In the equation below the digits 1, 2, 3, 4, 5, 6, 7, 8 and 9 have been replaced by stars.

$$*** + ** - ** - ** = 100$$

One possible solution is

$$123 + 89 - 67 - 45 = 100$$

Use this solution to help you find six other solutions.

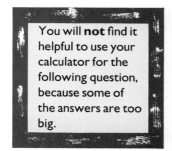

7 The following is a list of the powers of 2.

$$2^1 = 2$$
$$2^2 = 2 \times 2 = 4$$
$$2^3 = 2 \times 2 \times 2 = 8$$
$$2^4 = 2 \times 2 \times 2 \times 2 = 16$$
$$\ldots$$

(*a*) What is 2^5?

(*b*) List the first ten powers of 2. What pattern is made by the last digit of each of the powers of 2?

(*c*) What digit does 2^{12} end with?

(*d*) What digit does 2^{40} end with?

(*e*) What digit does 2^{157} end with?

(*f*) What do you think 2^0 is?

You can use your calculator to help you find powers of a number. One way is to use the constant facility on your calculator. For example, to find 4^5 you may need to press either

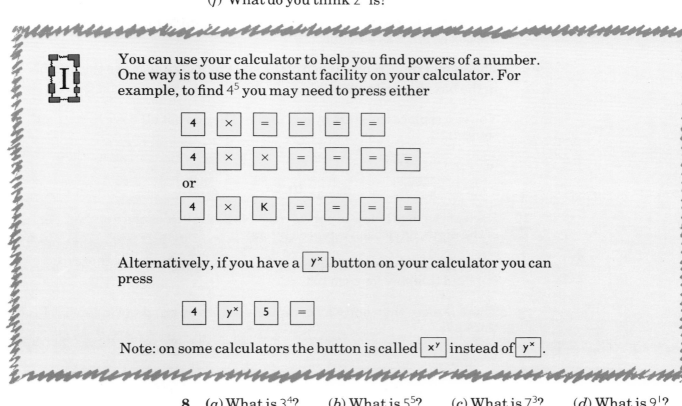

| 4 | × | = | = | = | = |

| 4 | × | × | = | = | = | = |

or

| 4 | × | K | = | = | = | = |

Alternatively, if you have a $\boxed{y^x}$ button on your calculator you can press

| 4 | y^x | 5 | = |

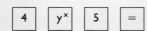

Note: on some calculators the button is called $\boxed{x^y}$ instead of $\boxed{y^x}$.

8 (*a*) What is 3^4? (*b*) What is 5^5? (*c*) What is 7^3? (*d*) What is 9^1?

(*e*) The last digit of a power of 5 is always 5. There are other numbers which are similar to 5, in that the last digit of any of their powers is always the same. Two of these are positive whole numbers less than 10. Which numbers are they?

(*f*) What digit does 9^{17} end with?

In the calculation below digits have been replaced by stars.

*7 − ** = | ** |

There is no way of knowing what the missing digits are. There are several different possibilities for the number in the box.

Suppose we want to make the number in the box as **large** as possible. Then we can replace the stars as follows.

97 − 10 = | 87 |

Suppose now we want to make the number in the box as **small** as possible. The smallest it can be is 10. There are several ways of getting this. One of them is as follows:

57 − 47 = | 10 |

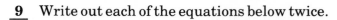

9 Write out each of the equations below twice.

The first time, replace each of the stars by a digit to make the number in the box as *large* as possible.

The second time, replace each of the stars by a digit to make the number in the box as *small* as possible.

You can replace the stars by *any* digits. They do not all have to be the same digit.

(a) ** + ** = | *** | (b) *9 + 4* = | *** |

(c) (**)² = | ***6 | (d) *86 − *7 = | ** |

10 Each of the lists below is part of a list of the multiples of a number. Some of the digits have been replaced by stars.

There is only one way of replacing stars by numbers in the list (a), (b) and (c). Find this way for each list.

There is more than one way of replacing stars by numbers in list (d). Find the ways.

(a)...	(b)...	(c)...	(d)...
350	289	1*5	***
***	***	***	***
***	***	***	***
***	***	***	667
***	***	38*	***
***	***	...	...
**9	***	...	...
...	...	...	...
	...		

11 Get the worksheet '*Investigating numbers*'.

Put any three-digit number on the top line in the '*start*' box. Fill the correct numbers in the other boxes.

Repeat, putting different three-digit numbers in the '*start*' box until all the lines are used up.

What do you notice?

Algebra can be used to help explain what is happening. Suppose the number in the '*start*' box is ABC. This does not mean A × B × C (as it usually does in algebra). Instead, A is the hundreds digit, B the tens digit and C the units digit.

So the number is really 100A + 10B + C. Make sure you understand why.

Now reverse the digits. What number do you get now?

Now subtract the smaller number from the larger, assuming that A is greater than B. Show that the number obtained is 99A–99C. This can be written as 99(A–C), which shows that the number is a multiple of 99.

Write out the 99 times-table. If a multiple of 99 is written as X9Y, explain the connection between X and Y.

Now explain why you get 1089.

12 Repeat question 11, but this time put a two-digit number in the '*start*' box. Use algebra to explain what happens.

What happens when you use a four-digit number?

SECTION B

This chapter began by looking at lists of multiples. A **factor** is the opposite of a multiple.

12 is a multiple of 4.
So 4 is a factor of 12.

1 (*a*) Write down all the factors of 12.

(*b*) Why can you not write down all the multiples of 12? Write down three multiples of 12.

(*c*) Write down all the factors of 17.

(*d*) Write down all the factors of 1.

2 Copy and complete the table shown below

Number	Type of number	Factors	Number of factors
1	odd, square, cube	1	1
2	even, prime	1,2	2
3			
4		1,2,4	3
5			
6	even		
7			
8	even, cube		
9			
10			
11			
12			

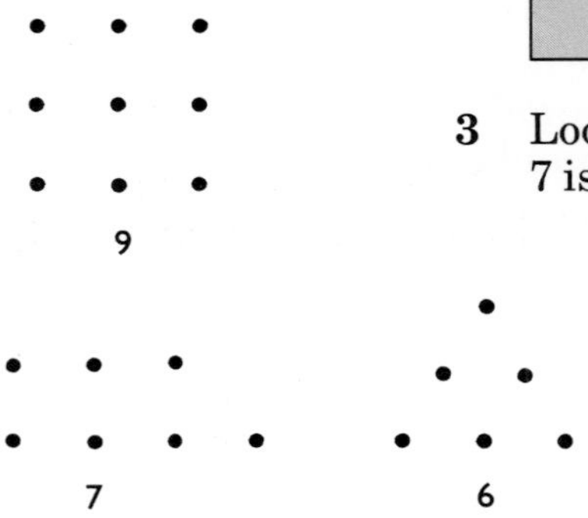

3 Look at figure 2. These pictures explain why 9 is called a square number, 7 is called an odd number and 6 is called a triangular number.

Draw pictures to explain why:

(a) 10 is an even number.

(b) 16 is a square number.

(c) 21 is a triangular number.

(d) 15 is **not** a prime number.

(e) 8 is a cube number.

Figure 2

4 Write down all the prime numbers less than 100.

The number 24 has 8 factors. These are 1, 2, 3, 4, 6, 8, 12 and 24. 24 can be written as the product of some of its factors in many different ways. For example:

$$24 = 4 \times 6$$
$$24 = 8 \times 3$$
$$24 = 4 \times 2 \times 3$$
$$24 = 12 \times 2 \times 1 \times 1$$

Two of the factors of 24 are **prime factors** (factors which are prime numbers). These are 2 and 3.

24 can be written as the *product of prime factors* in only one way (apart from order).

$$24 = 2 \times 2 \times 2 \times 3$$

This can be shortened by using index notation.

$$24 = 2^3 \times 3$$

5 Write the following numbers as a product of prime factors, using index notation where appropriate.

(a) 12   (b) 50   (c) 9   (d) 75   (e) 35

(f) 32   (g) 53   (h) 144   (i) 1001

Here is the list of the multiples of 6.

6	even
12	even
18	even
24	even
30	even
36	square
42	even
...	...
...	...
...	...

Only one thing has been said about each of the numbers. Thus, although 36 is even this has not been mentioned.

---

6 Look at each of the lists below. For each list try to find a list of the multiples of a number which matches it. If it is impossible to find a list of multiples which matches, say so, and explain how you *know* it is impossible. The first one is done for you.

(a)
prime	2
square	4
even	6
cube	8
...	
...	
...	

(b)
| odd |
| even |
| odd |
| even |
| ... |
| ... |
| ... |

(c)
| prime |
| even |
| odd |
| even |
| ... |
| ... |
| ... |

(d)
| odd |
| odd |
| odd |
| odd |
| ... |
| ... |
| ... |

(e)
| prime |
| even |
| prime |
| even |
| ... |
| ... |
| ... |

(f)
| even |
| square |
| even |
| square |
| ... |
| ... |
| ... |

(g)
| square |
| even |
| cube |
| square |
| ... |
| ... |
| ... |

(h)
| odd |
| square |
| odd |
| even |
| ... |
| ... |
| ... |

7 (a) How many multiples does 0 have?   (b) What are the factors of 0?

Finding the prime factors of a number is a good way of finding all its factors.

Suppose we want to find all the factors of 45.
We can write 45 as the product of prime factors. $45 = 3^2 \times 5$

To find all the factors we combine the prime factors in every possible way.

$3 \times 3 \times 5 = 45$
$3 \times 3 = 9$
$3 \times 5 = 15$
3
5
1

So 45 has six factors.

8 (a) Write 66 as the product of prime factors. Find all the factors of 66.

(b) Write 406 as the product of prime factors. Find all the factors of 406.

(c) Give a reason why 66 and 406 have the same number of factors.

(d) Find a number greater than a million which has the same number of factors as 406.

9 (a) Write 60 as the product of prime factors. Find all the factors of 60.

(b) Find a number greater than a million which has the same number of factors as 60.

(c) Find a number greater than a million such that the highest factor it shares with 60 is 15.

SECTION C

One way of finding a multiple of 9 is to multiply a whole number by 9.

The diagram gives a picture of what happens.

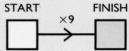

1 What number do you get in the **finish** box if you put each of the following numbers in the **start** box?

(a) 3   (b) 7   (c) 37   (d) 889

2 Look at figure 3. It shows that, when 8 is multiplied by 13, the answer is 104.

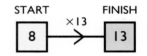

Figure 3

What numbers should go in place of the question mark in the diagrams below?

(a)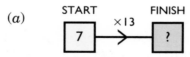

(f)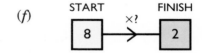

(b)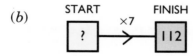

(g)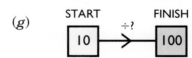

(c)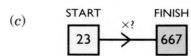

(h)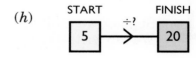

(d)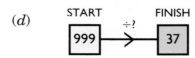

(i)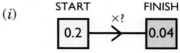

(e)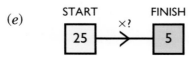

(j)

In the diagram below the process is longer.

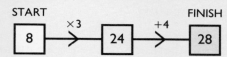

8 has been put into the starting box and this produces 24 in the middle box, and then 28 in the finishing box.

3 Look at figure 4.

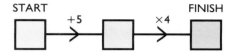

Figure 4

What number do you get in the **finish** box if you put each of the following numbers in the **start** box?

(*a*) 5   (*b*) 17   (*c*) 300

4 (*a*) Look at figure 5.

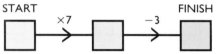

Figure 5

What number do you get in the **finish** box if you put each of the following numbers in the **start** box?

(i) 8   (ii) 63   (iii) 0   (iv) −7

(*b*) What number do you have to put into the **start** box to get 25 in the **finish** box?

(*c*) What number do you have to put into the **start** box to get 137 in the **finish** box?

(*d*) What number do you have to put into the **start** box to get 620 in the **finish** box?

(*e*) If you put the number *x* in the start box what number do you get in the **finish** box?

5 (*a*) Look at figure 6. Choose 5 whole numbers as **start** numbers. Show what **finish** number you get for each of your **start** numbers.

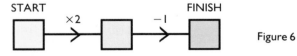

Figure 6

(*b*) What kind of numbers are *all* the **finish** numbers?

6 (*a*) Look at figure 7. Choose 5 odd numbers as **start** numbers. Show what **finish** number you get for each of your **start** numbers.

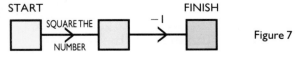

Figure 7

(*b*) What kind of numbers are *all* the **finish** numbers?

7 (*a*) Look at figure 8. Choose 5 triangular numbers as **start** numbers. Show what **finish** number you get for each of your **start** numbers.

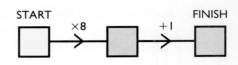

Figure 8

(*b*) What kind of numbers are *all* the **finish** numbers?

8 Look at figure 9. What number do you have to put into the **start** box to get the following numbers in the **finish** box?

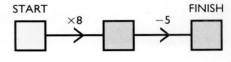

Figure 9

(*a*) 35 (*b*) −53 (*c*) 103

As explained in chapter 2 a rule for getting from one number (the **start** number) to another number (the **finish** number) is called a function.

Suppose the function *f* is described by the following diagram.

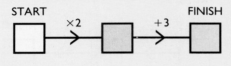

To find *f*(3) put 3 in the start box.

So *f*(3) = 9. In the same way, *f*(8) = 19 and *f*(−4) = −5.

If the number *x* is put in the **start** box this will produce the number $2x+3$ in the **finish** box. So the function *f* can be defined as $f: x \longrightarrow 2x+3$

9 The function *g* is defined by figure 10.

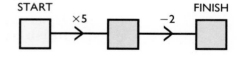

Figure 10

(*a*) What is

   (i) *g*(6)?   (ii) *g*(3.5)?
   (iii) *g*(0)?   (iv) *g*(−10)?

(*b*) What number do you get in the **finish** box if you put *x* in the **start** box?

(*c*) Write the function *g* in the form $g: x \longrightarrow$

Look at the first diagram

We could draw a second diagram to show how to get from the **finish** box to the **start** box.

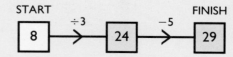

10 Look at figure 11.

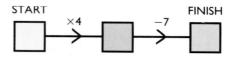

Figure 11

(a) What number do you finish with if you start with 6?

(b) What number do you finish with if you start with x?

(c) Draw a diagram to reverse the process.

11 Look at figure 12.

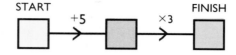

Figure 12

(a) What number do you finish with if you start with 7?

(b) What number do you finish with if you start with x?

(c) Draw a diagram to reverse the process.

FURTHER COURSEWORK TASKS

1〉 Write down a four-digit number.

Now write down the largest and smallest numbers you can get from using these four digits.

Subtract the smallest number from the largest number.

Repeat the process on the answer. Keep going until there is no point in going any further.

7342

$$
\begin{array}{ccccccc}
7432 & 8550 & 9972 & 7731 & 6543 & 8730 \\
2347- & 0558- & 2799- & 1377- & 3456- & 0378- \\
\hline
5085 & 7992 & 7173 & 6354 & 3087 & 8352
\end{array}
$$

Try the same process on several other four-digit numbers. What appears to be happening? Does it matter if any of the digits are the same?

Investigate the same situation using three-digit numbers or five-digit numbers.

2〉 Figure 13 shows a picture of a billiard table with six pockets.

This billiard table is 8×5. The dotted line is the path of a ball starting from the bottom left-hand corner pocket and moving at 45° to the cushion. Eventually the ball enters the bottom middle pocket.

Figure 13

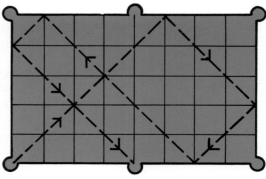

Which pocket does the ball enter if it is started from different pockets?

In each case, how many times does the ball bounce off the cushion before it goes into the pocket?

How long is the path in each case?

Explore these questions for rectangular tables of different sizes.

Investigate whether it is true that a ball enters a pocket if it starts from anywhere on the table.

Investigate other different rules for the movement of the ball.

Explore similar problems for a hexagonal table.

3〉 Run the computer program '*Counter*'.

Press *N* to select two counters.

Press *F* to choose the first numbers. Make these 10 and 50.

Press *S* to select the step sizes. Make these 3 and 1. Start the counters and see what happens.

Now put the counters back to 10 and 50 and choose step sizes so that eventually the counters show the same number at the same time.

Do this in as many ways as you can.

What different step sizes make the counters meet at the same number?

Choose any number. Can you now choose step sizes to make the counters meet at this number?

4〉 Copy the following

Sum	Product
$8 + 4 = 12$	$8 \times 4 = 32$
$5 + 7 = 12$	$5 \times 7 = 35$
$11 + 1 = 12$	$11 \times 1 = 11$
$3 + 4 + 5 = 12$	$3 \times 4 \times 5 = 60$
$9 + 1 + 1 + 1 = 12$	$9 \times 1 \times 1 \times 1 = 9$

Add further lines of your own. Investigate how you can obtain the largest possible product.

Now try the same thing for numbers whose sum is 16 instead of 12.

Try other numbers.

What happens if the numbers do not have to be integers?

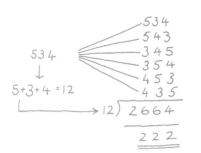

5) Write down three digits.

Now write down all the different numbers which can be made from these three digits.

Add all these numbers up. Divide the total by the sum of the three digits.

Repeat, choosing three different digits to start with.

What happens? Explain what you find.

What happens if the three digits are not all different?

What happens if you use two digits? Or four digits? Or N digits?

6) Look at the following:

$$2 + 4 = 6 \qquad \text{24 is a multiple of 6}$$
$$4 + 0 = 4 \qquad \text{40 is a multiple of 4}$$
$$1 + 2 + 6 = 9 \qquad \text{126 is a multiple of 9}$$
$$3 + 7 = 10 \qquad \text{37 is } not \text{ a multiple of 10}$$

Which numbers are a multiple of the sum of their digits and which are not? Look for patterns in your results. Explain some of the patterns.

7) The numbers 1, 2, 3, 4, 5, 6, 7, 8, 9, 10, 11 and 12 are put into a bag (figure 14).

You can take any of the numbers in the bag, as long as one of the factors of that number is *also* in the bag.

After you have taken a number, all the factors of that number are removed from the bag and you lose these.

Figure 14

Suppose for example you take 10. This is allowed because there are factors of 10 in the bag. You then have 10 and the numbers 5, 2 and 1 are removed from the bag. You lose these numbers. (See figure 15).

You can now take another number provided that at least one of its factors is also in the bag.

You keep taking numbers until you are not allowed to take any more. You then find the sum of all the numbers you have taken to give your score.

Figure 15

Investigate how to get the highest possible score.

Start with a different set of numbers in the bag: for example, all the numbers between 1 and 9, or all the numbers between 1 and 16. Investigate how to get the highest score now.

Write about the strategies you use.

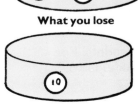

What you lose

What you have taken

4 GROWING CUBES

Figure 1

Figure 1 shows three models of 'double staircases' made from interlocking cubes.

- Make each of the models shown.

- Make the next two models in the sequence.

- Make the model which comes before the three models shown.

- How many cubes are used to make each model?

  Predict how many cubes are used to make each of the next 4 models.

- What is the surface area of each model? What is the pattern to this sequence of surface areas?

- How many faces does each model have? What is the pattern to this sequence?

- How many vertices does each model have? What is the pattern to this sequence?

- Starting with one model in the sequence, explain what you need to add to it to make the next model in the sequence.

  How many faces are added by doing this? Where are they added?

  Use methods like this to help you to explain some of the number sequences you found earlier.

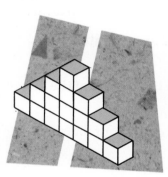

Figure 2

1   Figure 2 shows the first four models in a different sequence of models.

   (a) Find the number of cubes in each of the models. Predict the answers for the next three models in this sequence without making the models.

   (b) Find the surface area of each of the models. Predict the answers for the next three models.

   (c) Find the total length of all the edges of each of the models. For example, the total length of the edges of the first model is 16.

   Predict the answers for the next three models.

2 Figure 3 shows the first four models in another sequence.

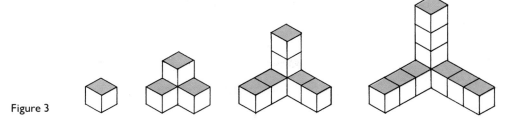

Figure 3

(a) Find the number of cubes in each of the models. Predict the answers for the next four models.

(b) Find the surface area of each of the models. Predict the answers for the next four models.

Look at your answer to question 1.

The surface areas of the first eight models are

10, 16, 22, 28, 34, 40, 46, 52

These numbers go up in 6s. We could show this by writing 6s underneath the sequence, like this:

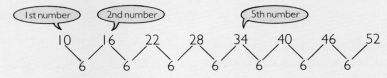

This is called a **table of differences**.

Between the 1st number and the 5th number there are 4 steps of 6.

3 The number sequence in the box above is

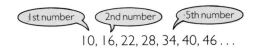

(a) What is the difference between the 1st number and the 5th number of this sequence?

(b) How many steps of 6 are there between the 1st number and the 9th number?

(c) What is the difference between the 1st number and the 9th number?

(d) How many steps of 6 are there between the 1st number and the 21st number?

(e) What is the difference between the 1st number and the 21st number?

(f) What is the 21st number?

4 Look at your answer to question 2(*b*). The surface areas of the first seven models are

6, 18, 30, 42, 54, 66, 78

(*a*) What steps do the numbers go up in?

(*b*) What is the 11th term of this sequence?

(*c*) What is the 41st term of this sequence?

(*d*) What is the 100th term of this sequence?

Look at each of the models in the sequence of 'single staircases' shown.

These are the numbers of cubes in the first 8 models in this sequence:

1, 3, 6, 10, 15, 21, 28, 36

If we work out the table of differences, as in the box before question 3, this is what we get:

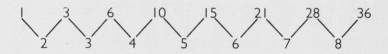

All the differences are different, but there is a clear pattern. We could add another line to the table of differences to show the differences of the differences.

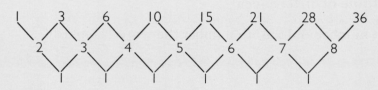

These differences are all 1.

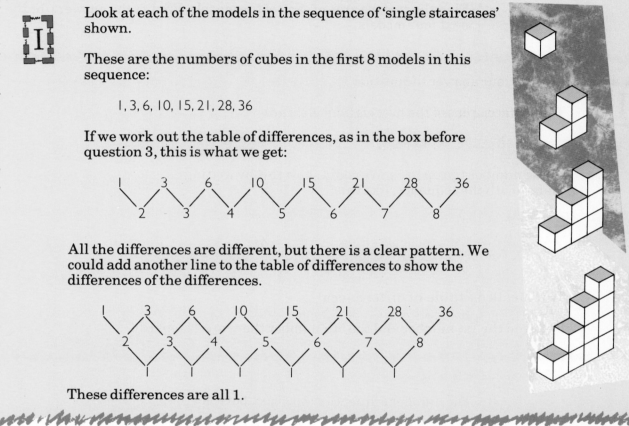

5 (*a*) Extend the table in the box above to work out the next few numbers in the sequence. Start at the bottom and work upwards.

(*b*) What is the 11th number?

(*c*) What is the 15th number?

6 (*a*) Find the surface area of each of the first eight models in the sequence of 'single staircases' described in the box above.

(*b*) Write down a table of differences for these surface areas, as explained in the box above.

(*c*) Extend the table to work out the next few numbers of the sequence.

(*d*) What is the surface area of the 13th model in the sequence?

(*e*) What is the surface area of the 17th model in the sequence?

7 (a) Make each of the models shown in figure 4.

Figure 4

(b) Use the method of question 5 to find the number of cubes in the 10th model of the sequence.

8 Look at the sequence you obtained for the number of vertices of the 'double staircases' at the start of this chapter. This sequence is

8, 16, 24, 32, 40 . . .

(a) Explain how you would work out the 10th number in this sequence.

(b) Give a rule for working out any term of the sequence.

 The Nth term means the number that comes in position N in the sequence.

(c) Give a formula for the Nth term of this sequence.

Look at the sequence you obtained for the number of faces of 'double staircases' at the start of this chapter. This sequence is

6, 10, 14, 18, 22 . . .

Here is the table of differences for this sequence.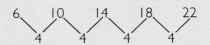

This is how to find a formula for the Nth term. The numbers go up in 4s, so the formula is

$4N$ + something

To find the 'something' look at the first term. The first term is 6 and $N = 1$. So

4×1 + something $= 6$

The 'something' must be 2.

So the Nth term of this sequence is $4N + 2$.

Here is a way of showing that the formula is correct.

1st term $N = 1$ $4 \times 1 + 2 = 6$
2nd term $N = 2$ $4 \times 2 + 2 = 10$
3rd term $N = 3$ $4 \times 3 + 2 = 14$

9 (*a*) Make sure that the formula in the previous box is correct by checking it with the fifth term.

(*b*) Use the formula to find the 20th term.

10 (*a*) The sequence of surface areas of the models in question 1 is

$$10, 16, 22, 28, 34, 40, 46$$

(i) Use the method explained in the previous box to find the Nth term of this sequence.
(ii) Which of the models has a surface area of 88?

(*b*) The sequence of surface areas of the models in question 2 is

$$6, 18, 30, 42, 54, 66, 78$$

(i) Find the Nth term of this sequence.
(ii) Does any of the models have a surface area of 150? If so, which model is it?

(*c*) The sequence of surface areas of a set of models is

$$6, 22, 38, 54, 70, 86, 102$$

(i) Find the Nth term of this sequence.
(ii) Does one of the models have a surface area of 550? If so, which model is it?

Look at the sequence you obtained for the number of cubes used to make the models in the *Introductory Task*. This sequence is

$$1, 4, 9, 16, 25 \ldots$$

These numbers are the square numbers.

The Nth term of this sequence is N^2.

Here is the table of differences for this sequence:

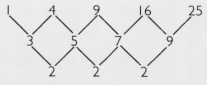

In the second row of differences the numbers are all the same. They are all 2.

Here is the table of differences for the sequence for which the Nth term is $2N^2$.

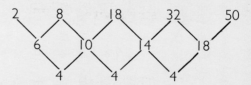

This time the second differences are all 4.

11 (*a*) Write out a table of differences for the sequence for which the Nth term is $5N^2$.

(*b*) Without writing out the table, say what number will be repeated in the second row of differences for a sequence if the Nth term is

(i) $3N^2$ (ii) $\frac{1}{2}N^2$ (iii) $\frac{11}{2}N^2$

12 (*a*) Write out the table of differences for a sequence if the Nth term is $2N^2 + N$.

What number is repeated in the second row of differences this time?

(*b*) Write out the table of differences for a sequence if the Nth term is $3N^2 + N$.

What number is repeated in the second row of differences this time?

(*c*) Write out the table of differences for a sequence if the Nth term is $4N^2 - 3N + 2$.

What number is repeated in the second row of differences this time?

(*d*) What conclusions can you draw from your answers to parts (*a*), (*b*) and (*c*) of this question?

Look at the sequence you obtained for the surface areas of the 'double staircases' in the *Introductory Task*.

This sequence is

6, 18, 34, 54, 78 ...

Here is one way of finding a formula for the Nth term of this sequence.

First write out the difference table for the sequence.

6   18   34   54   78
  12   16   20   24
     4   4   4

The second row of differences contains repeated 4s. This shows that the formula for the Nth term starts with $2N^2$. Why?

There are several ways of getting the rest of the formula. One way is to subtract $2N^2$ from the sequence.

```
   6   18   34   54   78
-  2    8   18   32   50
   4   10   16   22   28
```

This new sequence goes up in steps of 6. You can use the method in the box before question 9 to show that the formula for this new sequence is $6N - 2$.

Therefore the Nth term of the original sequence

6, 18, 34, 54, 78 ...

is $2N^2 + 6N - 2$.

It is sensible to check formulas obtained in this way. For example, you can check this formula by putting $N = 2$ to find the second term of the sequence. The formula gives $2 \times 2^2 + 6 \times 2 - 2 = 18$ and this is correct.

---

13 The sequence of surface areas of the 'single staircases' is

6, 14, 24, 36, 50, 66

Use the method in the box above to find the Nth term of this sequence.

14 The numbers of cubes required to make the first six models of question 7 are

1, 6, 15, 28, 45, 66

Use the method in the box above to find the Nth term of this sequence.

15 The numbers of cubes required to make the first six 'single staircases' are

1, 3, 6, 10, 15, 21

(a) Use the method in the previous box to find the Nth term of this sequence.

(b) Does any 'single staircase' require exactly 300 cubes? If so, which one?

(c) You have 500 cubes and decide to make the largest possible 'single staircase'. How many cubes will you have left over?

16 (a) Make two copies of one of the 'single staircases' described in the box before question 5.

Put these two copies together to make a 'rectangle'. What is the connection between this rectangle and the answer you obtained for question 15?

(b) Make two consecutive models in the sequence of 'single staircases'. Put them together to make

(i) a 'square'
(ii) one of the 'double staircases'.

Explain why this will always work, whichever pair of consecutive models you take. Hence explain why the numbers of cubes required to make the 'double staircases' are always square numbers.

17 Make each of the models shown in figure 5.

Figure 5

(a) How many cubes are needed for each of the models?

(b) Use a difference table to find the 7th term of this sequence.

(c) Find the Nth term of this sequence.

SECTION B

You would find a graphical calculator or a graph plotter on a computer useful to help you explore several of the ideas in this section.

1 Look at the sequence of models shown in figure 6.

Figure 6

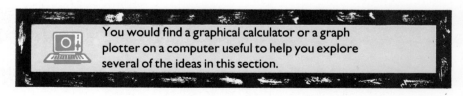

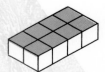

If the length of the model is 3 then 6 cubes are used to make the model. How many cubes are used to make the model if its length is 5?

Copy and complete the table below, showing the length of a model (L) and the corresponding number of cubes (C).

L	1	2	3	4	5	6	7	8
C			6				14	

On squared paper draw a graph of the number of cubes (C) plotted against the length of the model (L). Use 1 cm to represent 1 unit on each of the scales.

2 Look at the sequence of models shown in figure 7.

Figure 7

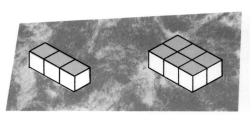

Copy and complete the table, showing the length of a model (L) and the corresponding number of cubes (C).

L	1	2	3	4	5	6
C		6			15	

Draw a graph of the number of cubes (C) plotted against the length of the model (L) on the same axes which you used for question 1.

3 Look at the graphs you drew for questions 1 and 2. In each graph the points lie on a straight line.

Which line is steeper?

One way of measuring the steepness of the lines is to use a difference table. Here is the difference table for question 1.

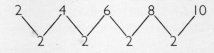

The differences are all 2s.

To describe the steepness of a line the word **gradient** is used. The gradient of this line is 2.

4 Write out a difference table for the sequence in question 2. What is the gradient of the graph for question 2?

5 Look at the sequence of models in figure 8.

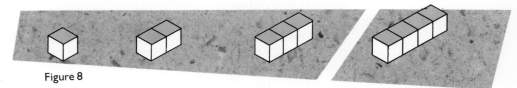

Figure 8

(a) Copy and complete the table below, showing the length of the model (*L*) and the corresponding surface area (*A*).

L	1	2	3	4	5
A		10			22

(b) Using a horizontal scale of 1 cm to represent 1 unit and a vertical scale of 1 cm to represent 2 units, draw a graph of the surface area (*A*) of a model plotted against its length (*L*).

(c) Find the gradient of this graph. (To do this, you might find it helpful to look at the difference table.)

(d) You should have discovered that the gradient of the graph in this question is bigger than the gradients of the graphs drawn for questions 1 and 2.

But the graphs drawn for questions 1 and 2 look steeper than the graph drawn for this question. Why is this?

6 This chapter began with 'double staircases'.

Here is a table showing the number (*N*) of a 'double staircase' and the corresponding number of faces (*F*).

N	1	2	3	4	5
F	6	10	14	18	22

(a) Draw a horizontal axis for *N* (with 1 cm representing 1 unit) and a vertical axis for *F* (with 1 cm representing 4 units).

(b) Draw a graph of the number of faces (*F*) plotted against the number of the model (*N*).

(c) Find the gradient of your graph.

(d) The formula for the number of faces, *F*, is $F = 4N + 2$.

(i) What is the connection between the gradient of your graph and the formula for *F*?
(ii) Join the points of the graph up with the straight line and extend it until it meets the vertical axis.

Now explain the significance of the number 2 in the formula in terms of your graph.

7 Here are three formulae for use in connection with three sequences of models.

(1) $A = 6N + 4$
(2) $A = 12N - 6$
(3) $A = 16N - 10$

Each formula tells you how to find the surface area, A, of the Nth model.

(a) Using a horizontal scale of 1 cm to represent 1 unit draw an axis for values of N from 0 to 4. Using a vertical scale of 1 cm to represent 4 units draw an axis for values of A from -12 to 56.

(b) Draw graphs of these formulae. Draw all three graphs on the same set of axes.

(c) What is the connection between the gradient of each of your graphs and the formula for A?

(d) Explain the significance of the number at the end of each of the formulae in terms of your graphs.

8 The number of cubes, C, needed to make the Nth 'double staircase' is N^2.

$$C = N^2$$

(a) Using a horizontal scale of 1 cm to represent 1 unit draw an axis for values of N from 0 to 5. Using a vertical scale of 1 cm to represent 4 units draw an axis for values of A from 0 to 28.

(b) Draw a graph of the number of cubes (C) plotted against the number of the model (N).

FURTHER COURSEWORK TASKS

Skeleton cubes

1〉 Investigate the number of cubes needed for sequences of skeleton cubes,

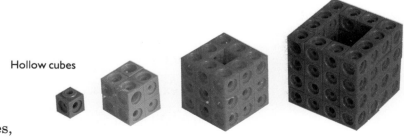

Hollow cubes

hollow cubes,

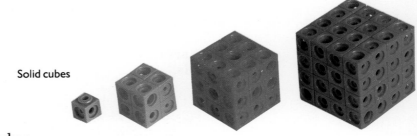

Solid cubes

and solid cubes.

Try to explain the sequences of numbers which you obtain.

2⟩ Investigate sequences of models. If you are using *Multilink* you might want to use prisms as well as cubes to make the models in your sequence.

Figure 9 shows two possible sequences.

First sequence

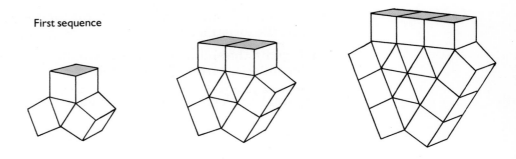

Figure 9

Second sequence

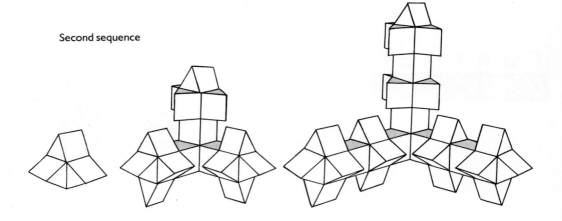

You might look at the number of cubes and the number of prisms required to make the models. You might look at the surface areas of the models, remembering that a triangular face is not the same area as a square face. You might look at the total length of the edges of each model.

Try to explain the sequences you obtain.

You might want to write out difference tables or to find formulae.

5 DESIGN FOR LIVING

- Measure your bedroom. Measure the size and the position of the bed and other furniture.

- Draw a plan of your bedroom on squared paper. Label your plan, and show the scale clearly.

- Draw pictures of what your bedroom looks like from different viewpoints.

- Instead, you might prefer to draw a plan of how you would like your bedroom to be.

> You will need a calculator to help you answer most of the questions in this chapter. Give all your answers as sensible approximations of your calculated answers. If you want help with giving sensible approximations then look at the section called 'Approximating' on page 249.

SECTION A

1 The top of the desk or table you are working on is probably a rectangle. How long is each of its four sides?

Divide the length of each side by 10. Make a plan of the top of your desk or table which is $\frac{1}{10}$th of the size of the original.

If you made lots of copies of the plan of your desk and cut them out, how many would you need to cover the whole of the top of your desk?

2 The three rectangles in figure 1 are all accurate scale drawings of desk tops.

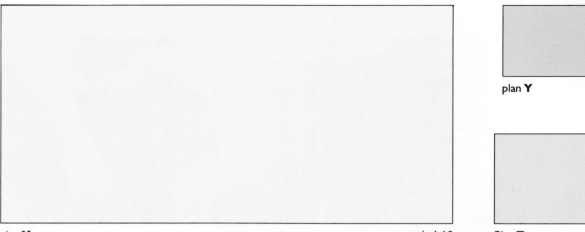

plan **X**   scale 1:10

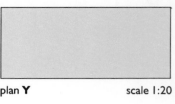

plan **Y**   scale 1:20

Plan **Z**   scale 1:25

Figure 1

(a) Two of these rectangles are scale drawings of the '*same*' desk top. By measuring the rectangles find out which two.

(b) Explain the reasoning you used to answer part (a).

3 Look at the bathroom plan shown in figure 2. This shows only the size of the room and the size of the bath. Other details have been left out.

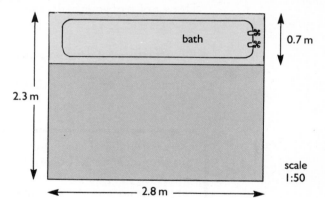

Figure 2

scale 1:50

(a) Estimate from the plan, *without calculating*, what fraction of the bathroom floor is covered by the bath and its surround.

(b) Check that the area of the whole bathroom floor is about 6.4 m².

(c) Check that the area of floor covered by the bath is about 2.0 m².

(d) To calculate the percentage of bathroom floor which is covered by the bath you do the following.

First Put the area covered by the bath into your calculator.

Second Divide by the area of the floor.

Third Multiply by 100.

Do this now. What percentage of the floor does the bath cover?

You should discover that the bath covers about 31% of the floor. If you do not get this answer talk to someone about the method you are using.

(e) Is 31% more or less than a quarter?

Is 31% more or less than a third?

Was the estimate you gave as the answer to (a) too big or too small?

4 Look at the plan of the garage shown in figure 3, showing a car parked in the garage.

Figure 3

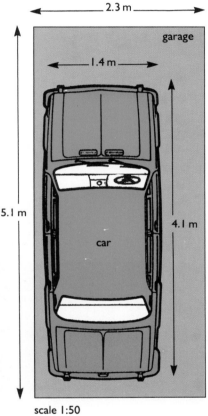

scale 1:50

(a) Estimate, without calculating, the fraction of the garage floor which is covered by the car.

(b) Estimate, without calculating, the percentage of the garage floor which is covered by the car.

(c) What is the area of the garage floor?

(d) What is the area of floor covered by the car?

(e) Use the method of question 3 to calculate the percentage of the floor covered by the car. Give your answer correct to the nearest whole number.

(f) Was the estimate you gave as the answer to (b) too big or too small?

(g) What percentage of the floor of the garage is **not** covered by the car?

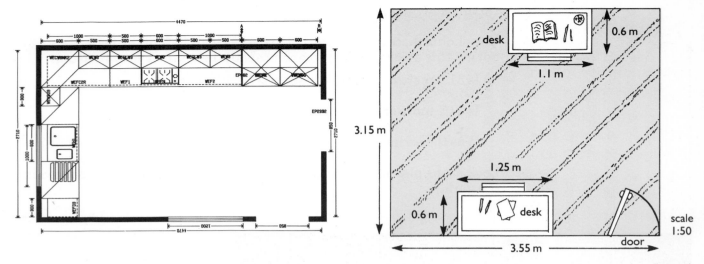

Figure 4

5 Look at the plan shown in figure 4. It is the plan of a study.

There are two desks in the study. These are shown on the plan.

(a) Estimate, without calculating, the percentage of the floor of the study covered by the two desks together.

(b) Calculate the area of the study floor.

(c) Calculate the total area of the two desktops.

(d) Calculate the percentage of the floor covered by the two desks together. Give your answer correct to the nearest whole number.

6   Figure 5 shows a plan of a back garden.

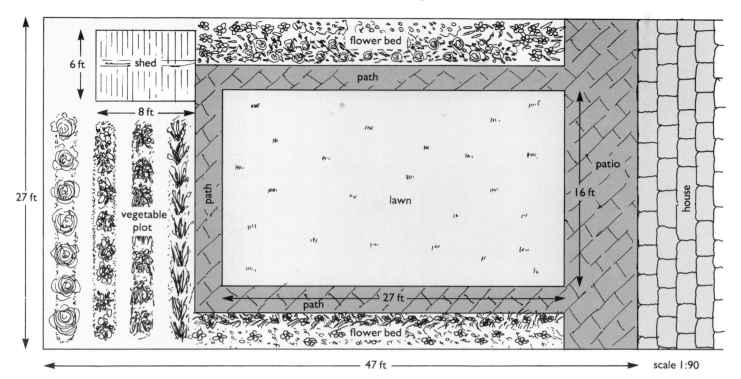

Figure 5

(a) Estimate, without calculating, the percentage of the garden that is lawn.

(b) Estimate, without calculating, the percentage of the garden covered by the shed.

(c) Calculate the area of the garden.

(d) Calculate the area of the lawn.

(e) Calculate the percentage of the garden that is lawn. Does the lawn cover more or less than half of the garden?

(f) Calculate the percentage of the garden covered by the shed.

(g) What is the percentage of the garden **not** covered by the shed?

7   Look at the bedroom plan shown in figure 6 on page 52. It is drawn accurately to a scale of 1:25 (one twenty-fifth of the real size).

Use your ruler to help you answer the following questions. Be as accurate as you can.

(a) How long (in mm) is the bedroom on the plan?

(b) How long (in m) is the bedroom really?

(c) How wide is the bedroom on the plan?

(d) How wide is the bedroom really?

(e) How wide is the window on the plan? (The width of the window does **not** mean how thick the glass is!)

(f) How wide is the window really?

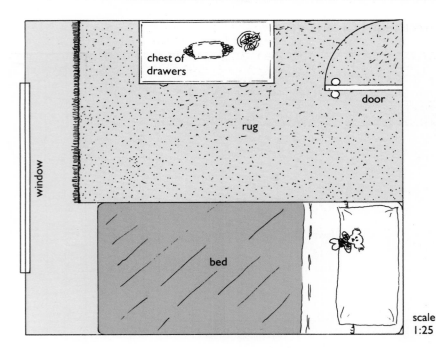

Figure 6

(g) What is the area of the bedroom floor on the plan?

(h) What is the area of the bedroom floor really? (This is **not** 25 times the answer to (g).)

(i) What is the length and the width of the bed on the plan?

(j) What is the length and the width of the bed really?

(k) What area of the floor does the bed cover?

(l) Part of the floor has been covered by a large rug. What is the actual length of the rug? What is its width? What is its area?

8   (a) What percentage of the floor of the bedroom in question 7 is covered by the rug?

(b) Approximately what fraction of the floor is covered by the rug?

(c) What percentage of the floor is covered by the bed?

9   Look at the bedroom plan shown in figure 7.

(a) Copy this plan which is drawn accurately to a scale of 1:25. Make sure your copy is exactly the same size as this plan.

Figure 7

(b) Someone wants to move the bed and chest of drawers from the bedroom of question 7 into this bedroom. They also want to put two wardrobes in this bedroom. The first wardrobe is 1.22 m wide, 0.41 m deep and 1.63 m high. The second wardrobe is 0.94 m wide, 0.55 m deep and 1.87 m high.

Think of a sensible arrangement of the bed, the chest of drawers and the two wardrobes in the bedroom. Show the positions of these items of furniture on the plan you have just drawn.

10　(a) What is the area of the floor of the bedroom in question 9?

(b) What percentage of the floor is covered by the bed?

(c) Why is your answer to question 10(b) smaller than your answer to question 8(c)?

(d) What percentage of the floor of the bedroom is not covered by *any* furniture?

11　The height of the bedroom in question 9 is 2.3 m. Find the percentage of the volume of the bedroom which is taken up by the two wardrobes.

SECTION B

1　A shop is advertising a television costing £299.99. A similar television can be rented for £10.99 a month.

After how many months will the money paid out in rental be more than the cost of buying the television?

2　In 1988 a shop was advertising a colour television and video package which could be rented for £18.99 a month. There was a special offer; the second month would be free: no rent would be charged that month.

(a) How much would it cost to rent this television and video for a year?

(b) What is the average monthly cost over this year?

3　Electricity bills are usually sent four times a year. You pay for the electricity you have used in the previous three months.

(a) If somebody is sent electricity bills in March, June, September and December which bill is likely to be the biggest? Why?

(b) Which bill is likely to be the smallest? Why?

4　When someone receives an electricity bill they might check it to make sure a mistake has not been made.

Someone receives the bill shown in figure 8.

(a) How much is the bill for?

(b) What does **standing charge** mean?

(c) One way of checking the bill is to see if it is reasonable. Which of the following facts would make you think that a mistake had been made with this bill?

If you want to design pleasant surroundings in which to live you need to think, not only about the space available, but also about heating, decorating and furnishing it.

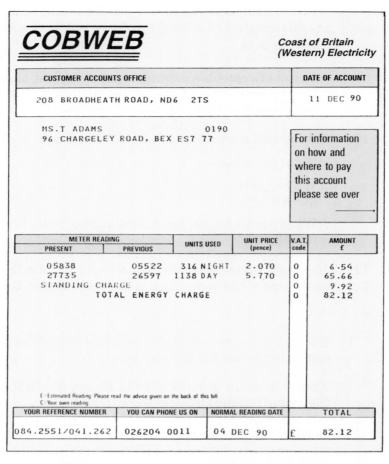

Figure 8

A The final reading shown on the bill is not the same as the reading on the meter on the day the bill is received.

B The bill for the previous three months (sent in September 1990) was only £27.

C The bill for December 1989 was only £42.

D The standing charge was only £9.92.

(*d*) What mistake do you think might have been made with the bill?

5   The electricity bill shown in figure 9 is for a household which pays less for electricity used at night than for electricity used during the day.

(*a*) How much is being charged for electricity used at night?

(*b*) How much is being charged for electricity used during the day?

(*c*) Suppose the people in this house had been able to change the times they did certain things, like washing clothes. Suppose they used 100 units **more** electricity at night and 100 units **less** electricity during the day. By how much would their electricity bill be reduced?

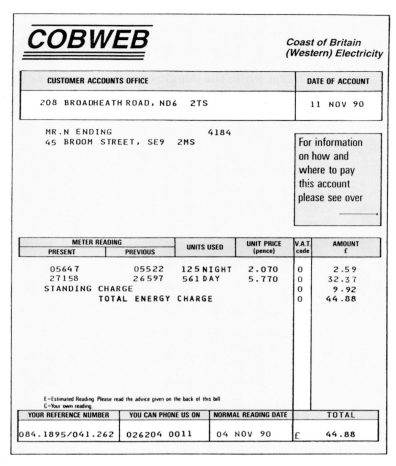

COBWEB

*Coast of Britain
(Western) Electricity*

CUSTOMER ACCOUNTS OFFICE	DATE OF ACCOUNT
208 BROADHEATH ROAD, ND6 2TS	11 NOV 90

MR. N ENDING 4184
45 BROOM STREET, SE9 2MS

For information
on how and
where to pay
this account
please see over

METER READING		UNITS USED	UNIT PRICE (pence)	V.A.T. code	AMOUNT £
PRESENT	PREVIOUS				
05647	05522	125 NIGHT	2.070	0	2.59
27158	26597	561 DAY	5.770	0	32.37
STANDING CHARGE				0	9.92
	TOTAL ENERGY CHARGE			0	44.88

E=Estimated Reading. Please read the advice given on the back of this bill.
C=Your own reading.

YOUR REFERENCE NUMBER	YOU CAN PHONE US ON	NORMAL READING DATE	TOTAL
084.1895/041.262	026204 0011	04 NOV 90	£ 44.88

Figure 9

6 Get the resource sheet called '*Dials*'.

A house has an immersion heater to heat the water. The immersion heater is fitted with a timer switch. This switch has a dial. There are two copies of this dial labelled question 8 on the resource sheet.

The switch is controlled by placing pins in the holes in the dial. A pin in the inside ring turns the heater on, and a pin in the outside ring turns the heater off.

(*a*) In the house the first person to get up in the morning gets out of bed at 7 a.m. The first person back in the evening arrives home at 5 p.m.

The people in the house decide to have the water coming on for 1 hour in the morning and for 2 hours in the evening. They want it to come on half an hour before the first person gets up or comes home.

Mark on the first dial where the pins should be placed.

(b) After a while the people in the house decide that the immersion heater is not on for long enough. It needs to come on a quarter of an hour earlier in the morning and go off three quarters of an hour later in the evening.

Mark on the second dial where the pins should now be placed.

7 Look at the plan of the bedroom shown in figure 10. The height of this bedroom is 2.3 m. The height of the window is 1.15 m and the height of the door is 2 m.

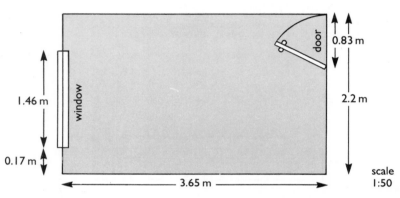

Figure 10

(a) The walls of the bedroom are to be painted with an emulsion paint. Find the approximate area of the walls to be painted.

(b) It says on a tin of emulsion paint that 1 litre of paint covers approximately 10 square metres of wall.

How many litres are required to give the walls of the bedroom two coats of paint?

8 The cash price of a television is £299.99. The shop selling it also offers credit. The terms of the credit are as shown:

★ A deposit ★ of £29.99
24 monthly payments of £15.08

(a) What is the total credit price?

(b) How much extra do you pay for the television if you buy it on credit?

(c) What percentage of the cash price is the extra amount paid for credit?

(d) You finish paying for your television after two years. So if you divide the answer to (c) by 2 you might think this would give you the annual rate of interest for your credit loan.

But the shop has, by law, to give the annual rate of interest. This is actually 34.2%. Explain why it is a lot more than half the answer to (c).

9   It is found that heating bills for a house amount to £300 per year.

One way of reducing heating bills would be to improve the insulation of the house which is very poor at present.

20% of heat is lost through the roof, and loft insulation would cost about £150.

25% of the heat is lost through windows and this could be halved by installing double glazing at a cost of about £2000.

(*a*) How long would it take to recover the cost of loft insulation in the form of reduced heating bills?

(*b*) How long would it take to recover the cost of double glazing in the form of reduced heating bills?

(*c*) If both were installed how long would it take to recover the cost in the form of reduced heating bills?

(*d*) Why do your answers to (*a*), (*b*) and (*c*) probably significantly overestimate the time taken to recover the cost of insulation?

10   Instead of being painted the walls of the bedroom described in question 7 are to be papered. The wallpaper to be used comes in rolls which are 52 cm wide and 10.05 m long.

How many rolls are required to paper the bedroom?

11   The cost of a particular carpet is given in figure 11.

SOLD IN 4m WIDTHS
(of any length).
Price is £12.99
per square yard.

Figure 11

How much would it cost to carpet the floor of the bedroom described in question 7 with this carpet?

(1 metre = 1.09 yards)

FURTHER COURSEWORK TASKS

1⟩   Redesign your bedroom.

Choose furniture from catalogues, find how much it costs and plan where it will fit. Find out the cost of carpets, paint, wallpaper and light fittings.

2⟩   Choose one of your hobbies which regularly costs you money. Suitable hobbies include keeping a pet, keeping a horse, running a moped, fishing or playing in a pop group.

Find the average monthly cost of your hobby. To do this, make a list of all your expenses in connection with the hobby. Collect bills if possible. Don't forget expenses such as transport costs or vet's fees.

3) Choose a cuddly toy, such as a teddy bear, and design clothes for it.

Clothes can be either knitted or sewn. Make sure that they fit.

4) Measure your garden and draw a plan. Redesign your garden and work out what the cost for your new garden will be.

You may want to include lawns, paths, patios, flower beds, vegetable plots, a greenhouse, a garden shed, garden furniture and ornaments.

You will probably need to visit a garden shop or garden centre to find out prices. For example, seeds and fertiliser (and perhaps bean sticks or soft fruit netting) will need to be bought for a vegetable garden. Paving slabs might be bought for a path or a patio.

5〉 Measure each of the rooms in your house.

Draw a plan of each floor of your house as accurately as possible. Think carefully about how much detail you are going to show.

either

Make a scale model of your house out of cardboard.

or

Draw plans for your 'ideal house'. Say how and why your ideal house differs from the house you live in.

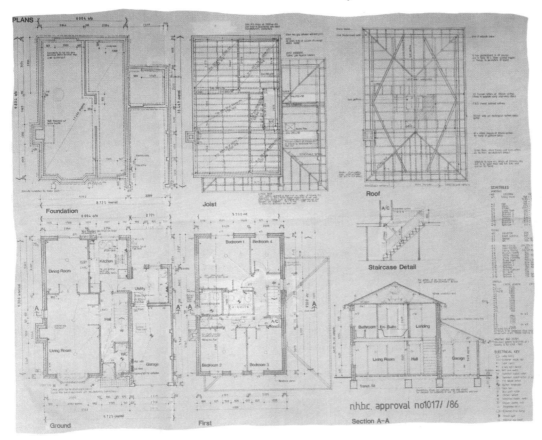

6〉 Work out the running costs of the house in which you live. You will need to look at bills for items such as rent or mortgage, fuel (electricity, gas, oil, solid fuel) and repairs.

You might be able to compare the cost of running your house with the cost of running another house, such as your grandparents' house.

You might want to look at the insulation you have at present, and to consider ways of improving it. You could find out the cost of hot tank insulation, roofing insulation, double glazing, draught-proofing and wall insulation. You could estimate the savings to your heating bills as a result of improved insulation. You might also want to investigate the hazards that might arise from insulation which is too effective, if this results in houses which are not adequately ventilated.

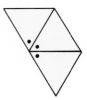

Get the resource sheet 'Regular polygons'.

Alternatively, use the computer program 'Tilekit'.

● Trace an equilateral triangle. Mark one of the corners clearly. Draw another equilateral triangle next to it touching the marked corner; and another; keep going.

You will finish up with this.

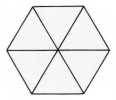

● Try the same idea with other regular polygons, squares, pentagons, hexagons, septagons, octagons, . . .

For pentagons you will get this

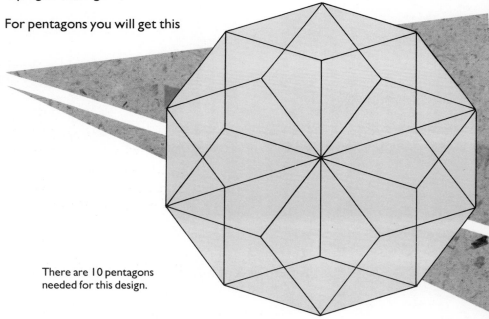

There are 10 pentagons needed for this design.

Be careful to make your drawings accurate. Otherwise you will not know when the pattern is complete.

● For each polygon you use, record how many times you need to draw the polygon to complete the pattern. Try to explain your findings.

SECTION A

Look at the pattern of squares below.

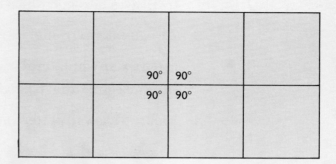

The reason why squares fit together to give this pattern is that the angle at the corner of a square is a right angle (or 90°). You need four right angles (or 360°) to fill the space around a point.

1 (a) Look at the pattern of equilateral triangles in figure 1.

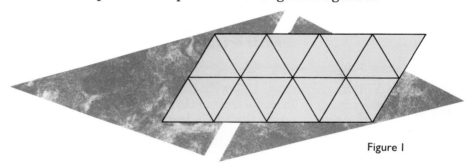

Figure 1

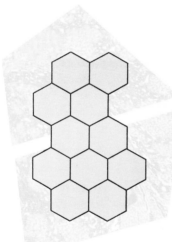

Figure 2

How many triangles are needed to fill the space around a point? What is the angle at the corner of an equilateral triangle?

(b) In the pattern of regular hexagons seen in figure 2, how many hexagons are needed to fill the space round a point? What is the angle at the corner of a regular hexagon?

A **regular polygon** is a polygon which has all sides the same length *and* all angles equal.

The picture below shows a hexagon. All its sides are the same length. But it is **not** a regular hexagon, because its angles are not all equal.

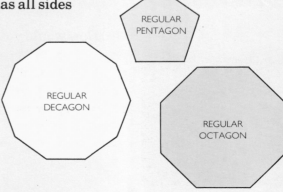

2 (a) Draw a different hexagon which has all its sides equal but which is not regular.

(b) Draw a hexagon which has its angles equal but which is not regular.

3 An equilateral triangle is a triangle which has all its sides equal.

(a) Draw an equilateral triangle.

(b) Is an equilateral triangle always a regular polygon?

4 Figure 3 shows a pattern of regular octagons and squares.

Figure 3

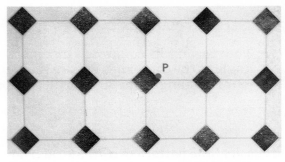

How many octagons and how many squares are used to fill the space round the point P? Use this to calculate the angle at the corner of a regular octagon.

You might be familiar with the *Logo* 'turtle' which is controlled by a computer. To move the turtle around the floor you give it commands such as the following:

```
FD    100
RT     70
FD     80
LT    120
```

The first command tells the turtle to move forward 100 units. The second command tells the turtle to turn to the right through 70°. The fourth command tells the turtle to turn to the left through 120°.

Turtles usually have 'pens' so that they can draw their path as they move along.

5 (a) How would you get the turtle to draw the path shown in figure 4?

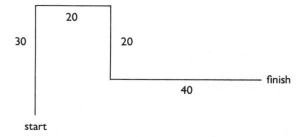

Figure 4

(b) If you gave the turtle the following set of instructions draw accurately what the turtle would draw.

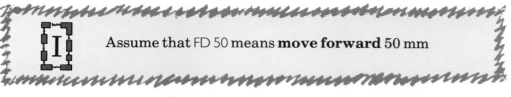

Assume that FD 50 means **move forward** 50 mm

FD	50
RT	90
FD	40
LT	60
FD	30
LT	140
FD	60

Use *Logo* on a computer when answering the questions 6 to 10

 6 What set of instructions could you give to a turtle so that it draws a square and ends up facing in the same direction as it started?

7 What instructions would you give to a turtle so that it draws an equilateral triangle and ends up facing in the same direction as it started?

 8 (a) What instruction could you give the turtle so that it rotates round once and ends up facing in the same direction as it started?

(b) What instruction could you give the turtle so that it rotates enough to turn round three times?

 9 What instructions could you give the turtle to get it to draw a regular hexagon and end up facing in the same direction as it started?

10 What instructions would you give the turtle to get it to draw a regular pentagon?

 11 Look at figure 5.

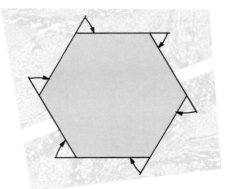

If the turtle were to draw this hexagon the angles it would turn through are marked.

Figure 5

(a) What is the total amount the turtle turns through altogether?

(b) What angle does the turtle turn through at each corner?

(c) What does this tell you about the angle at the corner of a hexagon?

The angle the turtle turns through when drawing a polygon is called the **exterior angle**. The angle at the corner of the polygon is called the **interior angle**.

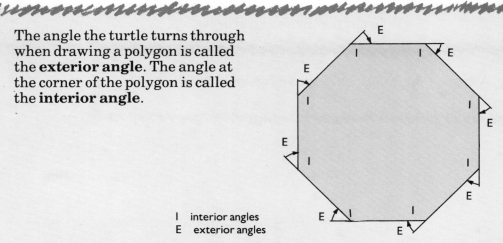

I   interior angles
E   exterior angles

12 (a) All the exterior angles of a regular octagon are equal. How big is one of them?

(b) All the interior angles of a regular octagon are equal. How big is one of them?

13 (a) Copy and complete the table below by finding the exterior and interior angles of the polygons listed.

	exterior angle	interior angle
equilateral triangle square regular pentagon (5 sides) regular hexagon (6 sides) regular septagon (7 sides) regular octagon (8 sides) regular nonagon (9 sides) regular decagon (10 sides) regular polygon with 11 sides regular dodecagon (12 sides)		

(b) (i) What is the exterior angle of a regular polygon with N sides?
(ii) What is the interior angle?

14 (a) Draw a graph showing the size of an interior angle (I) of a regular polygon plotted against the number of sides (N). Use 1 cm for one unit on the horizontal axis and 1 cm for 10° on the vertical axis.

(b) Write down a formula connecting I to N. Check the formula by using a graphical calculator or a graph plotter on the computer.

15 (a) Join up the points on the graph you drew for question 14 with a smooth curve. What is the value of I on this curve when N is 2? Can you interpret this result in terms of polygons?

(b) Look at the point on your curve at which N is $2\frac{1}{2}$. What is the value of I? If you use your formula rather than the graph you should get a more accurate answer.

Is it possible to have a regular polygon with $2\frac{1}{2}$ sides? Try drawing it. You should be able to do this. After all, you know the size of the angle at the corner of this polygon.

(c) Now draw a regular polygon with $2\frac{2}{3}$ sides.

(d) In chapter 2 circle patterns were explained. What number of points and what rule would produce a circle pattern with $2\frac{1}{2}$ sides?

(e) What number of points and what rule would produce a circle pattern with $2\frac{2}{3}$ sides?

SECTION B

For several of the questions in this section you will either need the resource sheet 'Regular polygons' or you will need regular polygons (triangle, square, pentagon, hexagon, etc) to draw round.

Two regular hexagons and two triangles can be used together to fill the space round a point.

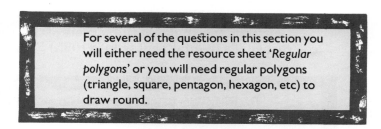
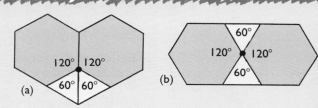

There are two ways in which the shapes can be arranged. Either the two hexagons can be next to each other, as shown in (a), or they can be opposite each other, as shown in (b).

1 One regular hexagon can be used together with equilateral triangles to fill the space round a point. Draw a picture to show this. Mark the sizes of the angles round the point in the same way as in the diagrams in the box above.

2 A mixture of squares and equilateral triangles can be used together to fill the space round a point. Figure 6 shows the start of this.

How many squares and how many triangles are needed if the space round a point is to be filled?

Draw pictures to show the different ways the squares and triangles can be arranged round the point. In each picture mark in the sizes of the angles round the point.

Figure 6

3 Squares, triangles and regular hexagons can be used together to fill the space round a point. Figure 7 shows one arrangement.

Draw the other arrangements which are possible.

Figure 7

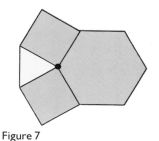

4 What regular polygons, other than squares and hexagons, can be used together with equilateral triangles to fill the space round a point? Draw pictures showing all the possible arrangements. In each picture mark in the sizes of the angles round the point.

5 Figure 8 shows a ring formed of six regular pentagons.

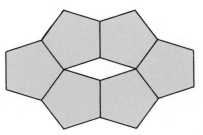

Figure 8

(a) Copy figure 8 and mark in the lines of symmetry.

(b) The shape in the middle of the ring is a rhombus, because its sides are all of equal length.

Calculate the angles at the corners of this rhombus. (The angle at each corner of a regular pentagon is 108°.)

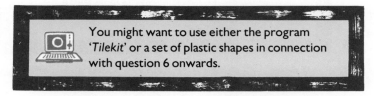

You might want to use either the program 'Tilekit' or a set of plastic shapes in connection with question 6 onwards.

6 (a) Draw a ring made from eight regular pentagons.

(b) Different rings can be made from ten regular pentagons. Draw pictures to show the possibilities.

7 Figure 9 shows a ring of six squares and six triangles.

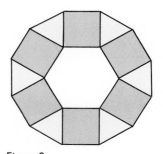

Figure 9

(a) Draw a ring of six squares and six hexagons.

(b) Draw a ring of four squares and four hexagons.

(c) Draw two different rings of six squares and three hexagons.

A ring can be named by describing the shape of the hole in the middle. For example, the ring made of squares and triangles, which is shown in figure 9, could be called a regular hexagon ring of size 1.

The picture adjacent shows a square ring of size 2.

8 (a) How many squares are required to make a square ring of size 3?

(b) How many squares are required to make a square ring of size N?

(c) Suppose that the number of squares needed for a square ring of size N is 100.

(i) Write down an equation satisfied by N.
(ii) Solve the equation to find N.

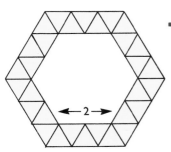

Figure 10

9 It is possible to make regular hexagon rings using only triangles. Figure 10 shows a regular hexagon ring of size 2.

(a) How many triangles are required to make a ring of size 1?

(b) How many triangles are required to make a ring of size N?

(c) Suppose that the number of triangles needed to make a ring of size r is 450.

(i) Write down an equation satisfied by r.
(ii) Solve the equation to find r.

10 Figure 11 shows how squares and triangles can be used to make a dodecagon ring of size 1.

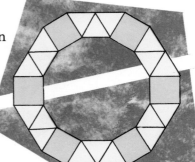

Figure 11

(a) How many squares and how many triangles are required to make a regular dodecagon ring of size 2?

(b) How many squares and how many triangles are needed to make a regular dodecagon ring of size N?

(c) When a dodecagon ring of size x is made it is found that the number of triangles needed is 60 more than the number of squares needed.

(i) Write down an equation satisfied by x.
(ii) Solve this equation to find x.

11 In a large collection of plastic squares and triangles there are exactly enough squares to make a square ring of size x and exactly enough triangles to make a regular hexagon ring, also of size x.

The rings are broken up and the shapes are rearranged to make a regular dodecagon ring of size y. All the squares are used in this ring, but there are 60 triangles left over.

(a) By considering the number of squares in each of the rings show that

$$4x + 4 = 6y$$

(b) By considering the number of triangles in each of the rings write down another equation connecting x and y.

(c) Solve the equations simultaneously, and hence find the total number of shapes in the collection.

There are more questions about simultaneous equations in section H of chapter 11 on page 164 and in Review Exercise 25, Equations 1, on page 235.

SECTION C

Look at the picture shown alongside.

This picture shows a design composed of a number of identical triangles.

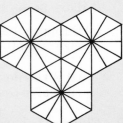

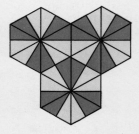 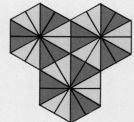

The pictures below show the same design coloured in.

Only one colour has been used for each little triangle. In the first picture the design has been coloured to show that kites will exactly cover the design. In the second case it has been coloured to show the design exactly covered by equilateral triangles.

> If you are not sure of the meanings of the shapes named in questions 1 and 2 look at the section called *'Triangles and quadrilaterals'* on page 246.

1 Get a copy of the resource sheet called *'Polygon designs'*. As well as kites and equilateral triangles there are other shapes which can be used to cover the design exactly. Colour in copies of the design on the resource sheet to show other shapes which can be used instead of kites or equilateral triangles. Find as many different shapes as possible which will do this. You can, for example, use rhombuses and trapeziums as well as several other shapes.

2 Look at figure 12.

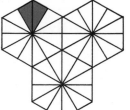 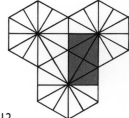

The area of the kite shown in the first picture is $\frac{1}{18}$ of the area of the whole design. The rectangle in the second picture is $\frac{1}{6}$ of the whole design.

Figure 12

The shapes referred to are shapes you can see in the design without adding extra lines to the design.

What fraction of the whole design are each of the following?

(a) the largest regular hexagon you can find.

(b) the smallest equilateral triangle.

(c) the largest equilateral triangle.

(d) the largest rectangle.

(e) the smallest rectangle.

(f) the largest rhombus.

(g) the smallest rhombus.

(h) the largest parallelogram.

(i) the largest trapezium.

(j) the largest hexagon (not necessarily regular).

3 Figure 13 shows one of the small triangles in the design coloured in. Calculate the size of each of the angles of this triangle.

4 Get the sheet called *'Parallel lines'*.

(a) Explain what parallel lines are.

(b) Look at the pattern labelled 1 on the *'Parallel lines'* sheet. One of the angles is labelled A. Colour in all the angles which are the same size as A.

(c) One of the angles is labelled B. Using a different colour, colour in all the angles which are the same size as B.

(d) In another grid of a similar type angle A is 50°. What is angle B?

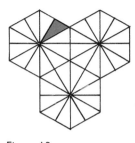

Figure 13

5 Look at figure 14. Find x and y.

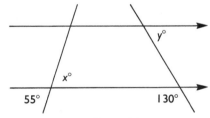

Figure 14

6

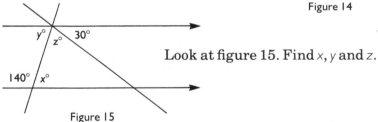

Look at figure 15. Find x, y and z.

Figure 15

7 (a) Look at the pattern labelled 2 on the *'Parallel lines'* sheet. One of the angles is labelled A. Colour in all the angles which are the same size as A.

(b) One of the angles is labelled B. Using a different colour, colour in all the angles which are the same size as B.

(c) One of the angles is labelled C. Using a different colour, colour in all the angles which are the same size as C.

(d) Look at the point on this pattern which is marked with a cross.

(i) How many angles of each colour fill the space round this point?
(ii) Using (i) and your picture, write down how you would explain to someone who did not know why the sum of the angles of a triangle is 180°.

Here is a different explanation that the sum of the angles of a triangle is 180°.

Imagine you are using a *Logo* turtle to draw a triangle. If the turtle draws the triangle and ends up facing the same way as it started the angles it turns through are the shaded angles in the picture.

When drawing the triangle the turtle turns right round once. So it turns through 360°. So the sum of the shaded angles is 360°.

You will provide the rest of the explanation by answering question 8.

8 (*a*) What do you know about the sum of the angles marked *a* and *b* in the drawing above? What do you know about *c* and *d*? *e* and *f*?

(*b*) What does this tell you about the sum of the angles of a triangle?

9 Use a method similar to the method used in question 8 to show that the sum of the angles of a quadrilateral is 360°.

SECTION D

Rangoli patterns are used by Hindu and Sikh families to decorate their homes during festivals such as Divali.

Here is how a Rangoli pattern is made.

Draw a few lines on a grid of square dots.

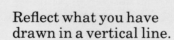

Reflect what you have drawn in a vertical line.

Now reflect in a horizontal line.

Now reflect in a diagonal line.

The final result can be coloured in some appropriate way.

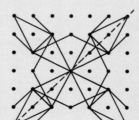

1   Using a sheet of square dot paper, choose some different starting lines and create a Rangoli pattern.

   A translation means a slide across the page without any rotation.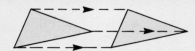

2   In which of the pictures seen in figure 16 is the shape on the right a translation of the shape on the left?

(a) 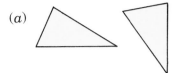   (b) (c) (d)

Figure 16

(e)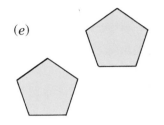

   Squares tessellate. You can change a square into another shape that tessellates like this.

First change one side of the square, like this.

Now translate this side across the square to produce this.

This gives a new shape.

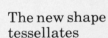

The new shape tessellates

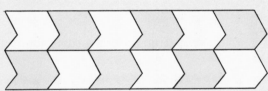

3   Carry out the process shown in the box above. Choose your own first change instead of the one shown in the box.

   The method explained in the previous box can be taken a step further.

First change two sides of a square, like this.

Now translate these sides across the square to produce this.

This gives a new shape. This new shape tessellates.

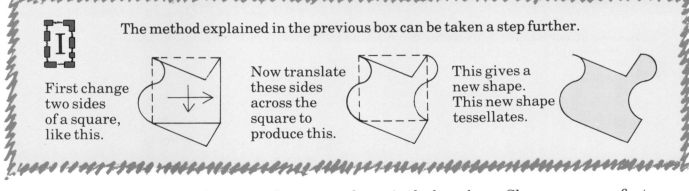

4   Carry out the process shown in the box above. Choose your own first change.

The artist, M.C. Escher, used this method to produce the tessellation shown opposite.

5 Repeat the process described in the box before question 4, but start with a parallelogram.

Choose your own first move.

6 Repeat the process described in the box before question 4 on a regular hexagon.

Choose your own first move. Your first move can be to change two of the sides of the hexagon, or even three of the sides if you want.

7 The hexagon you use for the process described in the box before question 4 does not have to be regular, but the sides do have to satisfy certain conditions. What are these?

8 Why can you not apply the process described in the box before question 4 to an equilateral triangle?

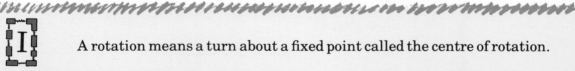

A rotation means a turn about a fixed point called the centre of rotation.

9 Get a copy of the resource sheet called '*Rotations*'. In each diagram the shaded shape is a rotation of the unshaded shape.

Mark the centre of rotation in each case. Also write down the angle through which the shape has been rotated.

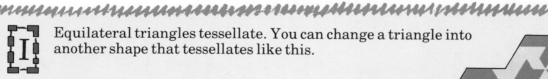

Equilateral triangles tessellate. You can change a triangle into another shape that tessellates like this.

First change one side of the triangle, like this.

Now rotate this side through 60° about one of its ends. You get this.

This gives a new shape.

The new shape tessellates

10 Carry out the process shown in the previous box. Choose your own first change.

This is the shape described in the box before question 10.

 What happens if you rotate the side again?

 The shape produced in this way does not tessellate.

But you will produce a tesselating shape if the changed side has rotational symmetry about its mid-point.

This new shape tessellates.

11 Carry out the process shown in the box above, but choose your own first change. Remember that your new side must have rotational symmetry about its mid-point.

1⟩ The photographs below show Islamic mosaics which use tessellations.

Draw accurately some tessellations. The mosaics shown in figure 17 might provide some ideas to get you started.

Use what you know about the size of the angles of the polygons to check that they fit together exactly round each point.

You might want to colour your tessellations systematically, and to explain the colouring systems you use.

You might want to find out more about Islamic mosaics.

2⟩ Produce some artistic tessellations by using the methods explained in *Section D*.

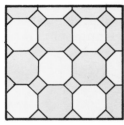
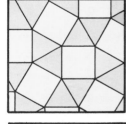
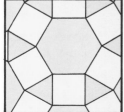

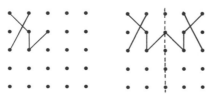 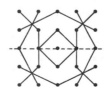 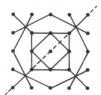

Figure 17

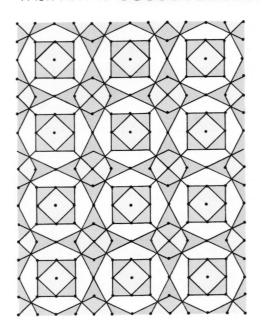

If you are able to use *Logo* which has multiple turtles you might want to use it to create your Rangoli patterns. The resource sheet called *'Rangoli patterns with multiple turtles'* might help you to get started.

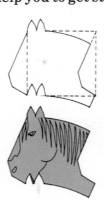

Explain clearly the methods you use to produce the tessellations.

3⟩ A deltahedron is a solid, all the faces of which are equilateral triangles.

A tetrahedron is a deltahedron with 4 faces (see figure 18).

Can you make a deltahedron with 5 faces?
Can you make a deltahedron with 6 faces?

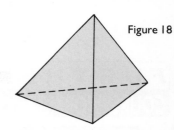

Figure 18

What number of faces can a deltahedron have? Make deltahedra which are different from one another but still have the same number of faces.

4⟩ Figure 19 shows a ring of 10 pentagons.

 Use *'Tilekit'* to investigate rings of pentagons. Are there other rings of 10 pentagons? How many different rings are there of 12 pentagons? What about other numbers of pentagons?

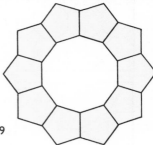

Figure 19

Figure 20 shows a ring of squares and octagons.

 Use *'Tilekit'* to investigate rings consisting of two, or three different shapes. Some possibilities are:

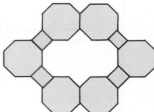

Figure 20

squares and hexagons
squares and pentagons
triangles, squares and hexagons

You might want to look at the shapes of the holes in the middle of your rings. You might also want to investigate the symmetry of your rings.

7 STATISTICAL EXPERIMENTS

You are going to do an experiment to measure how fast your reactions are. For this experiment you will need a 30 cm ruler and a partner.

If you are going to be first to have your reactions measured, sit comfortably with your right elbow on your desk or table (or your left elbow if you are left-handed). Put out the thumb and finger of your hand, ready to catch the ruler.

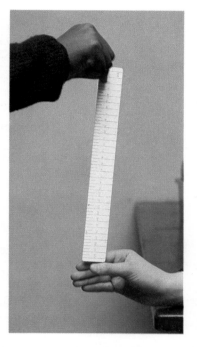

If you are the other person, hold the 30 cm ruler so that the bottom of it is level with your partner's hand.

When your partner is ready you will let the ruler drop, *without* telling your partner exactly when you are going to do this. Your partner will catch the ruler as quickly as possible. You can read the scale on the ruler to decide the distance the ruler fell before it was caught.

You and your partner will need to discuss what points to watch out for to make the experiment as accurate and reliable as possible. For example, how accurately are you going to measure? How far apart will your fingers be at the start?

Working in pairs:

- do the ruler experiment ten times, so that you have ten distances written down;

- now change places with your partner and repeat the process.

Both of you will now have ten measurements.

There are several different things you can now do.

- Decide which of you has quicker reactions.

- Repeat the experiment, but this time use your other hand. How much better are you with one hand than you are with the other?

- Collect together a list of results for about six people. *You will need these for the questions in Section A.*

- Use the results to find out how much different people vary in their reactions.

- Discuss with other people in the class a fair way of comparing different people's speeds of reaction.

SECTION A

Here are the results six students obtained when they did the ruler experiment with a 30 cm ruler. Each number in the table records the distance the ruler dropped, measured in cm.

Ha	Sue	Sam	Gurjeet	Mehreen	Clive
13.5	10	7.5	16	11.5	14
5.5	1	16	21	6.5	9
5.5	21	8	8	12	7.5
13.5	8	10	3	9.5	3.5
3	7	2.5	11	11	3.5
9.5	12	2	5	14	6.5
11.5	10	17	11	9	3
11.5	17	14	17	4.5	8
2.5	5	10	16	10	8
4	7	2	9	15	6

1 Gurjeet's worst distance was 21 cm and his best distance was 3 cm.

(a) What was Ha's best distance?

(b) What was Ha's worst distance?

(c) What was Sam's second best distance?

(d) What was Mehreen's third worst distance?

(e) Who had the worst distance of all, and what was it?

(f) Who had the best distance of all and what was it?

2 Answer similar questions for the sets of results you have collected for people in your class.

The ten results for a particular person are not all the same. Sometimes your reactions are quicker because you are concentrating more, or because you are lucky perhaps.

One way of measuring how consistent you are with your ten tries is to work out the **range** for your results. You do this by subtracting the smallest result from the largest.

Gurjeet's largest result is 21 cm and his smallest result is 3 cm. So the range for Gurjeet's results is 21 − 3 = 18 cm.

3 (a) What is Mehreen's largest result? What is her smallest result? What is the range for Mehreen's results?

(b) What is the range for Ha's results?

4 Look at the results you collected for people in your class.

(a) What is the range of each set of results?

(b) The most consistent person is the person whose results vary least. (This means the results have the smallest range.) Which person is most consistent?

(c) Which person is least consistent?

To see who has the fastest reactions you need to be able to compare the results for one student with the results for another student.

You could compare people's *best* results. Or you could compare their *worst* results. Most people think it is fairer to compare their *middle* results. You might decide to do this because the best results might have been luck and the worst results might have been due to a sudden loss of concentration. So you might decide that the middle result gives the best indication of what someone can really do.

The *middle* result is often called the **median** result.

Here are Sue's 10 results arranged in order of size:

1, 5, 7, 7, 8, 10, 10, 12, 17, 21

In this case, because there are 10 results (an even number) there is no middle result. There are two results in the middle: 8 and 10. To find Sue's *median* result you take the number which is half way between these two: 9.

5   Look at the results you collected for people in your class.

(*a*) Find the median of the results for each person.

(*b*) If you decide to use the medians to compare people's reactions:

(i) which person has the fastest reactions?
(ii) which person has the slowest reactions?

Another method of comparing reaction speeds is to use the **mean** result for each student. (Sometimes people call this the average.)

To calculate the mean of a set of results you add all the results up and then divide by the number of results.

If you add up all Sue's results you get 98 cm. There are ten results, and so you divide by 10. So the *mean* of Sue's results is $98 \div 10 = 9.8$ cm.

6   Look at the results you collected for people in your class.

(*a*) Find the mean of the results for each person.

(*b*) If you decide to use the means to compare people's reactions:

(i) which person has the fastest reactions?
(ii) which person has the slowest reactions?

7 Mary's first nine results are

   11, 4, 12.5, 8, 14, 5.5, 14.5, 15, 8.5

What would Mary's tenth result need to be for Mary's average to be the same as Sue's average, which is 9.8?

8 Here are Sanjay's first eight results:

   11, 17, 14, 12, 20, 18, 10, 4.

The mean for Sanjay's ten results is 14.2. The median for Sanjay's ten results is 14.5.

What are Sanjay's last two results?

Dave	Tina
6	9.5
7	12.5
—	3
25	10
4	8
7	8.5
18	7.5
16	
14	
16	

Here are the results Dave and Tina got when they did the experiment with a 30 cm ruler.

The dash means that on one of the trials Dave dropped the ruler completely.

Tina only had seven results because she had to leave school early to play for a sports team.

9 Look at Tina's results.

   (a) What is the median of Tina's results?

   (b) What is the mean of Tina's results?

   (c) What is the range of Tina's results?

   (d) Does the result for (c) tell you clearly that Tina is more consistent than Ha, Sue, Sam, Gurjeet, Mehreen and Clive? Give a reason for your answer.

10 Look at Dave's results. There are only nine real results, because the tenth result could not be recorded.

   (a) Do you think that a fair way of comparing Dave's results with the others would be to ignore the drop and pretend that Dave had only had nine tries?

   Give a reason for your answer.

   (b) What do you think should be the median of Dave's results?

   (c) What can you say about the mean of Dave's results?

   (d) What can you say about the range of Dave's results?

11 Which is a fairer way of comparing people's reactions: to compare the medians, or to compare the means?

Give a reason for your answer.

Questions 3 and 4 were about finding the *range* of sets of results by subtracting the smallest result from the largest.

Some people might not think that this is a very good way of measuring how consistent people are. After all, one of the results might have been a real fluke. Or you might have lost your concentration completely for one, but really be quite consistent otherwise.

So some people use a different method of calculating how spread out results are which ignores the results at either end. They calculate something called the **interquartile range**. If you have a list of the results in order of size, the interquartile range is the difference between the results one quarter of the way down the list and the result three quarters of the way down.

Here are Sue's results.

```
   bottom 25%      middle 50%      top 25%

   1   5   7   7   8   10   10   12   17   21
               ↑                    ↑
```

The interquartile range is $12 - 7 = 5$ cm.

12 Look at the results you collected for people in your class.

(*a*) Find the interquartile range for each set of results.

(*b*) If interquartile range is used as the measure of consistency, which person is most consistent and which person is least consistent?

13 Ha's and Sue's results have already been entered in the table below. Copy and complete it so that it shows all 60 of the results of Ha, Sue, Sam, Gurjeet, Mehreen and Clive.

> This interval includes all measurements of 5 or more but less than 10

Distance dropped (cm)	Tally	Frequency
0 –	IIII	
5 –	⊞ II	
10 –	⊞	
15 –	I	
20 –	I	
25 –		

> This means the number of measurements in the interval

Now copy and complete the histogram seen in figure 1 which shows the 60 results which you have entered in your table.

14 Draw a histogram to show the results you collected for people in your class.

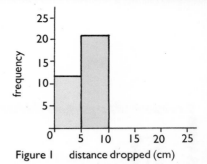

Figure I distance dropped (cm)

The table below shows all the results for all the eight students: Ha, Sue, Sam, Gurjeet, Mehreen, Clive, Dave and Tina.

Distance dropped (cm)	0 –	5 –	10 –	15 –	20 –	25 –	30 –
Frequency	15	28	19	11	2	1	1

To estimate the mean from this table you do the following.

A For each interval you need a typical result for that interval. (Usually the midpoint of the interval is used to give the typical result. For example, in the interval 15 cm to 20 cm the typical result is taken to be 17.5 cm.) Multiply this by the frequency for that interval.

B Add all these products up.

C Divide by the total number of results (which is the sum of the frequencies)

So an estimate for the mean of the results in the table above is

$$(15 \times 2.5 + 28 \times 7.5 + 19 \times 12.5 + 11 \times 17.5 + 2 \times 22.5 + 1 \times 27.5 + 1 \times 32.5) \div 77$$

$$= 10.2 \text{ correct to one decimal place.}$$

<u>15</u> (a) The table below shows the results for the four girls: Ha, Sue, Mehreen and Tina.

Distance dropped (cm)	0 –	5 –	10 –	15 –	20 –
Frequency	6	14	14	2	1

Calculate an estimate of the mean of these results.

(b) Someone decides to use an interval of 3 instead of 5 when making a table of the *same results*.

Distance dropped (cm)	0 –	3 –	6 –	9 –	12 –	15 –	18 –	21 –
Frequency	2	7	7	12	6	2	0	1

Calculate an estimate of the mean from this table.

(c) Here are the 37 results for the girls:

13.5, 5.5, 5.5, 13.5, 3, 9.5, 11.5, 11.5, 12.5, 4, 10, 1, 21, 8, 7, 12,
10, 17, 5, 7, 7.5, 16, 8, 10, 2.5, 2, 17, 14, 16, 2, 9.5, 12.5, 3, 10, 8, 8.5, 7.5

Calculate the mean of these 37 results.

(d) Compare your answers to parts (a), (b) and (c) and comment on what you notice.

16 Construct a table of the results you collected for people in your class. You can choose whether to use intervals of 5 or intervals of 3.

Calculate an estimate of the mean of these results.

17 Here are Ha's results:

13.5, 5.5, 5.5, 13.5, 3, 9.5, 11.5, 11.5, 2.5, 4.

Ha calculated the mean of her results to be 8.

It is clear that each of Ha's results was measured correct to the nearest 0.5 cm. This means that each result could *actually* have been as much as 0.25 cm larger or smaller than the result recorded.

(a) What is the largest total possible for Ha's *actual* results?

(b) What is the largest possible mean for Ha's *actual* results?

(c) What is the smallest possible mean for Ha's *actual* results?

There is yet another method used to calculate how much a set of results is spread out. This method involves calculating the **standard deviation** of a set of numbers and is used a great deal by statisticians.

This is how you calculate the standard deviation for Sue's results.

You first need the *mean* for Sue's results which is 9.8.

You then work out the following

Result	Difference between result and mean	Square of difference
10	0.2	0.04
1	−8.8	77.44
21	11.2	125.44
8	−1.8	3.24
7	−2.8	7.84
12	2.2	4.84
10	0.2	0.04
17	7.2	51.84
5	−4.8	23.04
7	−2.8	7.84

You then add the numbers in the right-hand column.

In this case you get 301.6.

You then divide by the number of results (in this case, 10) to get 30.16.

You then take the square root of this number: in this case, 5.5

5.5 is the standard deviation. It provides a measure of how far, on average, results are from their mean.

<u>**18**</u> (a) Calculate the standard deviation for each set of results you collected for people in your class.

(b) Using standard deviation as a measure, which person was most consistent?

Do people with big hands also have big feet?

One way of finding out is to collect the shoe sizes and handspans of all the people in the class.

Think about how to do this as accurately and reliably as possible.

• Collect shoe sizes and handspans of all members of the class.

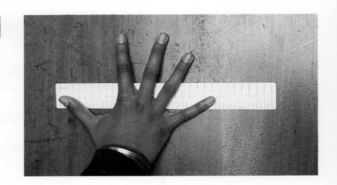

SECTION B

1 (a) Look at the shoe sizes in your set of data. Draw a bar chart which shows how many people have each shoe size. Give the bar chart a suitable title.

If you want to know which shoe size is the most common you look at the longest bar. The most common shoe size is called the **mode**.

(b) Which shoe size is the mode for your set of data?

2 For this question you will need data for both boys and girls.

(a) What is the median handspan for girls?

(b) What is the median handspan for boys?

(c) Do girls have bigger hands on average than boys? Give a reason for your answer.

3 Calculate the mean handspan for your set of data.

(If there are both girls and boys in your class you might want to calculate the mean handspan for girls and for boys separately. You can then compare them.)

4 *'On average, 14-year-olds have bigger handspans than 12-year-olds. Therefore a 14-year-old boy is bound to have a bigger handspan than a 12-year-old girl.'*

Is this true? Give a reason for your answer.

5 Make a scattergram of your data, showing handspans plotted against shoe sizes. The axes for the scattergram are shown in figure 2.

The cross on the scattergram shows someone who has shoe size 9 and a handspan of 215 mm. (Don't include this cross on your diagram unless you have someone with shoe size 9 and a handspan of 215 mm!)

6 Look at your scattergram. Would you say that people with large feet usually have large hands? Give a reason for your answer.

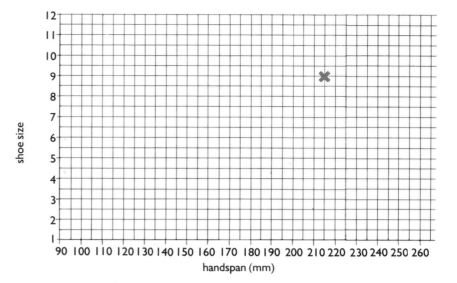

Figure 2

Look at the scattergram. The crosses in the scattergram do not all lie on a straight line, but a straight line has been drawn to fit as closely to the crosses as possible.

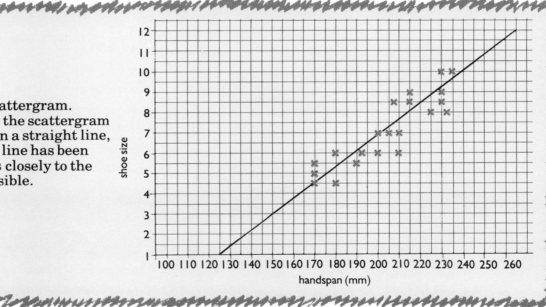

7 (a) Draw your own straight line on your scattergram which fits as closely as possible to the crosses you have put on the scattergram.

(b) Use your straight line to predict the shoe size for someone with a handspan of 260 mm.

(c) Use your straight line to predict the handspan for someone with shoe size 1.

(d) How accurate do you think your predictions are? Give a reason for your answer.

8 Complete the following table for the handspans in your set of data.

Handspan (mm)	140 –	150 –	160 –	170 –	180 –	190 –	200 –	210 –	220 –	230 –	240 –
Frequency											

Use the table to draw a histogram and give it a suitable title.

> **I** The **modal class** for a set of grouped data is the class (or group) which has most members.

9 What is the modal class of your data for handspans?

I The list below shows the handspans (in mm) for a group of 22 students.

300, 230, 190, 237, 215, 205, 180, 170, 170, 210, 210, 234, 230, 215, 224, 230, 207, 170, 200, 200, 192, 180

The results can be entered into a table of the type shown below.

Handspan (mm)	Cumulative frequency
⩽ 160	0
⩽ 170	3
⩽ 180	5
⩽ 190	6
⩽ 200	10
⩽ 210	14
⩽ 220	16
⩽ 230	20
⩽ 240	22

This means that 5 people have a handspan of 180 mm or less.

All 22 students have a handspan of 240 mm or less

From this table a graph can be drawn, called a cumulative frequency graph.

The graph shows the number of people who have handspans of less than a given length.

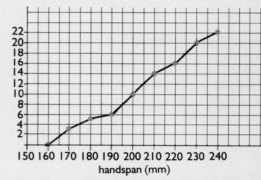

For example, 16 of the 22 people have a handspan of 220 mm or less.

10 Complete the table below for the handspans in your set of data.

Handspan (mm)	Cumulative frequency
⩽ 160	
⩽ 170	
⩽ 180	
⩽ 190	
⩽ 200	
⩽ 210	
⩽ 220	
⩽ 230	
⩽ 240	

Use the table to draw a cumulative frequency graph for your set of data. The axes for your graph will be similar to the axes shown in the box above. (Be careful! You will probably have a different number of people in your set of data.)

11 Figure 3 shows a cumulative frequency graph for the handspans of 215 15-year-olds.

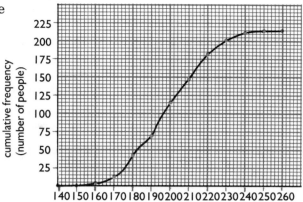

Figure 3

The **median** value is the value which 50% of people are above and 50% of people are below.

The **interquartile range** is the difference between the value that 25% of people are below and the value that 75% of the people are below.

(*a*) What is the median value for the handspans of the students shown in the cumulative frequency diagram shown in figure 3?

(*b*) What is the interquartile range for the handspans of these students?

(*c*) What percentage of these students have handspans which are bigger than your handspan?

It can be seen from figure 3 that 115 students have a handspan of 200 mm or less. So, if one of the 215 students is picked at random, the probability that he or she will have a handspan of less than 200 mm is

$$\frac{115}{215} = 0.53$$

The probability that he or she will have a handspan of more than 200 mm is

$$1 - 0.53 = 0.47$$

12 (*a*) How many of the 215 students have a handspan which is 180 mm or less?

(*b*) If one of the 215 students is picked at random what is the probability that he or she will have a handspan of 180 mm or less?

(*c*) If one of the 215 students is picked at random what is the probability that he or she will have a handspan of more than 220 mm?

13 The table shows the handspans of a group of 106 girls.

Handspan (mm)	Cumulative frequency
≤ 150	1
≤ 160	4
≤ 170	12
≤ 180	39
≤ 190	55
≤ 200	90
≤ 210	97
≤ 220	105
≤ 230	106

(a) Draw a cumulative frequency graph for this data.

(b) Estimate the median for this data.

(c) Estimate the interquartile range for this data.

(d) If one of these 106 girls is picked at random what is the probability that she will have a handspan of more than 200 mm?

Computer experiment

For this experiment you will need the computer program '*Estimating time*'. By using this program you can find out how good you are at estimating time.

- Use the computer program to estimate ten time intervals. Write down the results which are displayed on the screen at the end.

SECTION C

1 (a) How many of your ten estimates were too small?

(b) How many of your estimates were too big?

2 (a) Arrange your estimates in order. What is the median of your estimates?

(b) Arrange the actual times in order. What is the median of the actual times?

(c) Using your answers to (a) and (b) say whether you tend to underestimate or overestimate time.

Give a reason for your answer.

3 (a) Find the mean of your estimates.

(b) Find the mean of the actual times.

(c) Using your answers to (a) and (b) say whether you tend to underestimate or overestimate time.

Give a reason for your answer.

(d) Did you come to the same conclusion in question 3(c) as in question 2(c)?

If an actual time interval was 2.3 secs and you estimated that it was 1.9 secs your error would be 0.4 secs. To get your percentage error do the following.

A Calculate your error (in this case, 0.4).

B Divide your error by the actual time interval (in this case, 0.4 ÷ 2.3 = 0.17).

C Multiply by 100 to get the percentage error (in this case, 17%).

4 (*a*) Calculate the percentage errors of each of your ten estimates.

(*b*) Are you better at estimating long intervals of time or short intervals of time? Give a reason for your answer.

FURTHER COURSEWORK TASKS

1) Carry out a more thorough investigation into people's speeds of reaction.

You might want to continue using the ruler experiment for your investigation. Or you might want to devise your own test.

Here are some of the things you might want to do.

- Find out whether girls have faster or slower reactions than boys.

- Find out whether older children have faster or slower reactions than younger children. Find out whether adults have faster or slower reactions than children.

- Find out whether performance at the test improves with practice.

- Find out whether people are significantly better with their stronger hand than they are with their other hand.

- Find out whether people lose concentration if they have to do too many trials.

If you are using the ruler experiment you are measuring people's reaction times by seeing how far the ruler drops. If you want to know how *long* people take to react you need to find out how long it takes for the ruler to drop different distances.

- Test people's reaction using a computer program such as '*Times*', which measures accurately how long people take to react.

2) Design an experiment to discover how fit people are.

When you do exercise your pulse rate increases, you breathe more heavily and other changes happen to your body.

One way of deciding how fit you are is to measure how long it takes for your body to return to normal pulse rate, breathing and so on.

Before designing your experiments you might want to find out in more detail how fitness can be measured.

3) Investigate the bounciness of different balls, such as a tennis ball, a golf ball, a football, a squash ball, a ping-pong ball or a superball.

You might want to drop the balls from a measured height onto different surfaces and see how high they bounce, how many times they bounce, or how long they take before they stop bouncing.

4) Design a statistical experiment to investigate something of your own choice. Carry out the experiment and draw conclusions from the results.

JOINING MIDPOINTS

For this task you will need some centimetre squared paper.

- Draw a square of side 16 cm.

  Mark the midpoints of the sides and join them up.

- Describe the new shape you get.

  Find the area of the original shape and the new shape.

  How does the area of the new shape compare with the area of the original shape? Can you explain this by looking at your picture?

- Now mark the midpoints of the sides of your new shape and join them up.

- Answer the same questions about the new shape.

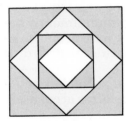

- Keep on joining the midpoints of the new shape. Describe what keeps happening to the area. Describe what keeps happening to the lengths of the sides. You might want to make a table of results to help you to explain what is happening.

- Keep repeating this idea until you can go no further.

  Imagine you could go on drawing until you had drawn 50 shapes inside the original shape.

  What can you say about your 50th shape?

- Now choose a different shape: a rectangle, a triangle or a kite, for example. Try out the same ideas with your chosen shape. Describe what happens.

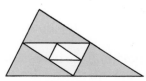

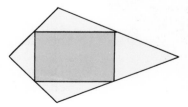

SECTION A Find the areas of these shapes. The shapes are not drawn here to their correct size. If you have difficulty with finding any of the areas, get a copy of the resource sheet called '*Areas of shapes*'.

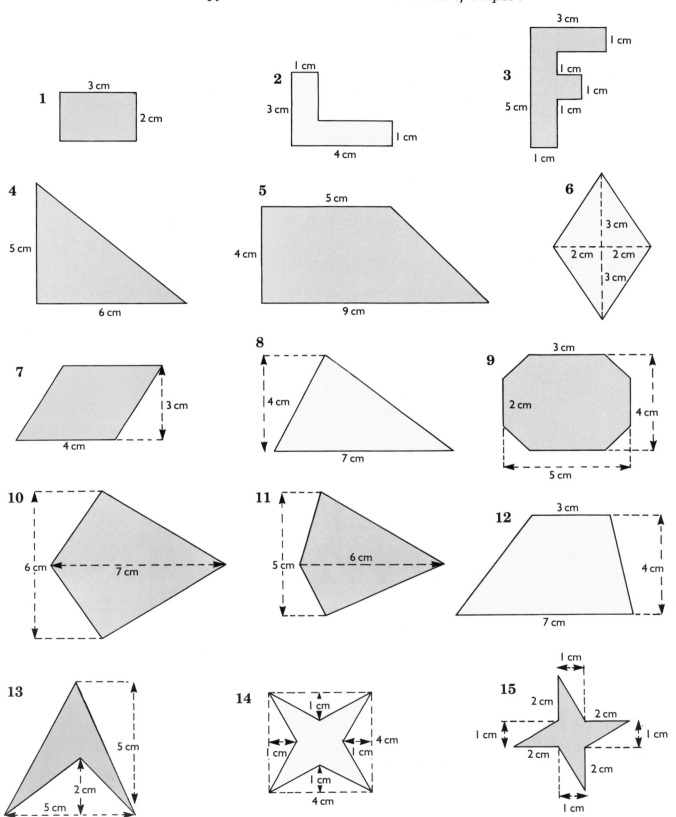

89

If the sides of a square are 8 cm long its area is 64 cm².

This is because $8^2 = 64$. In other words, 64 is the square of 8.

If the area of a square is 25 cm² what is the length of its sides? By trial and error we can find that the answer is 5 cm. This is because $5 \times 5 = 25$.

5 is called the square root of 25. This can be written as $\sqrt{25} = 5$.

If the edges of a cube are 3 cm long its area is 27 cm³.

This is because $3^3 = 27$. In other words, 27 is the cube of 3.

If the volume of a cube is 64 cm³ what is the length of its edges? By trial and error we can find that the answer is 4 cm. This is because $4 \times 4 \times 4 = 64$.

4 is called the cube root of 64. This can be written as $\sqrt[3]{64} = 4$.

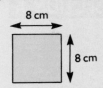

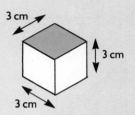

SECTION B

1 What are the lengths of the sides of the squares shown in figure 1?

Figure 1

2 What is

(*a*) $\sqrt{9}$?

(*b*) $\sqrt{25}$?

(*c*) $\sqrt{1}$?

3 What are the lengths of the edges of the cubes in figure 2?

Figure 2   8 cm³

125 cm³

216 cm³

1000 cm³

4 What is

(*a*) $\sqrt[3]{27}$?   (*b*) $\sqrt[3]{1}$?   (*c*) $\sqrt[3]{343}$?

5 (*a*) What is the area of the square shown in figure 3?

(*b*) A smaller square is obtained by joining the midpoints of the sides of this square.

What is the area of this smaller square?

16 cm

16 cm

Figure 3

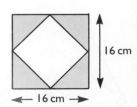

16 cm

16 cm

To find the length of the sides of the square in 5 (c) you need to find the square root of its area. There is no exact number for this so you need to use a calculator with a square root button.

(c) What is the length of the sides of this smaller square? Make sure you give your answer to a sensible degree of accuracy.

6   Using a calculator find the following:

(a) $\sqrt{10}$ (b) $\sqrt{2}$ (c) $\sqrt{289}$ (d) $\sqrt{1444}$

(e) $\sqrt{0.81}$ (f) $\sqrt{0.0196}$ (g) $\sqrt{0.4}$

7   Complete the table below, showing the length of the side of a square, given the area.

Area, A	0	5	10	15	20	25	30	35	40	45	50
Length of side of square, L			3.2						6.3		

On squared paper draw a graph of the length of the side of a square plotted against its area. (Let 1 cm represent 5 units on the horizontal axis for A and let 1 cm represent 1 unit on the vertical axis for L).

How does the length of the side change when the area goes up in equal steps? How is this shown by the graph?

Using a computer graph plotter or a graphical calculator, draw a graph similar to the one you have just drawn. What function will you need to use?

SECTION C

When you join the midpoints of the sides of a square this is the pattern you get.

The picture below shows the starting square and the third square.

The starting square is an enlargement of the third square.

To enlarge a shape you need a **centre** of enlargement and a **scale factor**.

In the picture above the centre of enlargement is the centre of the square. The scale factor is 2. This is because the black lines going from the centre to the corners of the larger square are 2 times the length of the lines going from the centre to the smaller square.

You can enlarge any shape using any centre you like and any scale factor.

This is how you enlarge the rectangle shown with scale factor 3.

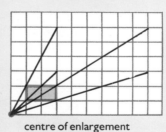

centre of enlargement

Join the centre to each corner of the rectangle and make the lines 3 times as long.

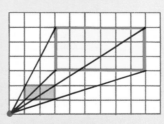

Now join up to get the enlargement. The sides of the enlarged rectangle are 3 times as long as the sides of the starting rectangle.

1 Copy each of the shapes in figure 4 onto squared paper. Enlarge each shape by the scale factor stated, using the centre C shown.

Figure 4

(a)

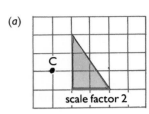

scale factor 2

(b)

scale factor 3

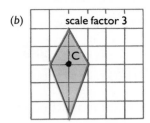

(c)

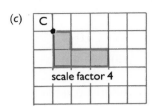

scale factor 4

(d)

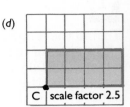

C | scale factor 2.5

One rhombus shown below is an enlargement of the other.

To find the centre of the enlargement draw lines joining the corners of one rhombus to the corresponding corners of the other. The centre is where the lines meet.

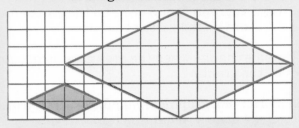

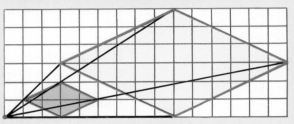

You can find the scale factor in two ways. Either you can measure the sides of the rhombus. Or you can measure the lengths of the lines joined to the centre. Using either method you can find that the scale factor in this case is 3.

(a)

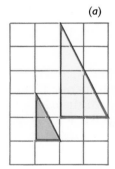

2 One of each of the pairs of shapes shown in figure 5 is an enlargement of the other.

Copy each of the pairs of shapes onto squared paper. Then find the centre of enlargement and the scale factor.

(c)

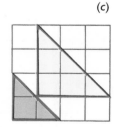

(d)

(b)

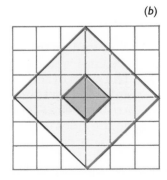

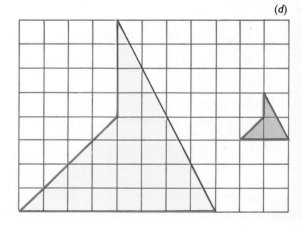

Figure 5

When you join the midpoints of the sides of a triangle you get another triangle inside.

When you draw lines joining a corner of one triangle to the corresponding corner of the other triangle you find that these lines meet at a point.

So the large triangle is an enlargement of the small triangle. But the enlargement has turned the triangle upside down.

When this happens a negative number is used for the scale factor. In this case the scale factor is -2.

The pictures below show how to enlarge a shape using a scale factor of -3.

Join the centre to a corner of the shape.

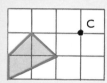

Continue the line 3 times as far in the opposite direction.

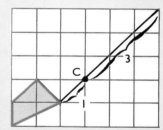

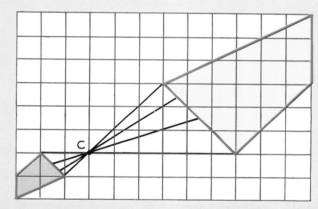

Do this for all corners of the shape and join up.

---

3 Copy each of the shapes shown in figure 6 onto squared paper. Enlarge it by the scale factor stated, using the centre shown.

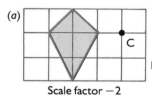

(a) Scale factor -2

(b) Scale factor -3

Figure 6

It is still called an enlargement even when the new shape is smaller than the shape you started with. But to get a new shape which is smaller the scale factor must be less than 1.

This rectangle can be 'enlarged' using the centre shown, with scale factor 0.5, as above.

4 Copy each of the shapes shown in figure 7 onto squared paper. Enlarge it by the scale factor stated, using the centre shown.

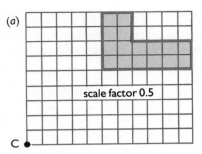

scale factor 0.5

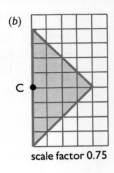

scale factor 0.75

Figure 7

5 Draw a regular pentagon. Join the midpoints of its sides.

Show that the new shape is an enlargement of the original shape. Estimate the scale factor by making suitable measurements on your drawing.

6 Copy each of the hexagons shown in figure 8 onto squared paper. For each hexagon join midpoints twice.

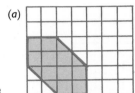

(a)

(b)

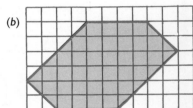

Figure 8

For which hexagon is the final shape obtained an enlargement of the starting shape?

When you enlarge a shape the new shape is the same shape as the shape you start with but a different size. Two shapes which are the same shape but a different size are called **similar**.

All squares are similar. Squares are different sizes but they are all the same shape.

But rectangles are not all the same shape.

These two rectangles are not similar.

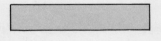

There are various methods of finding out whether rectangles are similar. Here are two methods.

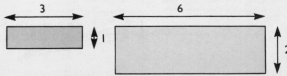

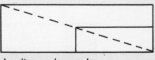

in *both* rectangles one side is 3 times the other (it does not have to be 3)

the diagonals match

7 Which pairs of the rectangles seen in figure 9 are similar?

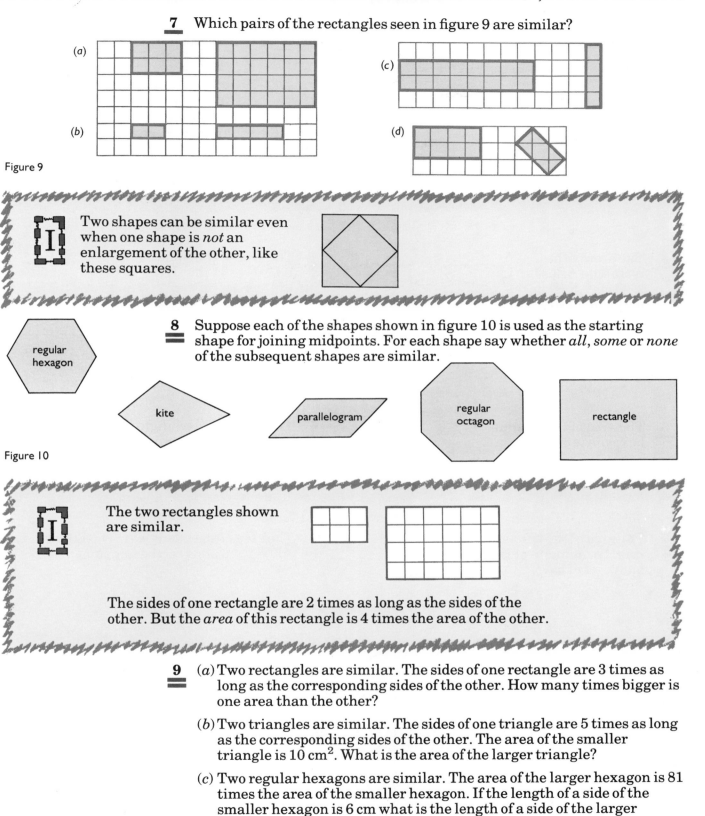

Figure 9

Two shapes can be similar even when one shape is *not* an enlargement of the other, like these squares.

8 Suppose each of the shapes shown in figure 10 is used as the starting shape for joining midpoints. For each shape say whether *all*, *some* or *none* of the subsequent shapes are similar.

regular hexagon

kite

parallelogram

regular octagon

rectangle

Figure 10

The two rectangles shown are similar.

The sides of one rectangle are 2 times as long as the sides of the other. But the *area* of this rectangle is 4 times the area of the other.

9 (a) Two rectangles are similar. The sides of one rectangle are 3 times as long as the corresponding sides of the other. How many times bigger is one area than the other?

(b) Two triangles are similar. The sides of one triangle are 5 times as long as the corresponding sides of the other. The area of the smaller triangle is 10 cm^2. What is the area of the larger triangle?

(c) Two regular hexagons are similar. The area of the larger hexagon is 81 times the area of the smaller hexagon. If the length of a side of the smaller hexagon is 6 cm what is the length of a side of the larger hexagon?

10 The length of a side of square A is 11 cm. The area of square B is 3 times the area of square A. What is the length of a side of square B?

SECTION D

In each of the following diagrams find the area of the shaded portion. Explain as clearly as possible why your method works.

1 The area of the kite is 38 cm².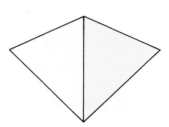

2 The area of the square is 16 cm². Midpoints of the sides of the square have been joined.

3 The area of the rectangle ABCD is 60 cm². E is the midpoint of AB.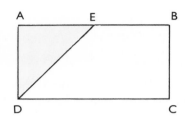

4 The area of the square KLMN is 64 cm². KL = 4PL, LM = 4QM, MN = 4RN and NK = 4SK.

5 The area of the regular hexagon is 36 cm².

6 The area of the triangle XYZ is 60 cm². W is the midpoint of XZ.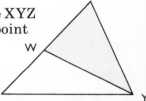

7 The area of the triangle HIJ is 48 cm². K is the midpoint of HJ and L is the midpoint of IJ.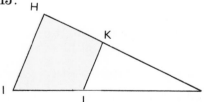

8 The area of the triangle ABC is 60 cm². AE = $\frac{1}{3}$ AB and D is the midpoint of AC.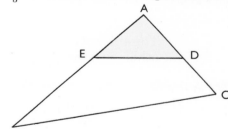

9 The area of the square ABCD is 60 cm². AB = EA = FB = GC = HD.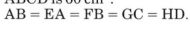

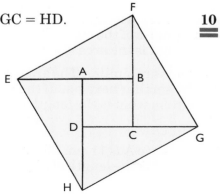

10 The area of the rhombus PQRS is 80 cm². T is the midpoint of PQ and U is the midpoint of QR.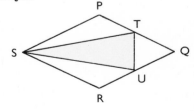

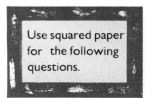

One way of describing a shape you have drawn on squared paper is to use vectors, see figure 11.

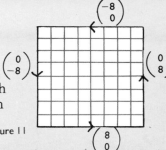

The vector marked on each side tells you how each side is drawn. The arrow tells you which direction it was drawn in.

Figure 11

Use squared paper for the following questions.

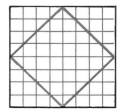

Figure 12

1 Figure 12 shows the same square. This time the square formed by joining the midpoints of the sides has been drawn. Write down vectors for the sides of this square.

2 On dotty paper, draw a square one side of which is the vector $\begin{pmatrix} 6 \\ 4 \end{pmatrix}$. Find suitable vectors to label the other sides of the square.

Join the midpoints of the sides of the square. Write down vectors for the sides of this new square. Explain clearly the connection between these new vectors and the vectors that describe the original square.

3 Do the same if one side of the starting square is the vector $\begin{pmatrix} 8 \\ 4 \end{pmatrix}$, but this time try to find all the vectors without drawing the square.

4 Suppose you start with a square and join the midpoints of its sides. One of the sides of the new square is the vector $\begin{pmatrix} 3 \\ 5 \end{pmatrix}$. What vectors can describe the sides of the square you started with?

Any line drawn on dotty paper can be marked by two different vectors. Which vector is used depends on which way the arrow is drawn.

5 If a line can be marked by the vector $\begin{pmatrix} 4 \\ 3 \end{pmatrix}$, what other vector can it be marked by?

What is the other vector which can mark a line which is marked by the vector $\begin{pmatrix} -3 \\ 2 \end{pmatrix}$?

6 In figure 13 the sides of the quadrilateral have been marked by arrows which follow on in the same direction (anti-clockwise) round the quadrilateral.

Copy this drawing and label the sides with vectors. Add the four vectors together. What do you notice?

Join the midpoints of the sides of the quadrilateral. Write down vectors for the sides of the lines you have just drawn. What is the connection between these four vectors and the original vectors?

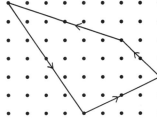

Figure 13

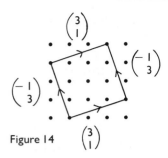

Figure 14 $\begin{pmatrix} 3 \\ 1 \end{pmatrix}$

7 Figure 14 shows a square marked by its vectors

If you multiply all the vectors by 2 they are suitable for marking the sides of a larger square.

What do you need to multiply the lengths of the sides of the first square by to get the lengths of the sides of the second square?

What do you need to multiply the area of the first square by to get the area of the second square?

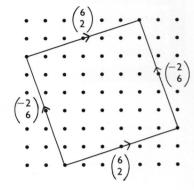

8 Draw the triangle whose sides have the vectors $\begin{pmatrix} 3 \\ 2 \end{pmatrix}$, $\begin{pmatrix} -4 \\ 1 \end{pmatrix}$ and $\begin{pmatrix} 1 \\ -3 \end{pmatrix}$.

Multiply each of these vectors by -3 and draw a triangle whose sides have these new vectors.

How do the lengths of the sides of the second triangle compare with the lengths of the sides of the first?

How does the area of the second triangle compare with the area of the first?

FURTHER COURSEWORK TASKS

1〉 Figure 16 shows you just a few of the designs you can produce by repeatedly joining midpoints.

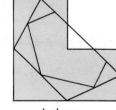
L-shape

regular pentagon

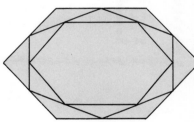
irregular hexagon

Figure 16

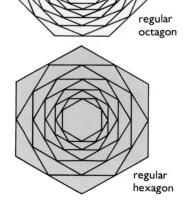
regular octagon

regular hexagon

Try to produce some of these designs, or use some other designs of your own.

You might, or might not, want to use squared paper for this task.

In which of your designs do shapes reproduce themselves?

In which designs are new shapes produced?

What happens to the area?

What happens to the lengths of the sides?

You may notice other things to write about.

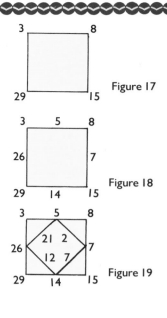

Figure 17

Figure 18

Figure 19

2) Write four numbers at the corners of a square as in figure 17. (Your numbers can be different from the numbers in figure 17.)

On each side of the square write the number which is the difference between the numbers at its two ends (figure 18).

Join the midpoints of the sides. Repeat the process (figure 19).

What happens eventually? Does it still happen if you start with different numbers?

Try starting with a triangle. What happens now?

Try starting with a hexagon. Or an octagon. Or a pentagon.

Explain clearly how different things happen when you start with different shapes.

3) Instead of using midpoints you can use points which divide the sides in thirds, quarters, etc.

In figure 20 the points chosen are one-third of the way along the sides of the previous shape.

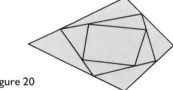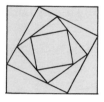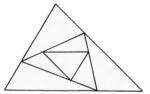

Figure 20

Investigate what happens this time. Try the same idea with other shapes or use something other than thirds.

You might want to use midpoints on some sides and thirds on others.

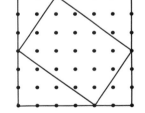

4) What polyhedron is produced by joining the midpoints of the faces of a cube?

What happens when you join the midpoints of the faces of this polyhedron.

You can use either wire or wooden sticks or straws and pipe cleaners to make models. You can use cotton to attach sticks or straws to the centre of a face.

Investigate what happens if instead of starting with a cube you start with a different polyhedron.

You might want to investigate the sizes of the polyhedra produced.

Instead of joining the midpoints of faces of a cube you could join the midpoints of edges.

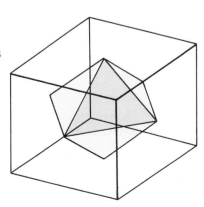

III REVIEW EXERCISES A

EXERCISE I Arithmetic of whole numbers

1 Add two hundred and forty seven to three thousand seven hundred and sixty five, giving your answer in figures.

2 Before our holiday the mileometer on the car read 48458. After the holiday it read 49372. How far did we drive on our holiday?

3 There are four members of a family. When a box of favourite chocolates is bought it is shared out equally and each person gets 12 chocolates.

   On one occasion a box of these chocolates was bought and shared while one member of the family was away. How many chocolates did each person get?

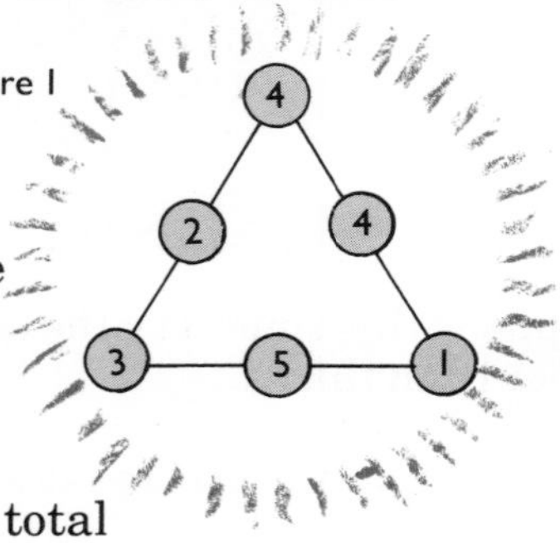

4 Figure 1 shows a magic triangle.

   It is magic because the total of the numbers along each of the three sides of the triangle is the same. (In the case shown the total for each side is 9.)

   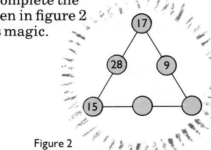

   Figure 1

   Figure 2

   (a) Copy and complete the triangle seen in figure 2 so that it is magic.

   (b) Make up a magic triangle which uses each of the numbers 15, 16, 17, 18, 19, 20 once.

5 Three years ago Sheila was exactly half as old as her mother. She is now 22. How old is her mother?

6 On a Saturday night 768 people went to see a play. A third of these were children. How many adults saw the play?

7 There are 11 players in a hockey team.

   At a large hockey tournament several teams were taking part. Some of the teams brought one reserve player; others did not. Altogether there were 150 players at the tournament.

   (a) How many teams were taking part in the tournament?

   (b) How many of the teams sent reserves?

8 A train stopped at Sheffield where 86 passengers got off and 145 passengers boarded. When the train left Sheffield it had 329 passengers. How many passengers were on the train when it arrived in Sheffield?
   NEA Syllabus C, May 1988, Paper 3

9 What is the remainder when 5000 is divided by 51?

10 Ann is Mike's daughter and Mike is less than twice as old as Ann.

   In four years time Mike will be 50.

   Which of the following statements are true?

   A Six years ago Mike was 40.

   B In four years time Ann will be 25.

   C Ann is no longer a teenager.

   D In four years time Ann will be as old as Mike is now.

   E Mike is due to retire at the age of 65. By that time Ann will be more than double her present age.

   F There was a time when Mike was exactly twice as old as Ann.

11 A metal rod of length 65 cm is cut into 10 pieces, each piece being 1 cm longer than its predecessor. Find the length of the shortest piece.
   NEA Syllabus C, May 1988, Paper 4

EXERCISE 2 Symmetry

1 Copy each of the shapes shown in figure 3 and draw their lines of symmetry.

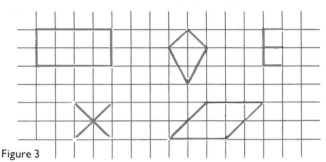

Figure 3

2 (a) Copy and complete the picture shown in figure 4 so that the dotted line is a line of symmetry.

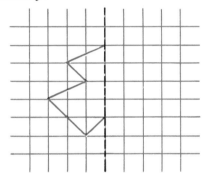

Figure 4

(b) Copy and complete the picture shown in figure 5 so that both the dotted lines are lines of symmetry.

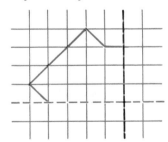

Figure 5

3 Which of the following letters have

S T A G E F O U R

(a) rotational symmetry,

(b) exactly one line of symmetry,

(c) more than one line of symmetry?

4 Simon wants to arrange two 3-inch square photographs in a frame like this:

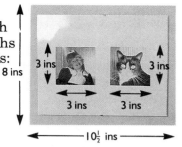

(a) He wants the gaps at the top and bottom to be the same. Work out how big the gaps should be.

(b) He also wants the gaps at the sides and in the middle to be the same.

Work out how big these gaps should be.

MEG Leicestershire Mode 3, Syllabus B, May 1988, Paper 1

5 In each of the following diagrams shade two squares so that the completed diagram has the symmetry stated.

(a) Just one line of symmetry.

(b) Rotational symmetry of order 2 but no line of symmetry.

MEG, May 1989, Paper 1

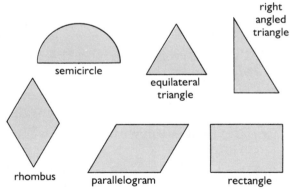

Figure 6

6 Write down the name of the shape shown in figure 6 above which has

(a) 3 lines of symmetry,

(b) just 1 line of symmetry,

(c) no line of symmetry but has rotational symmetry,

(d) no line of symmetry and no rotational symmetry.

MEG, June 1986, Paper 4

7 (a) Draw a letter of the alphabet with 1 line of symmetry.

(b) Draw a letter of the alphabet with rotational symmetry of order 2 and 2 lines of symmetry.

(c) Draw a letter of the alphabet with rotational symmetry of order 2 and no lines of symmetry.

(d) Draw a letter of the alphabet with 4 lines of symmetry.

(e) Draw a letter of the alphabet with no symmetry.

8 (a) Copy figure 7 and shade it so that it has rotational symmetry of order 3.

(b) Copy figure 7 and shade it so that it has one line of symmetry.

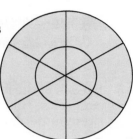

(c) Copy figure 7 and shade it so that it has rotational symmetry of order 2.

(d) Copy figure 7 and shade it so that it has rotational symmetry but no line of symmetry.

Figure 7

9 (a) Draw a triangle with exactly one line of symmetry.

(b) Draw a triangle with more than one line of symmetry.

(c) Draw a quadrilateral with rotational symmetry but no line of symmetry.

(d) Draw a hexagon with exactly two lines of symmetry.

(e) Draw a hexagon with exactly three lines of symmetry.

10 (a) Describe completely the symmetry of the pattern of shaded squares in the crossword puzzle seen in figure 8.

Figure 8

Helen is compiling a crossword puzzle. She wants the pattern of the shaded squares to have the same type of symmetry as the pattern in part (a) about the centre square *which is unshaded.*

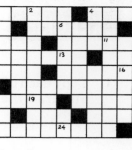

Figure 9

(b) Copy figure 9 onto squared paper.

(i) Complete the shading on the crossword puzzle.

(ii) Complete the numbering of the squares in the puzzle.

NEA Syllabus C, May 1988, Paper 3

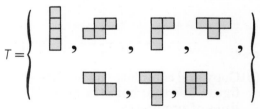

$n(S)$ means the number of elements in the set S.
So, if $S = \{1, 3, 5, 7, 9\}$
$n(S) = 5$

11 L and R are subsets of the set of patterns T.

$T = \{$ ... $\}$

$L = \{$patterns with at least one line of symmetry$\}$.

$R = \{$patterns with rotational symmetry of order 2$\}$.

(a) Show by drawing,
(i) the members of set L,
(ii) the members of set R.

(b) Write down the value of $n(R)$.

MEG June 1987, Paper 3

12 (a) How many axes of symmetry does each of the following shapes have:

(i) a cone?
(ii) an equilateral triangular prism?
(iii) a cylinder?

(b) Describe a polyhedron with one axis of symmetry and with two planes of symmetry.

EXERCISE 3 Rounding off

Significant figures

Sometimes you are asked to give a number correct to 3 (or some other number of) significant figures. This means the number you give should contain 3 figures. If the first figure you *don't* want to use is 5 or more, then round up.

For example, when rounded to 3 significant figures:

3.4527 becomes 3.45
643.6 becomes 644

If there are zeros at the beginning of the number don't count these as figures.

For example, when rounded to 3 significant figures:

0.05678 becomes 0.0568
0.0045832 becomes 0.00458

If the number is large you will need to replace the figures you do not need by zeros.

For example, when rounded to 3 significant figures:

34 623 becomes 34 600
735 800 becomes 736 000

Sometimes when you round up a number with a 9 in you may appear to lose a figure.

For example, when rounded to 3 significant figures:

3596 becomes 3600

If the last figure you want to keep is zero and is after the decimal point you must write it.

For example, when rounded to 3 significant figures:

3.4024 becomes 3.40

Don't write this as 3.4

To find a number to 2 significant figures, or 4 significant figures, etc, the same principles apply.

---

1 Write the following correct to 3 significant figures:

(*a*) 23.47   (*b*) 4.3634   (*c*) 0.87357

2 Write the following correct to 2 significant figures:

(*a*) 123   (*b*) 487   (*c*) 7682

3 Write the following correct to 1 significant figure:

(*a*) 4.39   (*b*) 2740   (*c*) 697   (*d*) 0.0038

4 Write the following correct to 3 significant figures.

(*a*) 0.004256   (*b*) 60.041   (*c*) 98 654 321
(*d*) 3.798

Decimal places

Sometimes you are asked to give a number correct to 2 (or some other number of) places of decimals. The principles here are similar to those for significant figures, but you count only figures after the decimal point.

For example, when rounded to 2 decimal places:

3.534 becomes 3.53
42.6571 becomes 42.66

You count the figures after the decimal point even if they are zeros.

For example, when rounded to 2 decimal places:

0.045 becomes 0.05
0.0027 becomes 0.00

If the last figure you want to keep is zero and is after the decimal point you must write it.

For example, when rounded to 2 decimal places:

304.498 becomes 304.50

Don't write this as 304.5

To find a number to 1 decimal place or to 3 or 4 decimal places, etc, the same principles apply.

5 Write the following correct to 2 decimal places:

(*a*) 5.346   (*b*) 17.234   (*c*) 0.0456

6 Write the following correct to 1 decimal place:

(*a*) 15.42   (*b*) 56.07   (*c*) 3.03   (*d*) 14.96

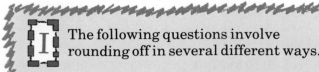

The following questions involve rounding off in several different ways.

7 The population of Leicester recorded in the 1981 census was 279 971. Give the population correct to the nearest thousand.

8 The external angle of a regular polygon with 7 sides is 360 ÷ 7. Give this angle correct to the nearest degree.

9 Find the cost of 43 litres of petrol at 39.2p per litre

(*a*) to the nearest penny,

(*b*) to the nearest pound.

10 Fuel consumptions of cars are often given in miles per gallon.

Round each of these fuel consumptions to the nearest 5 miles per gallon:

(*a*) Ford Fiesta Saloon   38 mpg

(*b*) Saab 900   27 mpg

(*c*) Fiat Panda 750L   45 mpg

11 The numbers of votes cast in the 1983 General Election in Bexhill were as follows:

Mr. I. Pearson	3587
Ms. A. Rix	538
Mr. P. Smith	10 583
Mr. C. Wardle	30 329

(*a*) Calculate the total number of votes cast.

(*b*) How many more votes did Mr. Wardle get than all the other three candidates combined?

(*c*) Write the number of votes cast for Mr. Smith correct to the nearest thousand.

(*d*) Write the number of votes cast for Mr. Wardle correct to 3 significant figures.

MEG June 1987, Paper 2 and Paper 3

12 Stamp collectors use a unit called 'perf'. A perf is the number of perforations in 2 cm on one edge of a stamp. It is rounded to the nearest whole number. What is the perf of a stamp 3.4 cm long with 23 perforations along that side?

MEG SMP 11–16, June 1988, Paper 4

EXERCISE 4   Types of Number I

1 One million, seven hundred and fifty six thousand five hundred and forty Fiat cars were sold in Western Europe in 1987.

Write this number in figures.

2 Every year in Britain one-and-a-half million tons of glass is thrown away in the form of bottles and jars.

Write this number in figures.

3 There are an estimated quarter of a million pigeon fanciers in Great Britain.

Write this number in figures.

4 Which of the following numbers is not a square number?

9, 24, 36, 49, 81

5 Write down from the following set of numbers

49, 50, 51, 52, 53, 54, 55, 56, 57, 58

(*a*) a prime number,

(*b*) a square number,

(*c*) three multiples of 3,

(*d*) a number which is double a square number,

(*e*) a number which is double a cube number,

(*f*) a number which is double a prime number.

6 The first six triangular numbers are

1, 3, 6, 10, 15, 21

(a) Write down from this list

   (i) one odd number;
   (ii) two numbers which are multiples of 5.

(b) Use diagrams to help you explain clearly why these numbers are called triangular numbers.

MEG Specimen, Paper 1

7 Write down five consecutive numbers between thirty and fifty, none of which is prime.

8 (a) Write down the factors of 64.
   (b) Which of these factors are square numbers?

9 Write down the smallest number greater than 20 which leaves a remainder of 2 when divided both by 5 and by 7.

10 Consider the numbers:

   10, 11, 12, 13, 14, 15, 16, 17, 18, 19

(a) Which are prime numbers?

(b) Which three of the numbers are factors of 910?

MEG SMP Mode 2, May 1988, Paper 2

11 From the following set of numbers

   11, 21, 31, 41, 231, 241, 321, 341, 421, 431

choose

(a) a number which is a multiple of 7,

(b) two numbers which are multiples of 3,

(c) a number which is a multiple of two other numbers on the list.

12 The table shows all the factors of the numbers from 1 to 9.

Number	Factors
1	1
2	1, 2
3	1, 3
4	1, 2, 4
5	1, 5
6	1, 2, 3, 6
7	1, 7
8	1, 2, 4, 8
9	1, 3, 9

(a) What is the next number to have exactly two factors?

(b) What name do we give to all those numbers with exactly two factors?

(c) Find the next number after 9 with exactly three factors (this will be the third such number).

(d) The fourth number with exactly three factors is 49. Find the fifth such number.

NEA Syllabus A, May 1988, Paper 3

13 (a) Express as a product of its prime factors

   (i) 126
   (ii) 420

(b) Find the smallest number of which 126 and 420 are factors.

SEG, Summer 1988, Paper 4

14 (a) How many consecutive zeros are there at the end of the number which is produced when all the integers from 1 to 10 inclusive are multiplied together?

(b) How many consecutive zeros are there at the end of the number which is produced when all the integers from 1 to 50 inclusive are multiplied together?

NEA Syllabus C, May 1988, Paper 4

EXERCISE 5   **Patterns and sequences**

1 Write down the next two numbers in each of the following sequences.

(a) 4, 7, 10, 13, 16,

(b) 3, 6, 12, 24, 48,

(c) 1, 3, 9, 27, 81,

(d) 2, 5, 10, 17, 26,

(e) 400, 200, 100, 50, 25,

(f) 12, 11, 9, 6, 2.

2 Figure 10 shows an equilateral triangle with sides 3 cm long. It has been tessellated with white and pink tiles which are equilateral triangles with sides 1 cm long.
The white tiles are base upwards and the pink tiles are base downwards.

Figure 10

(a) An equilateral triangle with sides 4 cm long is tessellated in a similar way with white and black tiles with sides 1 cm long. Using a triangular grid, or otherwise, find

    (i) the number of white tiles used,
    (ii) the number of black tiles used,
    (iii) the total number of tiles used.

(b) Complete the following table for equilateral triangles of various sizes.

Length of side (cm)	1	2	3	4	5
Number of white tiles (W)	0		3		
Number of black tiles (B)	1		6		
Total number of tiles (T)	1		9		

(c) Write down the special name which is given to the numbers that appear

    (i) in the B row of the table,
    (ii) in the T row of the table.

MEG June 1987, Paper 4

3 A gardener buys roses and decides to plant them one metre apart in triangles.

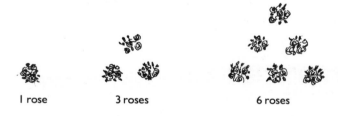

1 rose   3 roses   6 roses

(a) Draw a picture of a similar pattern using 10 roses.

(b) How many roses would he need if the triangle had 5 roses along each side?

He decides to form a triangular pattern using 15 roses.

(c) How long is each side of his triangle?

(d) Draw an accurate scale diagram of this pattern. (Use 1 cm to represent 1 metre.)

His son, who is keen on patterns, counts the number of equilateral triangles that can be drawn.

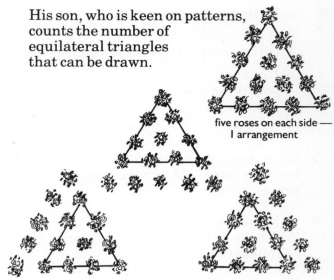

five roses on each side — 1 arrangement

four roses on each side — 3 arrangements

He continues by counting triangles with 3 roses on each side.

(e) How many equilateral triangles can be drawn with 3 roses on each side?

SEG, Summer 1988, Paper 1

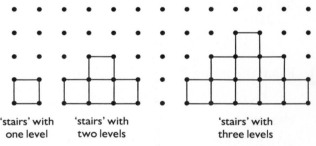

'stairs' with one level   'stairs' with two levels   'stairs' with three levels

Figure 11

4 A child is building sets of 'stairs' with some bricks. Figure 11 shows the view of the 'stairs' that the child has built for 1, 2 and 3 levels.

(a) Draw the view for the 'stairs' with 4 levels.

(b) Complete the table.

Number of levels	Number of bricks
1	1
2	
3	
4	

(c) How many bricks are needed to build a set of 'stairs' with 10 levels?

LEAG SMP Specimen 1991, Paper 1

5

$$3^2 - 4 = 5 \times 1$$
$$4^2 - 4 = 6 \times 2$$
$$5^2 - 4 = 7 \times 3$$
$$6^2 - 4 = 8 \times 4$$

(a) Write down the next two rows of this pattern.

(b) Complete the following row from the same pattern.

$$77^2 - 4 =$$

6 The numbers below are called Pascal's triangle

Row total

1
2
4

Each row starts and ends with a 1. The other numbers in the row are obtained by adding together the two numbers immediately above them.

(a) Write down the next two lines of Pascal's triangle.

(b) Find the totals of the numbers in each of the first 10 rows of Pascal's triangle. (The first three totals are shown next to Pascal's triangle above.)

(c) Find the totals of the ringed numbers in each of the first ten rows of Pascal's triangle.

(d) The total of the numbers in the 20th row of Pascal's triangle is 524 288. What is the total of the ringed numbers in the 20th row of Pascal's triangle?

7 Figure 12 shows some dominoes arranged in a pattern.

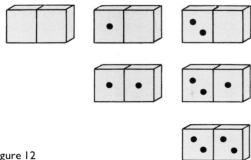

Figure 12

(a) Draw the next column of dominoes in the pattern.

(b) Write down the total number of spots in each of these four columns of dominoes.

(c) Divide each of these totals by 3 and write down the new sequence of numbers.

(d) Write down the next two numbers in the sequence you obtained in part (c).

(e) Using your previous answers, find the total number of spots in the column in which the double 6 domino appears.

(f) In which row and which column of the pattern above would this domino appear?

NEA Syllabus C, May 1988, Paper 3

8 A die is numbered in such a way that the sum of the numbers on opposite faces is the same for each pair of opposite faces.

Figure 13 shows two views of this die.

Figure 13

The pictures below show three more views of the same die. Copy these pictures and fill in the missing numbers.

(a)   (b)   (c)

9 This is a Fibonacci sequence

2, 5, 7, 12, 19, 31, . . .

because each new term of the sequence is obtained by adding the previous two terms.

The following are Fibonacci sequences of positive numbers.

3, 7, 10, a, b, . . .

c, 11, 16, 27, d, . . .

7, e, 24, f, g, . . .

2, h, i, 32, j, . . .

k, l, m, n, o, 44, . . .

Find the values of a, b, c, d, e, f, g, h, i, j, k, l, m, n and o.

EXERCISE 6 Using algebra

1 In a game of 'guess my rule' the following responses were given to numbers tried.

Saying 4 produced the response 9

Saying 7 produced the response 15

Saying 11 produced the response 23

Saying 20 produced the response 41

(a) Explain in words what rule is being used to produce the response.

(b) What response would you get to saying 37?

(c) What number would you say to get the response 99?

2 Figure 14 shows the first three of a set of patterns made from matchsticks.

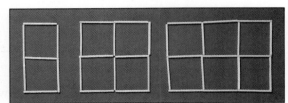

Figure 14

(a) Draw the fourth pattern.

(b) How many matches are needed to make each of the first four patterns?

(c) Without drawing the pattern write down how many matches are needed to make the fifth pattern.

(d) How many matches are needed to make the 20th pattern?

(e) How many matches are needed to make the xth pattern?

3 A temperature can be measured as °F (Fahrenheit) or °C (Celsius). The exact relationship between F and C is given by

$$F = \frac{9C}{5} + 32.$$

(a) Find the value of F when C = 20.

(b) Find the value of C when F = 14.

An approximate relationship between F and C is given by the following rule.

To find F, add 15 to C and double your answer

(c) Write this relationship as a formula.

(d) Use this relationship to find an approximate value of F when C = 20.

MEG, May 1988, Paper 5

4 Carol and Javed did an investigation together, in which they had to count the number of intersections in a series of diagrams. They got these results:

3, 8, 15, 24

Their teacher asked them, for homework, to see if they could find a pattern in their results. The next day the pupils returned with this:

Carol

Diagram	Number	Pattern
1	3	1 × 3
2	8	2 × 4
3	15	3 × 5
4	24	4 × 6
5		

Javed

Diagram	Number	Pattern
1	3	$1^2 + 2 \times 1$
2	8	$2^2 + 2 \times 2$
3	15	$3^2 + 2 \times 3$
4	24	$4^2 + 2 \times 4$
5		

(a) Their teacher asked each pupil to continue their pattern for diagram 5. Fill in what you would expect each to write in the tables above.

(b) Their teacher then asked each pupil to write down a formula for the number of intersections in diagram n. Write down the two formulas that the pupils would have given.

(c) Show that these two formulas are equivalent to one another.

MEG, May 1988, Paper 2

5 (a) The sum of 2 consecutive numbers is $2x + 7$. What is the larger of the two numbers?

(b) The sum of 3 consecutive numbers is $6y + 9$. What is the smallest of the numbers?

(c) The sum of 4 consecutive numbers is $4z - 10$. What is the smallest of the numbers?

6 (a) If n is a positive whole number explain why $2n - 1$ must be an odd number.

(b) Write down the next odd number after $2n - 1$.

(c) Add $2n - 1$ to the next odd number after $2n - 1$.

(d) Explain why the sum of two consecutive odd numbers is always a multiple of 4.

(e) Write down the next two odd numbers.

(f) Explain why the sum of four consecutive odd numbers must be a multiple of 8.

7 Nelson decides to plant vegetables in a piece of garden which is rectangular in shape. He uses a long cane to measure the land and finds that it is 5 cane lengths plus one stride by 3 cane lengths plus one stride. The plan of the land and the proposed vegetable plots is shown in figure 15. The unshaded area respresents a path.

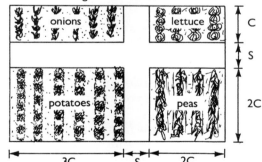

C = cane length   S = stride

Figure 15

(a) Find, in terms of c, the total area of land used for growing vegetables.

(b) Find, in terms of c and s the area of the path.

(c) The area of the potato plot is 216 square feet. Find c.

SEG A, Summer 1988, Paper 4

8 A computer has been programmed to produce a sequence according to this rule.

To produce the Nth term of the sequence multiply N by itself, add N and then divide by 2

(a) Write down the first four numbers the computer will produce.

(b) Write down a formula for the Nth term of the sequence.

(c) The computer has been programmed to stop after it has produced one number bigger than 1000. How many numbers will the computer produce?

1	2	3	4	5	6	7	8	9
10	11	12	13	14	15	16	17	18
19	20	21	22	23	24	25	26	27
28	29	30	31	32	33	34	35	36
37	38	39	40	41	42	43	44	45
46	47	48	49	50	51	52	53	54
55	56	57	58	59	60	61	62	63
64	65	66	67	68	69	70	71	72
73	74	75	76	77	78	79	80	81

Figure 16

9 Figure 16 shows a number square with an outline 'T' on it. The number at the base of the outline is 20 so we say that the outline is 'based on 20'. Using a translation, the outline can be moved so that it is based on a different number, but it must always remain upright and completely within the number square.

(a) Find the total of the five numbers in the outline when it is based on 40.

(b) If the outline is based on x, write down (in terms of x) the other four numbers in the outline and show that the total of the five numbers in the outline is $5x - 63$.

(c) Find the five numbers in the outline given that their total is 287.

(d) Explain why the total of the five numbers in the outline could not be

(i) 290,
(ii) 117.

MEG Specimen, Paper 6

10 A pink ball is placed on a table and is represented by T_1, as shown in figure 17(a).

It is then surrounded by white balls to form a triangular shape, T_2, as shown in figure 17(b).

Shape T_3 is formed by surrounding T_2 by pink balls, and so on.

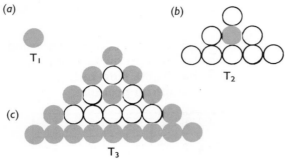

Figure 17

(a) What kind of triangles are formed by the centres of the outside balls?

(b) How many rows of balls will there be in

(i) shape T_7?
(ii) shape T_n?

(c) How many balls will there be in

(i) shape T_7?
(ii) shape T_n?

(d) What colour balls will be added

(i) to T_{17} to make T_{18}?
(ii) to T_{2n-1} to make T_{2n}?

(e) How many balls will be added to T_{n-1} to make T_n?

NEA Syllabus B, May 1988, Paper 4

EXERCISE 7 Drawing and interpreting diagrams

1 ABCDE represents the shape of the end wall of a house. It is drawn accurately on a 1 cm square grid in figure 18.

(a) (i) Name two edges of the shape that are parallel.
(ii) Name two edges of the shape that are perpendicular

(b) (i) Measure and write down the length of AB.
(ii) Find the perimeter of the shape ABCDE.

(c) Find the area of the shape ABCDE.

MEG SMP, May 1988, Paper 1

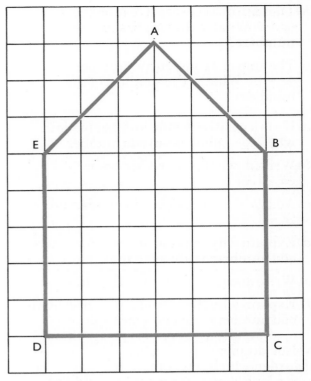

Figure 18

2 A photograph is to be mounted on a cardboard surround.

(a) The cardboard surround is a rectangle which is 150 mm by 180 mm. Draw this rectangle accurately on plain paper.

(b) The dimensions of the photograph are 100 mm by 150 mm and the photograph is to be placed symmetrically in the frame.

Draw the position of the photograph accurately on your drawing of the frame.

You will need to use a compass for the drawings in questions 3, 4, 7, 10 and 11.

3 Figure 19 shows a road sign which is not drawn to scale. The dimensions of the road sign are in metres.

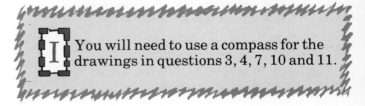

Figure 19

Make an accurate scale drawing of the outline of this road sign. Use a scale of 2 cm to 1 metre.

4 Figure 20 shows an accurate drawing of a triangle made from a loop of string.

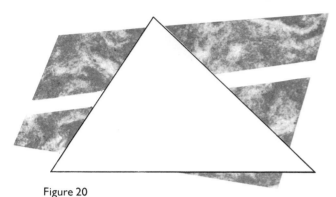

Figure 20

(a) How long is the loop of string?

(b) What is the size of the largest angle of the triangle?

(c) Draw accurately a different triangle which can be made from the loop of string, and whose largest angle is smaller than the answer to (b).

(d) Draw accurately a different triangle which can be made from the loop of string and whose largest angle is bigger than the answer to (b).

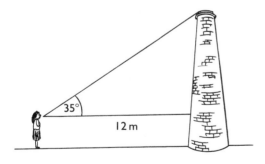

5 A girl whose eyes are 1½ metres above the ground, stands 12 metres away from a tall chimney. She has to raise her eyes 35° upwards from the horizontal to look directly at the top of the chimney.

Using a scale of 1 cm to represent 1 metre, find the height of the chimney by scale drawing.

MEG, May 1988, Paper 4

6 Figure 21, which is not drawn to scale, is of a lean-to shed which is to be built against the side of a house.

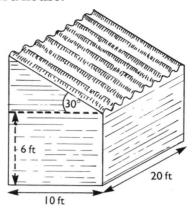

Figure 21

(a) Make a scale drawing, with a scale of 1 cm to 1 ft, of the end of the shed. Use this drawing to determine the length of the sloping edge of the roof in feet correct to one decimal place.

(b) Corrugated roofing sheets are 6 ft long and 3 ft wide. Each sheet is placed on the roof so that its length is in the same direction as the slope of the roof. Because only whole sheets are used there is some overlapping of the sheets when they are positioned on the roof. How many sheets would you use to make the roof?

NEA Syllabus C, May 1988, Paper 1

7 Figure 22 is a sketch of an irregular quadrilateral.

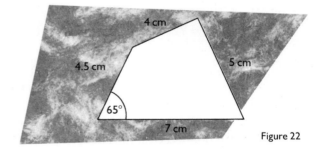

Figure 22

(a) Draw this quadrilateral accurately.

(b) Mark the midpoints of the sides of this quadrilateral, and draw a new quadrilateral inside it by joining the mid-points.

(c) Measure the angles of the new quadrilateral. Comment on what you notice.

8 An aircraft takes off from an airport at A. It travels 4 km to B while climbing at an angle of 42° to the horizontal ground and then a further 9.5 km to C at an angle of 10° to the ground. The aircraft then levels off and flies horizontally. The path of the aircraft is shown in figure 23.

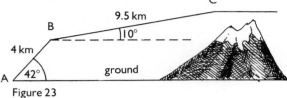

Figure 23

(a) Make an accurate scale drawing of the flight path showing A, B and C, using a scale of 1 cm to 1 km.

(b) When the aircraft reaches C use your scale drawing to find

(i) the distance of C from A
(ii) the height of the aircraft above ground level.

(c) When the aircraft reaches C it then flies over a mountain of height 3500 m. How many metres above the top of the mountain is the aircraft at this point?

(d) Another aircraft climbed steadily from A to C. What angle did its flight path make with the ground?

MEG SMP Mode 2, May 1988, Paper 2

9 Figure 24 shows a bicycle. When it stands on horizontal ground, CB is also horizontal and D is 26 cm above the ground.

Angle BCD = 72° and BA is parallel to CD.
AB = 5 cm, BC = 58 cm and CD = 50 cm.

(a) Make an accurate scale drawing of ABCD, one fifth of full size.

(b) Using your drawing, find the total length of tubing needed to construct ABCD.

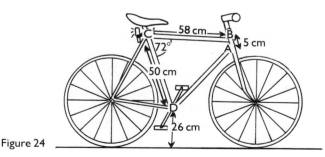

Figure 24

(c) A tall man requires a cycle with its saddle 1 m above the ground. The saddle of this cycle can be raised to be 22 cm vertically above BC. Is it big enough for him? Show the measurement which you take from your drawing to answer this.

MEG SMP Specimen, Paper 3

Figure 25

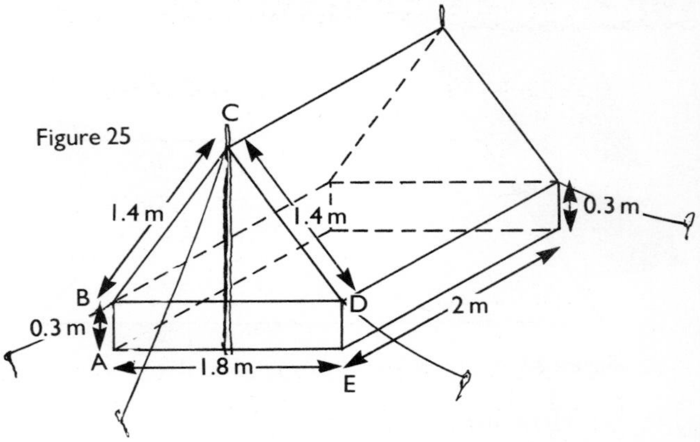

(tent diagram with measurements: 1.4 m, 1.4 m, 0.3 m, 0.3 m, 2 m, 1.8 m; labels A B C D E)

10 Figure 25 shows a tent. Using a scale of 5 cm to 1 m, construct accurately a scale drawing of the end ABCDE.

From your diagram find

(a) the height of the tent in metres,

(b) the angle which the sloping edge CB makes with the horizontal.

NEA Syllabus C, May 1988, Paper 3

11 Figure 26 shows the junction of two rivers. Some Scouts are asked to estimate the distance between the point C and the tree, T, on the opposite bank. The Scouts are at the point B and cannot cross either river. They mark the points A and D and make the measurements shown in the diagram. ABC and DBT are straight lines.

AB = 20 m, BD = 15 m, AD = 17 m, angle TAB = 41° and angle BDC = 36°.

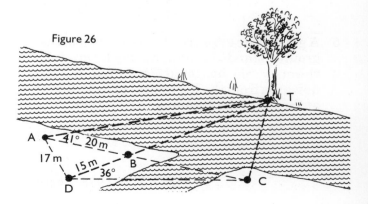

Figure 26

Using a scale of 1 cm to represent 5 metres, draw a scale diagram of the situation and find the distance CT, in metres.

MEG, May 1988, Paper 2

EXERCISE 8 Dials, clocks and time

A   B

1 How many grams of flour should be taken off pan A and placed on pan B so that the same weight of flour is on each scale?

NEA Syllabus C, May 1988, Paper 2

2 The pictures below show a dress-making tape. Say to what measurement the arrow is pointing in each picture, and give the units of measurement.

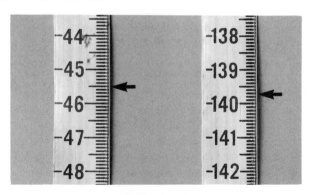

3 Roger weighs some rice. Figure 27 shows the weight in kilograms.

(a) What is the weight of the rice in kilograms?

(b) What is the weight of the rice in grams?

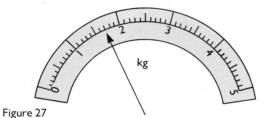

Figure 27

(c) Taking 1 kg to be 2.2 pounds calculate the weight of the rice in pounds.

SEG B, Summer 1988, Paper 2

4 Figure 28 represents the speedometer of a car. The speeds are given in miles per hour on the outer scale and kilometres per hour on the inner scale. There is also a fuel gauge.

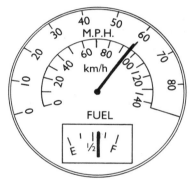

Figure 28

(a) Write down the speed, in m.p.h., that is shown on the dial.

(b) Estimate, as accurately as possible, the speed shown in km/h.

(c) What fraction, of a full tank of fuel, remains in the car?

LEAG SMP, May 1988, Paper 2

5 Before yogurt can be made the milk has to be heated up and then left to cool to a temperature of 49° C before it can be added to the 'live' yogurt.

The thermometer in the photograph on the next page shows the temperature of some milk at 10.56 a.m.

(a) What was the temperature of the milk at 10.56 a.m.?

(b) The milk cools down at one degree every three minutes. At what time will it be ready to add to the 'live' yogurt?

Roast Turkey

Allow ¾ lb per person.

Use a hot oven.

For turkey up to 12 lb, allow 15 minutes per lb and 15 minutes extra. For every extra 1 lb over 12 lb, allow 12 minutes more.

Oven temperature guide

Very cool	120°C
Cool	145°C
Moderate	175°C
Moderately hot	195°C
Hot	225°C
Very hot	245°C

6 Use the information in the tables above to answer the following questions.

(a) How many minutes does it take to roast a 9 lb turkey?

(b) If I want the 9 lb turkey to be ready by 1 p.m., at what time should I start to cook it?

(c) At what temperature should the oven be set?

(d) How many people will a 9 lb turkey be sufficient for?

(e) How many minutes does it take to roast an 18 lb turkey?

MEG November 1986, Paper 2

7 Wayne took 4 hours 37 minutes to run a marathon. The marathon started at 10.45 a.m.

At what time did Wayne finish?

8 Figure 29 gives the timings of BBC television programmes on Tuesday 18th July 1989.

BBC1	TV AT A GLANCE
6.00 Ceefax AM	
6.30 The Flintstones	
7.00 Breakfast Time	
9.05 Heathcliff	
9.25 Record Breakers	BBC2
10.00 Tom and Jerry	
10.30 Playbus	
10.55 Five to Eleven	**6.55** Open University
11.00 Popeye Double Bill	**7.20** Closedown
11.15 The O Zone	**9.00** Pages from Ceefax
11.25 Superman	**9.55** Castles of Scotland
11.50 Bananaman	**10.25** Energy Resources
12.00 Dallas	**10.50** Film: Take Me High
1.00 One O'Clock News	**12.20** Small World
1.30 Neighbours	**12.30** Oil
1.50 Antiques at Home	**12.55** Energy
2.20 Film: Morning Departure	**1.20** Bertha
4.00 Cartoon	**1.35** See Hear!
4.10 Ewoks	**2.00** The Man behind the Mask
4.35 Really Wild Show	**2.50** Holiday Outings
5.00 Newsround	**3.00** Musical Mariner
5.05 Gentle Ben	**4.00** Film: Dangerous Exile
5.35 Neighbours	**5.30** Goodbye to the Good Old Days
6.00 Six O'Clock News	**6.00** Film: Playmates
6.30 Regional magazines	**7.35** Business Matters
7.00 Tinniswood Country	**8.00** On the Line
7.30 EastEnders	**8.30** Ebony on the Road
8.00 The Paul Daniels Magic Show	**9.00** Studio 5B
8.45 Points of View	**9.50** The Home Front
9.00 Nine O'Clock News	**10.30** Newsnight
9.30 Shadow of the Cobra	**11.15** Open Golf 1988
11.00 An Ocean Apart	**12.00** Open University
12.05 Close	**2.30** Close

Figure 29

(a) How long were these programmes:

(i) *Energy* on BBC2?
(ii) the film *Morning Departure* on BBC1?

(b) What was the longest programme on BBC2?

(c) Someone watched *The Home Front* on BBC2. As soon as it was finished she turned over to BBC1 and watched it until the close.

How many minutes of *Shadow of the Cobra* did she watch?

9 (a) What is the smaller angle between the hands of a clock at 4 o'clock?

(b) What is the larger angle between the hands of a clock at 11 o'clock?

(c) What is the smaller angle between the hands of a clock at half past 2?

(d) How long does it take

(i) a minute hand to turn through 420°?
(ii) an hour hand to turn through 420°?

(e) Through how many degrees did a minute hand turn during the showing of the film *Playmates* on BBC2? (See question 8.)

10 In the 1988 Winter Olympics, the medals for the Women's 20 km cross country were all won by Soviet competitors. Their times were as follows:

1	T. Tikhonova	55 minutes 53.6 seconds
2	A. Reztsova	56 minutes 12.8 seconds
3	R. Smetanina	57 minutes 22.1 seconds

(a) How many seconds was Reztsova behind the winner?

(b) The British competitor, L. Mackenzie, finished 13 minutes 45.2 seconds behind Smetanina. What was her time?

MEG, May 1989, Paper 1

11 A hairdresser takes between 10 minutes and 15 minutes to cut a man's hair.

(a) He works, at most, 7 hours a day and charges £2.40 for each haircut. Calculate the greatest amount he can earn in one day.

(b) Mr. Smith arrives at 9.45 a.m. to have his hair cut. He finds one customer just starting to have his hair cut and three others waiting. Mr. Smith waits his turn.

Find

    (i) the earliest time
    (ii) the latest time

he can expect to have his haircut finished.

MEG June 1987, Paper 5

EXERCISE 9   Money

1 How many chocolate bars costing 22 p each could you buy for £2?

How much change would you get?

2 How much would it cost to place the following advert in the local newspaper if the charge is £1.40 plus 17 p per word?

> **Automatic washing machine** for sale. £95. Good as new. Launderette has opened next door. Phone 333444.

3 Veena does a part-time job, for which she gets £1.90 per hour.

(a) If she works for eight hours how much does she get?

(b) One week Veena could not remember how many hours she had worked, but she was paid £11.40. How many hours did she work?

(c) On the Saturday before Christmas Veena's boss agreed to pay her 'time and a half' for seven hours work. How much did she earn?

4 One shop is selling pens at 13 p each and a second shop is selling the same make of pen at £1.70 per dozen.

At which of these shops would you advise someone to buy this make of pen?

5 When the gas meter in a house was read in September the reading was 3664 units. When it was read again three months later the reading was 3901 units.

If there is a standing charge of £10.60 and gas costs 47 p per unit find the gas bill for the house for this three month period.

6 Ann went on a sponsored walk to raise money for Oxfam.

Here is her sponsor form.

SPONSOR	AMOUNT PER KM	AMOUNT PAID
Claire	3p	
Darren	2p	
Mum	25p	
Mrs Hawes	15p	
Fred	£2.50 altogether	
Paul	4p.	
NUMBER OF KILOMETRES WALKED		
TOTAL £		
SIGNED		

What Fred wrote means that Fred wanted to pay Ann £2.50 however far she walked.

Ann walked 17 kilometres.

What was the total amount of sponsor money she could collect?

7 In a greengrocer's shop apples cost ten pence each and oranges cost fifteen pence each.

(a) Ericka bought six apples and nine oranges. How much did she spend?

(b) Driss spent three pounds and bought an equal number of apples and oranges. How many of each did he buy?

SEG B, Summer 1988, Paper 1

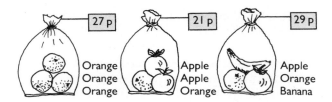

8 Work out the cost of 1 orange, the cost of 1 apple and the cost of 1 banana.

MEG, May 1988, Paper 4

9 To save money to buy Christmas presents, Mrs. Shaw made 40 weekly payments into a Christmas club.

(a) After the 40 weeks, Mrs. Shaw had paid in £160. How much did she pay per week?

(b) A bonus of 5 p in the £ was added to the £160 Mrs. Shaw had paid. How much was the bonus?

(c) What was the total amount in Mrs. Shaw's Christmas club account?

10 Vicky calculates how much money she has in her bank account as follows:

Date		Amount in Bank
January 1st		£50
January 14th	withdrew £15	£35
January 21st	withdrew £16.50	(A)
February 1st	paid in £11	(B)
February 15th	wrote cheque for £35	(C)

(a) How much money should Vicky enter at (A)?

(b) How much should she enter at (B)?

(c) Vicky uses her calculator to find the answer to (C). The calculator displays −5.5. Explain what this means.

NEA Syllabus A and B, May 1988, Paper 2

11 Steady Car Hire's charges for hiring a car are £70 per week plus 3 p per mile. Smart Cars just charge 14.7 p per mile.

Sharon and Ian want to hire a car for a two-week holiday. They expect to travel about 1400 miles during the holiday.

From which hire firm would you advise Sharon to hire the car?

12 Ann, Kuldip, Winston and Darren go out for a meal together. The total bill for the meal is £17.60.

They decide to pay the bill as quickly as possible and settle up with one another later.

Ann provides a £10 note, Winston provides a £5 note. Kuldip has some change and so she provides £2.60. Darren does not contribute at this stage.

Later they settle up so that they all pay the same amount for the meal.

(a) Darren gives his quarter of the bill to Ann. How much does he give her?

(b) How should Ann, Kuldip and Winston settle up between themselves so that each has paid the same amount?

13 A builder paid £167 000 for a 53-acre site.

What was the price of the land per acre, correct to the nearest £100?

14 Chris travels to work five days a week from Runcorn to Liverpool. A peak hour return ticket costs £2.80. A 13-week season ticket costs £145.20.

(a) How much does she save if she buys a 13-week season ticket instead of a peak hour return ticket each day?

(b) In one 13-week period Chris had a fortnight's holiday, and was at home sick for 3 days. Her friend, Alan, said that her season ticket had been a waste of money. Was Alan right? Show how you worked out your answer.

NEA Syllabus C, May 1988, Paper 1

15 Nadia used her camera while she was on holiday. She has one 36-picture film and two 24-picture films to be processed.

MEGAPRINT

IT'S EASY TO ORDER . . .

YES Please process my film(s)

	No. of films	Amount
Up to 24 pictures: £2.79 per film.	☐	£ .
36 pictures: £3.39 per film.	☐	£ .
Postage: 35p per film.		£ .
	Total £	.

(a) (i) How many pictures are there altogether on Nadia's three films?
(ii) The local chemist charges 14 p for processing each picture. How much would Nadia have to pay to have her three films processed?

(b) Alternatively, Nadia could send her films to 'Megaprint'. Their charges are shown on the order form.

Copy and complete the boxes on the form to show how much Nadia would have to pay 'Megaprint'.

(c) 'Megaprint' usually sell films at the following prices:

24 picture film	£1.55
36 picture film	£1.95
Postage	Free

This month they have a special offer of three 24 picture films for the price of two.

(i) How much cheaper is it this month to buy three 24 picture films than to buy two 36 picture films?

(ii) Taking costs of processing by 'Megaprint' into account, would you advise Nadia to use the special offer or to buy two 36 picture films? Show your calculations.

MEG, May 1989, Paper 4

16 A shop is selling a washing machine for £299.99. Alternatively, you can buy it for a down payment of £50 and 24 monthly payments of £12.70.

How much extra do you have to pay if you decide to pay for the washing machine over two years?

17 A cat is fed twice a day. At each feed it has one third of a tin of cat food. The cat also has biscuits and gets through one packet every two weeks.

The cat uses a cat tray and a new bag of cat litter is needed approximately once a month.

Tins of cat food cost 39 p each. Boxes of biscuits cost £1.18.

Bags of cat litter cost £2.45.

Estimate the cost of keeping the cat for a year.

EXERCISE 10 Angles, polygons and tessellations

1 What is the value of angle a?

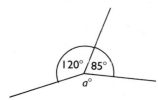

2 Find the angle marked y in figure 30.

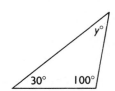

Figure 30

3 In figure 31 the lines l and m are parallel. Calculate the values of a, b, c and d.

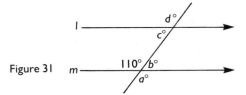

Figure 31

4 (a) Which two of the shapes seen in figure 32 can be joined without overlapping to make a rectangle?

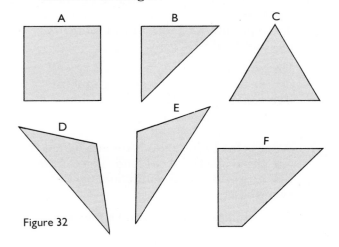

Figure 32

(b) Draw as accurately as possible, the rectangle that could be made with the two shapes you have chosen in (a).

MEG, May 1988, Paper 1

5 Figure 33 shows the side view of a house.

Work out the angle marked x, at the top of the roof.

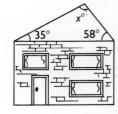

Figure 33

6 Copy the pentagon shown in figure 34 onto squared paper.

Draw a tessellation consisting entirely of pentagons of this shape

Figure 34

7 Copy the pentomino shown onto squared paper.

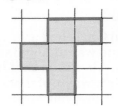

Draw a tessellation consisting entirely of pentominoes of this shape.

8 Figure 35 shows a step ladder. The length XY is equal to the length XZ.

Figure 35

The angle at the top hinge is 26°.

Calculate the size of the angle marked p.

9 PQR is an isosceles triangle and PR = QR.

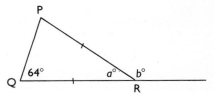

Calculate the values of a and b.

10 Three car registration plates shown in figure 36 have been cut in two. The drawings are not accurate.

Write down the three registration numbers on the plates before they were cut in two.

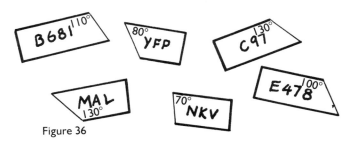

Figure 36

11 Figure 37 shows the view of a window from above. It is closed when in the position AB. It opens to the position AC and is held open by a latch BC which makes an angle of 68° with AB.

(a) (i) Give a reason why ABC is isosceles.
    (ii) Calculate the angle BAC.

(b) The latch BC is replaced with one which is the same length as AB. What is the size of angle BAC when the window is open?

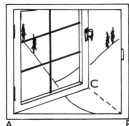

Figure 37

SEG A, Summer 1988, Paper 2

12 A piece of floor is covered with L shaped tiles. The design is repeated over its surface. It consists of the 3 colours red (R), blue (B) and yellow (Y) as shown in figure 38.

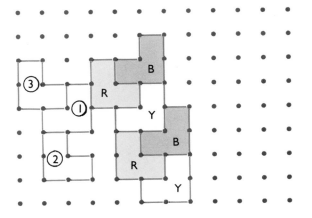

Figure 38

(a) What fraction of the pattern shown is coloured yellow?

(b) (i) Extend the pattern to the right by adding six tiles, showing the colour of each.
    (ii) What are the colours of the tiles numbered 1, 2 and 3?

SEG A, Summer 1988, Paper 2

13 Figure 39 shows the side view of a folding clothes airer made out of several straight pieces of covered wire, hinged at the joints.

(a) What type of quadrilateral is ABCD?

(b) State the size of each of the following angles:

angle *b*,
angle *h*,
angle *f*

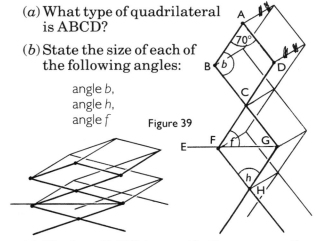

Figure 39

(c) The length EG is exactly the same as the length BG.
Given that AD = 26 cm, find the length of EG.

NEA Syllabus C, May 1988, Paper 2

14 Figure 40 shows a pattern of tiles made of 5 squares and 4 regular figures each of 8 sides.

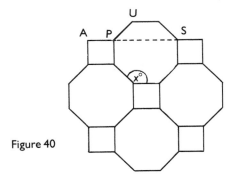

Figure 40

(a) Calculate the value of *x*.

(b) Calculate the sum of the interior angles of one regular figure of eight sides.

(c) Calculate angle UPS.

(d) Calculate angle APU.

MEG SMP Specimen, 1987, Paper 1

15 Part of a regular polygon is shown in figure 41.

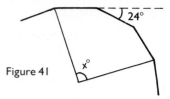

Figure 41

(a) How many sides does the polygon have?

(b) Calculate the angle marked x.

16 Figure 42 shows part of a ring of regular pentagons. The hole in the middle of the ring is a regular polygon.

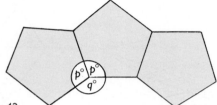

Figure 42

(a) Calculate the angles p and q.

(b) How many pentagons are there in the ring?

17 ABCD is a parallelogram.

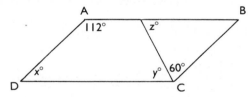

Calculate the values of x, y and z.

18 Figure 43 shows the frame of a bicycle. Angle EBC = 73°, angle BCD = 100° and angle BED = 65°. AB = BE and AE is parallel to BC. Find the values of x, y and z.

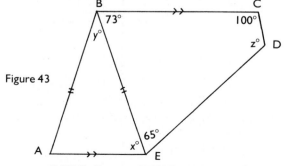

Figure 43

MEG, June 1987, Paper 2 and Paper 3

19 In figure 44 (not drawn to scale) ABCD is a parallelogram and ABE is an equilateral triangle.

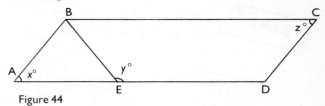

Figure 44

Work out the values of x, y and z.

LEAG SMP, May 1988, Paper 1

20 Find the size of the smallest angle in the triangle shown in figure 45.

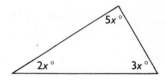

Figure 45

21 In figure 46 the lines l and m are parallel.

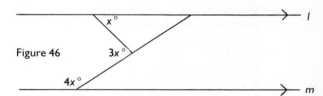

Figure 46

Find the value of x.

22 Figure 47 shows part of a floor covered with two kinds of tiles. All the tiles are regular polygons.

(a) Find the sizes of the angles of the triangular tiles.

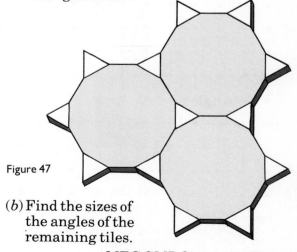

Figure 47

(b) Find the sizes of the angles of the remaining tiles.

MEG SMP Specimen, Paper 3

23 (a) One of the angles of an isosceles triangle is 130°. What are the other two angles?

(b) One of the angles of an isosceles triangle is 40°. What are the other two angles

(i) if the triangle is an acute-angled triangle?
(ii) if the triangle is an obtuse-angled triangle?

24 The interior angle of a regular polygon is 13x° and the exterior angle is 2x°.

(a) Calculate x.

(b) Find the number of sides of the regular polygon.

25 The drawing below shows a regular pentagon with one of its diagonals.

(a) Describe the symmetry of this drawing.

(b) The diagonal divides the pentagon into a triangle and a trapezium.
Find the four interior angles of the trapezium.

26 In the triangle ABC seen in figure 48, the sides of AB and AC are equal in length. The side BC is produced to D so that CD = AC.

(a) Taking angle ADC = x, find, in terms of x, the size of

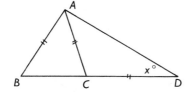

Figure 48

(i) angle ACB,
(ii) angle BAD.

(b) Given that AD = BD, find the value of x.

MEG November 1987, Paper 3

27 In the pentagon ABCDE, angle B = angle E = 144° and angle C = angle D = 108°.

(a) Calculate the size of angle A.

(b) Prove that AB is parallel to ED.

(c) Sketch the pentagon ABCDE given that it has one line of symmetry. Indicate clearly the pairs of sides of the pentagon which are parallel.

MEG, May 1988, Paper 6

28

Figure 49

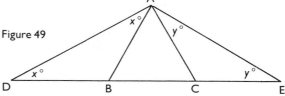

(a) In figure 49, which is not drawn to scale, angle BAD = angle ADB = x and angle CAE = angle CEA = y.

(i) Calculate, in terms of x, the size of angle ABC.
(ii) Calculate, in terms of x and y, the size of angle BAC.
(iii) Explain clearly why DE is equal in length to the perimeter of the triangle ABC.

(b) Use the results obtained in part (a) to construct a triangle ABC with perimeter 12 cm and with angle ABC = 60°, angle BCA = 70° and angle CAB = 50°.

(You may use a protractor to measure any angles you require.)

NEA Syllabus B, May 1988, Paper 4

EXERCISE 11 Transformations

1 (a) Copy figure 50.

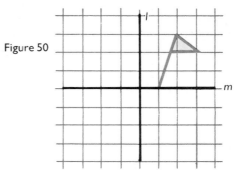

Figure 50

(b) Draw the reflection of the flag in the line *l*.

(c) Draw the reflection of the flag in the line *m*.

2 (a) Draw on squared paper the shape with corners at (3, 1), (6, 1), (4, 3) and (4, 2).

(b) Draw the shape obtained by enlarging this shape by scale factor 2 with the origin as centre of enlargement.

 In the picture below the shape labelled B is a translation of the shape labelled A.

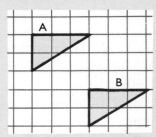

To get from any point of A to a corresponding point of B you move 4 to the *right* and 3 *down*. So the translation of A to B can be described using the vector $\begin{pmatrix} 4 \\ -3 \end{pmatrix}$.

3 (a) Copy the flag shown in figure 51 onto squared paper and label it F.

(b) Draw the flag obtained by translating the shape F by $\begin{pmatrix} 3 \\ 2 \end{pmatrix}$

Label this flag G.

(c) Draw the flag obtained by translating the flag F by $\begin{pmatrix} -4 \\ 1 \end{pmatrix}$

Label this shape H.

Figure 51

4 (a) Copy figure 52 onto squared paper.

(b) Draw the result of reflecting the F shape in the line *l*.

(c) Draw the result of rotating the F shape through half a turn about the point A.

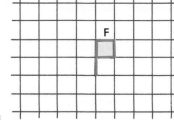

Figure 52

5 (a) In figure 53, four triangles P, Q, R and S are marked. For each of the following mappings, state whether it is a reflection, a rotation, a translation or an enlargement.

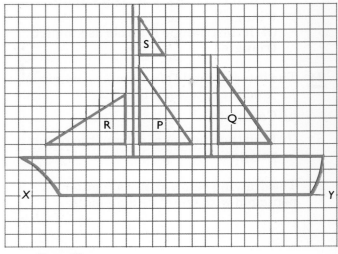

Figure 53

(i) triangle P → triangle Q
(ii) triangle P → triangle R
(iii) triangle S → triangle P

(b) What is the angle of the rotation in part (a)?

(c) What is the scale factor of the enlargement in part (a)?

(d) Draw the reflection of the whole diagram in the line *XY*.

MEG June 1987, Paper 4

6 Look at figure 54.
Describe, fully, the single transformation that maps

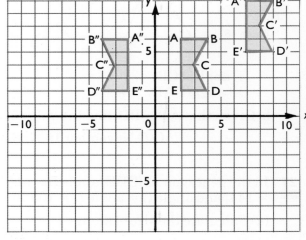

Figure 54

(a) ABCDE to A′B′C′D′E′,

(b) ABCDE to A″B″C″D″E″.

LEAG Specimen Paper, 1991, Paper 2

7 (a) Copy figure 55 onto squared paper.

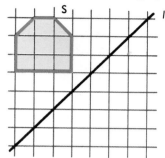

Figure 55

(b) Draw the reflection of the shape labelled S in the line *l*.

8 (a) Draw the rhombus with vertices at (0,0), (1,−2), (2,0) and (1,2). Label it A.

(b) Draw the rhombus with vertices at (2,0), (4,−4), (6,0) and (4,4). Label it B.

(c) Rhombus B is an enlargement of rhombus A.

(i) What is the scale factor?
(ii) What are the coordinates of the centre of enlargement?

9 (a) Copy figure 56 onto squared paper.

(b) The drawing is to be enlarged. The enlargement of the side labelled AB has already been drawn. Complete the enlargement.

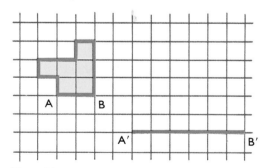

Figure 56

(c) Mark the centre of the enlargement.

(d) State the scale factor of the enlargement.

10 Figure 57, which is not drawn to scale, shows four photographs. The three on the right are all enlargements of the one on the left.

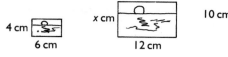

Figure 57

(a) Find *x* and *y*.

(b) The difference between *v* and *w* is 3. Find *v* and *w*.

11 (a) Copy figure 58 onto squared paper.

(b) L_1 is the image of L after a single transformation. Describe this transformation fully.

(c) L_2 is the image of L after another single transformation. Describe this transformation fully.

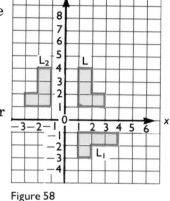

Figure 58

(d) L_2 is the image of L_1 after a reflection. Draw the mirror line for this reflection and label it **m**.

(e) Enlarge the shape labelled L using the scale factor 2 with the origin as centre of enlargement.

Label the enlargement L_3.

(f) What fraction of the area of L_3 is the area of L?

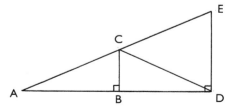

Figure 59

12 In figure 59, triangle ADE is the image of triangle ABC after an enlargement, scale factor +2, using A as the centre of enlargement.

(a) Write down the length of AE if AC = 7 cm.

(b) Write down the size of angle CED if angle ACB = 70°.

(c) Name an isosceles triangle in the diagram.

(d) Name two triangles in the diagram which are congruent to each other.

MEG Specimen, Paper 2 and Paper 3

13 Figure 60 shows a trapezium ABCD in which AB is parallel to DC.
The trapezium consists of four right angled triangles ADM, CMD, MCN and BCN, each with sides of length 3 cm, 4 cm and 5 cm.

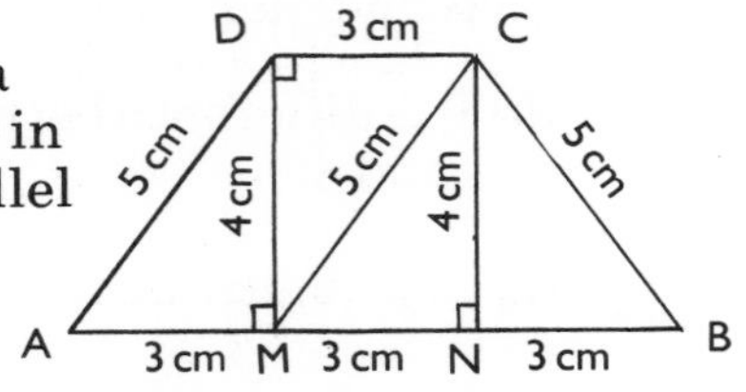

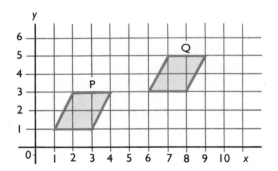

Figure 60

Describe fully the single transformation which will map

(a) triangle ADM onto triangle MCN

(b) triangle BCN onto triangle MCN

(c) triangle CMD onto triangle MCN.

MEG Specimen, Paper 5

14 Describe fully two different transformations which map the parallelogram labelled P to the parallelogram labelled Q in figure 61.

Figure 61

15 (a) Draw the triangle with vertices at the points (1,1), (3,1) and (3,2). Label the triangle A.

(b) Draw the image of A after the enlargement with centre (2,0) and scale factor 2. Label the image B.

(c) Draw the image of A after a translation of $\begin{pmatrix} -3 \\ 2 \end{pmatrix}$
Label the image C.

(d) Describe fully the transformation which maps B onto C.

16 (a) (i) On graph paper plot the following points (0,0); (0,1); (4,3); (7,3); (3,1); (3,0); (0,0), and join them up in the order given.
(ii) Label the figure P.
(iii) Label the point (7,3), A.

(b) The figure P is reflected in the y-axis to form the image Q.

(i) Draw this image and label it Q.
(ii) Write down the coordinates of the image of A.
(iii) Label this point B.

(c) The figure Q is enlarged by scale factor 2, with the centre of enlargement the origin, to form the image R.

(i) Draw this image and label it R.
(ii) Write down the coordinates of the image of B.
(iii) Label this point C.

(d) The figure R is translated six units in the negative direction, parallel to the y-axis, to form the image S.

(i) Draw this image and label it S.
(ii) Write down the coordinates of the image of C.
(iii) Label this point D.

(e) The figure S is enlarged by scale factor ½, with the centre of enlargement the origin, to form the image T.

(i) Draw this image and label it T.
(ii) Write down the coordinates of the image of D.
(iii) Label this point E.

(f) Which of the figures is congruent to T?

SEG B, Summer 1988, Paper 3

17 Look at figure 62. A and B are two points on the circumference of a circle whose centre is O.

Triangle ABO is translated to the new position A'B'O' so that B' coincides with O.

(a) Explain why

(i) O' lies on the circumference,
(ii) A'B' is parallel to AB,

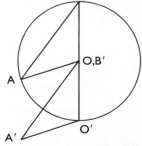

Figure 62

(iii) angle A'B'A = angle B'AB,

(iv) angle B'AB = angle B'BA.

(b) State a relationship between the angles AB'O' and ABO.

LEAG SMP, June 1988, Paper 3

18 An infinite strip pattern is to be created so that it has half-turn symmetry about points A and B. Two of the cells have already been filled with the design.

Figure 63

Copy figure 63 and put the appropriate design into the four empty cells.

19 Figure 64 shows a measuring scoop used for measuring soap powder for a washing machine. It has a diameter of 8 cm and a height of 10 cm.

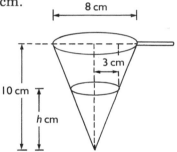

Figure 64

Calculate the height of the powder (h cm) in the scoop when the radius of the soap powder surface is 3 cm.

NEA Syllabus A, May 1988, Paper 4

EXERCISE 12 Statistics I

1 The table below shows the number of hours of sunshine in British holiday resorts on one July day.

Resort	Hours
Blackpool	8
Bournemouth	6
Clacton	8
Colwyn Bay	7
Great Yarmouth	9
Paignton	2
Scarborough	10

(a) Draw a bar chart to display this information.

(b) Find the median value of this data.

(c) Find the mean value of this data.

(d) In how many of these resorts was the temperature above the mean?

2 26 people were asked how many television sets they had at home. The information is displayed in the bar chart seen in figure 65.

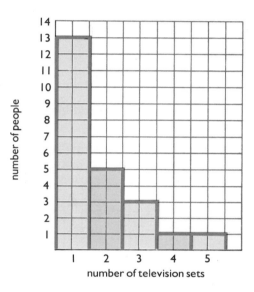

Figure 65

(a) What is the modal number of television sets?

(b) The person who collected the information did not record people who had no television set at home. How many people were there without a television set?

3 The midday temperature, in degrees Celsius, for ten July days in London were as follows:

18 20 22 23 26 28 22 18 18 17

(a) What is the range for this data?

(b) What is the median temperature?

(c) What is the mean temperature?

4 A girl did a part-time job for six weeks. Her average weekly earning was £23.50.

How much did she earn altogether during the six weeks?

5 25 golfers played in a competition. Their scores were

82	88	85	86	92
101	82	86	92	85
83	86	87	87	82
94	92	100	96	94
81	86	89	90	86

(a) Copy and complete the table below.

Score	Tally	Frequency
80–84		5
85–89		
90–94		
95–99		
100–104		

(b) How many of the golfers scored less than 90?

(c) Copy and complete the bar chart in figure 66 to show the information in your table.

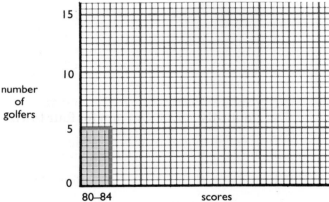

Figure 66

(d) What percentage of the golfers scored less than 85?

LEAG May 1988, Paper 1

6 The ages of the five members of the *'Pentagons'* pop group are given in the table below.

	Age	
	years	months
Abdul	17	3
Betty	18	6
Colin	19	0
Deborah	17	9
Errol	17	6

Errol says his age is the average age of the group. Is he right? Explain your answer.

NEA Syllabus C, May 1988, Paper 1

7 When the weights of eight bags of flour were checked, the following results were obtained:

1.53 kg
1.52 kg
1.49 kg
1.51 kg
1.53 kg
1.51 kg
1.53 kg
1.54 kg

(a) find the average weight of these eight bags of flour.

(b) Each bag is supposed to weigh 1½ kg. How much, in kilograms, is the heaviest bag overweight?

(c) Write your answer to part (b) in grams.

MEG, May 1989, Paper 1

8 The number of letters in each of the first sixty words of a newspaper article were as follows:

6, 9, 6, 4, 3, 2, 8, 4, 7, 3, 5, 5, 2, 6, 6, 6, 2, 5, 11, 2, 3, 7, 2, 2, 4, 2, 1, 3, 7, 2, 3, 7, 5, 4, 4, 5, 5, 6, 1, 7, 8, 2, 6, 3, 5, 14, 2, 8, 10, 6, 2, 3, 3, 6, 2, 3, 7, 2, 3, 3.

(a) Use a tally chart to record the number of words with 1 letter, 2 letters, 3 letters, and so on.

(b) What is the mode for this data?

(c) Find the total number of letters in the sixty words.

(d) What is the mean number of letters per word?

(e) What is the median number of letters per word?

9 In a recent survey of a certain area, the number of people living in each house was noted and the information represented by the bar chart shown in figure 67.
(a) From the bar chart find:

(i) how many houses had only two people living in them
(ii) how many houses had more than three people living in them
(iii) how many houses there were altogether in the area.

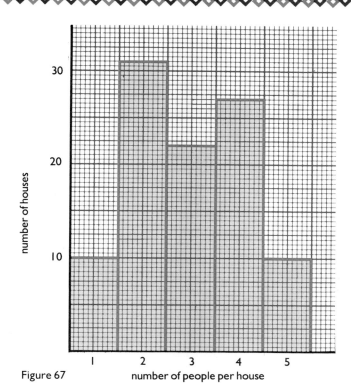

Figure 67   number of people per house

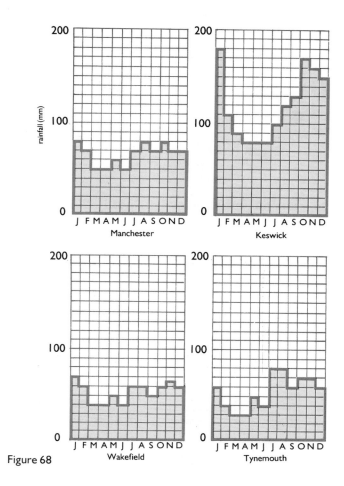

Figure 68

(b) Calculate:

(i) how many people were living in the area

(ii) the mean number of people per house.

LEAG June 1986, Paper 2

10 Write down three numbers which have a mean of 7 and a median of 5.

11 Four blocks of copper are weighed and their volumes are then measured.
Here are the results.

	mass (g)	volume (cm³)
1st block	310	30
2nd block	605	70
3rd block	908	100
4th block	1221	140

(a) Plot these results as points on a graph, using a scale of 1 cm for 10 cm³ on the horizontal axis and 1 cm for 100 g on the vertical axis.

(b) Draw the straight line which fits the points most closely.

(c) Give the approximate weight of a piece of copper whose volume is 80 cm³.

(d) Give the approximate volume of a piece of copper which weighs 1 kg.

12 The graphs shown in figure 68 show the mean monthly rainfall in mm for four towns over a twelve-month period.

(a) Which town had the driest January?

(b) Which town had the wettest summer?

(c) Calculate the mean monthly rainfall for the year for Manchester, giving your answer to the nearest mm.

(d) What is the range in monthly figures for the year in Keswick?

(e) During the month of July, Keswick had rain on 12 days. What is the probability that, during a one-day visit to Keswick in July, it will *not* rain?

NEA Syllabus C, May 1988, Paper 2

13 In an examination each candidate is awarded one of the grades A, B, C, D, E, F. Grade A is the highest and grade F is the lowest. The distribution of grades obtained by the 30 pupils in the class is shown in the table below.

Grade	A	B	C	D	E	F
Number of pupils	4	9	7	5	3	2

(a) Write down the mode of this distribution.

(b) Find the median of this distribution.

(c) Give a reason why it is not possible, using only the information given, to find a mean for this distribution.

MEG November 1987, Paper 2

14 The mean height of 6 girls is 1.62 m. The mean height of 5 of the girls is 1.59 m. What is the height of the sixth girl?

15 The results of two mathematics tests of a group of children are shown in the table below.

Names	Test A	Test B
Bill	60	35
Ritu	38	21
Mary	65	47
Elaine	Abs	31
George	75	56
James	48	40
Martine	67	54
Taran	23	11
Conrad	82	59
Claire	16	20
Brenda	92	62
Michelle	80	Abs

These results are plotted on the scatter diagram in figure 69. Copy this diagram

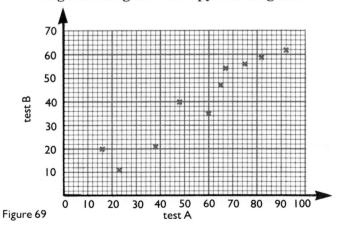

Figure 69

(a) Draw a line of best fit for these points.

(b) From your line estimate

(i) the score Elaine might have got on Test A,
(ii) the score Michelle might have got on Test B,
if they had not been absent.

NEA Syllabus A, May 1988, Paper 3

16 The village of Deep Snoring has 45 inhabitants. Their ages (in completed years) are as follows:

32, 30, 6, 2, 0, 64, 71, 55, 59, 45, 14, 12, 22, 24, 19, 47, 43, 16, 15, 37, 51, 53, 17, 11, 18, 36, 61, 57, 56, 51, 46, 50, 24, 31, 36, 40, 58, 51, 68, 70, 72, 69, 33, 31, 6.

(a) Copy and complete the following table.

Age (in completed years)	Tally marks	Frequency
0–9		
10–19		
20–29		
30–39		
40–49		
50–59		
60–69		
70–79		
Total =		45

(b) Copy figure 70 and draw a histogram to represent this information.

NEA Syllabus B, May 1988, Paper 3

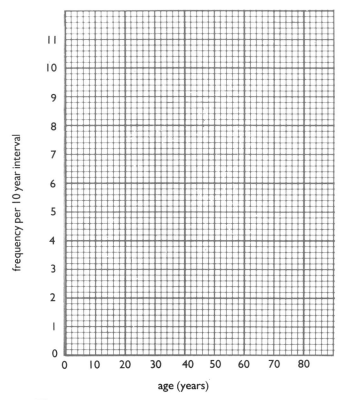

Figure 70

17 Class 1*E* collected information about the number of children in each of their families. They illustrated this information by a bar chart and also calculated the mean number of children per family.

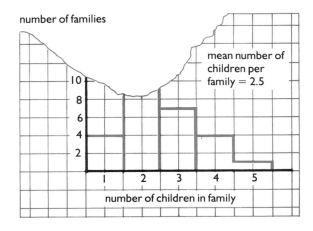

Figure 71

Charlene Roberts, a member of 1*E*, accidentally tore her paper. What was left of her work is shown in figure 71.

(*a*) How many families had 3 children in them?

(*b*) Find how many families had 2 children in them.

MEG June 1987, Paper 3

18 (*a*) Write down three numbers for which the median is 10, the mean is 8 and the range is 8.

(*b*) Write down five positive numbers for which the median is 3, the mean is 4 and the mode is 7.

19 The weights of new-born babies are given, to the nearest 10 g, in the following table.

Weight (kg)	Frequency
1.00 – 1.49	3
1.50 – 1.99	8
2.00 – 2.49	12
2.50 – 2.99	22
3.00 – 3.49	27
3.50 – 3.99	18
4.00 – 4.49	9
4.50 – 4.99	1

Weight	Cumulative frequency
Not more than 0.995 kg	0
Not more than 1.495 kg	3

(*a*) Complete the cumulative frequency table above.

(*b*) On graph paper, draw a cumulative frequency diagram to illustrate the data.

(*c*) From your diagram, and making methods clear, estimate

(i) the median weight,
(ii) the probability that a new-born baby chosen at random from this sample weighs between 2.4 kg and 3.2 kg.

NEA Syllabus C, May 1988, Paper 3

Number of weeks after 1 January 1985	0	10	20	30	40	50	60	70	80	90	100	110	120
Percentage of members still on diet	100	97	80	54	36	27	20	16	14	12	10	9	8

The members of a nationwide slimmers' club all started on a new diet on 1 January 1985. The percentage of members still on the diet was recorded at the end of each period of 10 weeks. The results are shown in the table above.

(a) (i) Find the percentage of members who had given up the diet by the end of 40 weeks after 1 January 1985.
(ii) Given that 2800 members had given up the diet by the end of 60 weeks, calculate the number of members who were still on the diet.

(b) Using a scale of 2 cm to represent 20 weeks on the horizontal axis and 2 cm to represent 10% of members on the vertical axis, draw a graph to show the percentage of members still on the diet for times up to 120 weeks after 1 January 1985.

(c) Using your graph and making your methods clear, estimate

(i) the median,
(ii) the interquartile range

for the length of time members were on the diet.

MEG June 1987, Paper 6

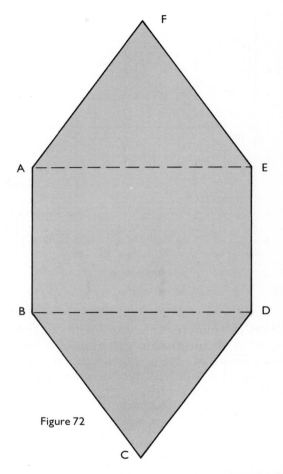

Figure 72

EXERCISE 13 Length, area and volume I

1 (a) Make the necessary measurements from figure 72 to answer the following questions. (Each of the measurements you require is a whole number of centimetres.)

(i) What are the lengths of AB and BC?
(ii) What is the perimeter of the hexagon ABCDEF?
(iii) What is the area of the rectangle ABDE?

(iv) What is the area of the triangle AEF?
(v) What is the area of the hexagon ABCDEF?

(b) By drawing four or more tiles of the same shape as the hexagon already drawn, show how to construct a tessellation.

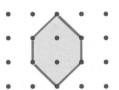

MEG June 1986, Paper 4

2 In the parallelogram ABCD shown in figure 73, AB = 10 cm, BC = 12 cm, BN = 8 cm, angle BAN = 53°, angle BND = 90°, angle BCD = x° and angle ADC = y°.

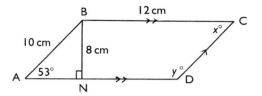

Figure 73

Calculate

(a) the value of x,

(b) the value of y,

(c) the area, in cm, of ABCD.

MEG Nov 1986, Paper 1A

3 Figure 74 represents the four interior walls of a room

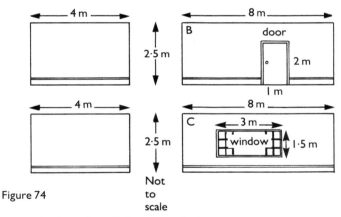

Figure 74

The height of the room is 2.5 m.

(a) Find the area, in square metres, of

    (i) wall A,
    (ii) wall B, excluding the door,
    (iii) wall C, excluding the window.

(b) Find the total area in square metres of the four walls, excluding the door and window.

(c) A 3 litre tin of emulsion paint covers 30 square metres of wall.
How many 3 litre tins of emulsion paint need to be bought to cover the area found in part (b)?

MEG June 1987, Paper 1 and Paper 2

4 Figure 75 shows the plan of a car park. Cars park in the marked bays.

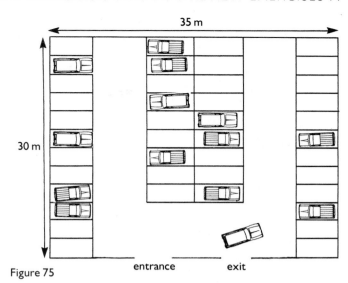

Figure 75

The car park measures 30 metres by 35 metres. Each parking bay measures 2.5 metres by 5 metres.

(a) How many parking bays are marked in the car park?

(b) Find the area, in square metres, of the whole car park.

(c) Find the area, in square metres, of one parking bay.

(d) Two thirds of the parking bays are full. How many parking bays are empty?

(e) The parking charge for each hour, or part of an hour, is 15p. Mr. Adams leaves his car in the car park at half past ten one morning. He drives it out again at quarter past three that afternoon. How much should he expect to pay?

MEG Nov 1987, Paper 4

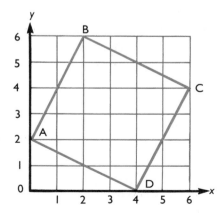

Figure 76

5 The one centimetre grid in figure 76 shows part of a wallpaper design requiring a square ABCD to be coloured yellow.

(a) Write down the coordinates of the points A and D;

(b) Find the area of the triangle AOD;

(c) Find the area of the square ABCD.

MEG, SMP specimen, Paper 1

6 A rectangle has an area of 48 cm².

(a) The length of each side is a whole number of centimetres. One possible rectangle would be 1 cm wide by 48 cm long.

(*Note*: 48 cm wide by 1 cm long is *not* a different rectangle).

(i) Write down the sizes of all the other possible rectangles.
(ii) Which of these answers gives the least perimeter for the rectangle?

(b) Another rectangle with the same area has a width of ½ cm.

(i) What is the length of this rectangle?
(ii) What is the perimeter of this rectangle?

SEG B 1988, Paper 1

7 Figure 77 is of a sheet of glass which has been cut to fit a large rectangular window.

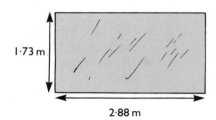

1·73 m

2·88 m

Figure 77

(a) Calculate the exact value of

(i) the perimeter of the glass,
(ii) the area of one side of the glass.

(b) Write down your answers to part (a) correct to the nearest whole number.

MEG May 1988, Paper 1

8 Figure 78 shows a matchbox measuring 5 cm by 4 cm by 2 cm.

2 cm

5 cm   4 cm

Figure 78

(a) Calculate the volume of the matchbox. 12 similar matchboxes fill a carton with base dimensions of 10 cm by 8 cm.

Calculate

(b) the volume of the carton,

(c) the height of the carton,

(d) the total number of matches in the carton, if each box contains 48 matches.

MEG May 1988, Paper 1

9 An isosceles triangle LMN is shown in figure 79.

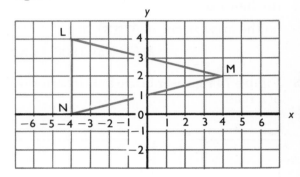

Figure 79

(a) Write down the coordinates of M.

(b) Find the area, in square centimetres, of triangle LMN.

MEG May 1988, Paper 1

10 (a) On a sheet of squared paper draw three rectangles each of which has an area of 24 cm², but having perimeters of different lengths.

(b) Calculate the perimeter of each of the rectangles you have drawn.

11 The area of a square is 15 m². Find the length of one of its sides, giving your answer correct to one decimal place.

12 The rectangular window in figure 80 (width 2.4 m and length 1.5 m) has to be glazed with three pieces of glass. Each of the pieces is the same size.

2·4 m

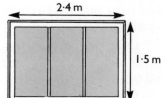

1·5 m

Figure 80

(a) Work out the width and length of one of the pieces of glass needed.

(b) Work out the area of the piece of glass whose dimensions you found in (a).

(c) Glass costs £2.40 per square metre. Calculate the total cost of glass needed to glaze the window.

LEAG, SMP May 1988, Paper 1

13 The box in figure 81 is filled with packets of tea. Each packet of tea is 5 cm by 5 cm by 12 cm. When full, the box contains 100 packets of tea. The packets of tea are stacked upright in the box.

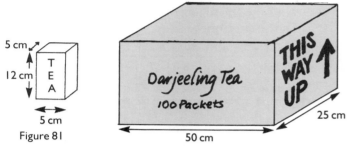

Figure 81

(a) How many packets of tea fit onto the base of the box?

(b) How many layers of packets of tea are there in a full box?

(c) What is the height of the box?

LEAG, SMP May 1988, Paper 1

14 A water tank is 70 cm high, 80 cm wide and 120 cm long.
An overflow pipe is fixed 15 cm from the top of the tank.

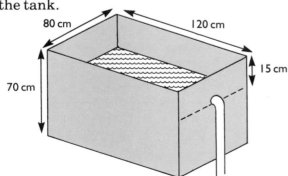

(a) At what height from the base is the pipe fixed?

(b) What is the greatest volume of water that the tank can hold?

MEG Leicestershire Mode 3, May 1989, Paper 1

15 The internal dimensions of a box are 24 cm by 21 cm by 18 cm.

(a) How many cubes of side 3 cm will fit into this box?

(b) How many cubes of side 5 cm will fit into this box?

16 (a) Figure 82 shows a corridor 2 m wide. Calculate the area of the floor of the corridor.

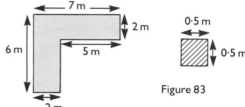

Figure 82   Figure 83

(b) The floor of this corridor is covered with square carpet tiles which have a side of 0.5 m as shown in figure 83.

(i) How many carpet tiles are needed to cover 1 square metre?
(ii) How many tiles are needed to cover the corridor?

SEG A May 1988, Paper 2

17 Figure 84 represents the end view of a garden shed. The edges AB and AE are equal in length, CD = 2.6 m and angle BAE = 66°.

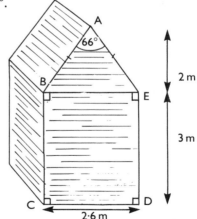

Figure 84

(a) Calculate the size of angle ABE.

(b) Calculate the size of angle ABC.

(c) Calculate the area of triangle ABE.

(d) Calculate the total area of the end of the shed.

NEA Syllabuses A and B May 1988, Paper 2

18 Figure 85 is a drawing of a rectangular petrol can. How many litres of petrol does it hold when full? (1 litre = 1000 cm³)

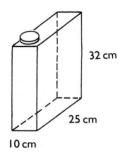

Figure 85

LEAG Specimen 1991, Paper 2

19 (a) Calculate the area of the room shown in figure 86.

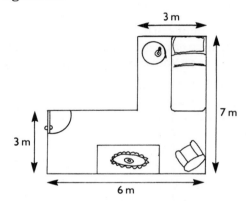

Figure 86

(b) The room is to be carpeted by carpet strips cut to any length from a roll 1.5 m wide.

What is the total length of carpet required?

20

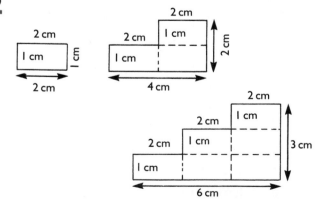

The diagram above shows the first three of a sequence of shapes made up of rectangles of height 1 cm and base 2 cm.

(a) (i) Copy and complete the following table to show the perimeters of the first five shapes in the sequence.

Height (cm)	1	2	3	4	5
Perimeter (cm)	6	12			

(i) Write down a formula for the perimeter (P cm) in terms of the height (H cm).

(ii) How many of the shapes in the sequence have a perimeter of less than 82 cm?

(b) (i) Copy and complete the following table to show the areas of the first five shapes in the sequence.

Height (cm)	1	2	3	4	5
Area (cm)	2	6			

(ii) How many of the shapes in the sequence have an area of less than 58 cm² ?

MEG June 1986, Paper 5

21 A rectangle has length 8 cm and breadth 5 cm. The midpoints of the sides of the rectangle are joined to form a rhombus ABCD, as shown in figure 87.

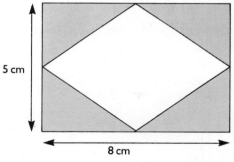

Figure 87

Calculate the area, in square centimetres, of the rhombus.

MEG November 1987, Paper 2 and Paper 3

22 The edge of a cube box is 1 m. How many cubes of edge 2 cm will fit into the box?

23

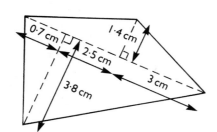

Figure 88

Calculate the area of the quadrilateral shown in figure 88.

24 A large cube is made up of 343 small cubes. How many of the small cubes are there along one of the edges of the large cube?

25 A square floor of side a has a square carpet of side b placed as shown in figure 89.

(a) Express the area of the floor not covered by the carpet in terms of a and b.

(b) If $a = 5.1$ metres and $b = 3.9$ metres find, in square metres, the area of floor not covered by the carpet.

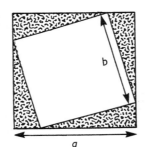

Figure 89

SEG A Summer 1988, Paper 4

26 The material for a lamp shade is cut from a trapezium as illustrated in figure 90.

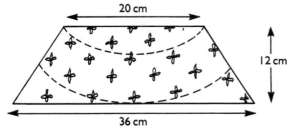

Figure 90

Calculate the area of the trapezium

(a) in cm^2

(b) in m^2.

SEG A Summer 1988, Paper 4

27 Figure 91 shows the end view of a greenhouse.

B is 2.5 m above ED
AB = BC
AE = CD = 2 m
ED = 3 m.

Figure 91

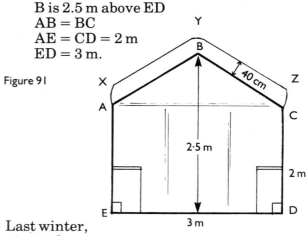

Last winter, 40 cm of snow settled on the roof.

(a) Calculate the area, in m^2, of

(i) the end of the greenhouse, ABCDE,
(ii) the end, XYZDE, including the layer of snow.

(b) Hence find the area of the snow section, XYZCBA.

(c) Explain why the answer to (b) should equal the width of the greenhouse multiplied by the depth of snow.

LEAG (SMP), June 1988, Paper 4

EXERCISE 14 Sines and cosines

Section C of chapter 2 explained how to find the coordinates of points on the circumference of a circle.

Drawing (*a*) below is a copy of the picture for question 9 on page 19.

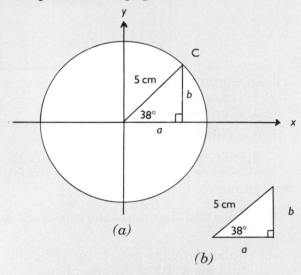

(a)

(b)

Drawing (*b*) above is the same, except that the axes and circle have not been drawn.

To find the length of the side labelled *a* you first put 38 into your calculator and press the ⬚ cos ⬚ button. The answer you get is 0.7880107. This is called the cosine of 38°. Frequently people write

$$\cos 38° = 0.7880107$$

To finish finding the length of *a* you multiply this number by 5.

You could write your method down like this.

$$a = 5 \times \cos 38°$$
$$= 5 \times 0.7880107$$
$$= 3.9400538$$

The value of *a* should be given as a sensible approximation. This might be 3.9 or 3.94 cm.

To find *b* you could write

$$b = 5 \times \sin 38°$$
$$= 5 \times 0.6156614$$
$$= 3.0783074$$

A sensible value of *b* might be 3.1 or 3.08 cm.

Drawing (*a*) below is similar to the picture for question 10 on page 20.

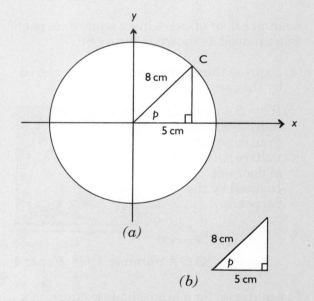

(a)

(b)

Drawing (*b*) above is the same, except that the axes and circle have not been drawn.

To find the angle marked *p* you divide 5 by 8 (which is the radius of the circle or the **hypotenuse** of the right-angled triangle) and then press ⬚ inv ⬚ ⬚ cos ⬚ or ⬚ cos^{-1} ⬚. You could write this as follows

$$p = \text{inv} \cos (5 \div 8)$$
$$= \text{inv} \cos 0.625$$
$$= 51.317813$$

A sensible answer for *p* might be 51°.

1 The ladder shown in figure 92 makes an angle of 70° with the ground. The ladder is 3.8 m long.

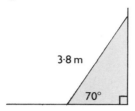

Figure 92

(a) How far up the wall does the ladder reach?

(b) How far is the bottom of the ladder from the bottom of the wall.

2 A ladder 4.2 m long is placed against a wall so that it reaches 3.7 m up the wall.

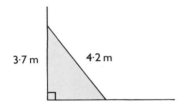

Find the angle the ladder makes with the ground.

3 Susan is flying a kite. The string is 93 m long and the angle between the string and the horizontal ground is 62°.

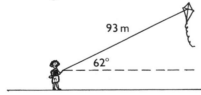

How high is the kite above Susan's hand?

4 A kite is flying on the end of a string which is 75 m long.

The kite is 4 m lower than it would be if the string was vertical.

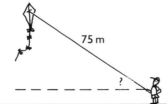

What angle does the string make with the ground?

5 The triangle ABC in figure 93 is an equilateral triangle whose sides are 8 cm long.

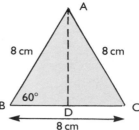

Figure 93

(a) Find the length of the line AD.

(b) Find the area of the equilateral triangle ABC.

6 Four rods are jointed together so that they can make a quadrilateral. Two of the rods are 8 cm long and two are 6 cm long.

(a) Figure 94 shows the rods with an angle of 90° between them, so that they form a rectangle.

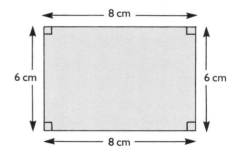

Figure 94

What is the area of the rectangle?

(b) The rods are now moved so that the angle between them is 50°, as shown in figure 95.

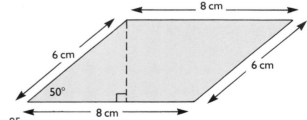

Figure 95

(i) What is the length of the dotted line?
(ii) What is the area of the parallelogram formed by the rods?

(c) What should be the angle between the rods to make the area of the parallelogram they form exactly half the area of the rectangle?

7 A regular hexagon has sides of length 10 cm.

Another regular hexagon is drawn inside by joining the midpoints of the sides of the first hexagon.

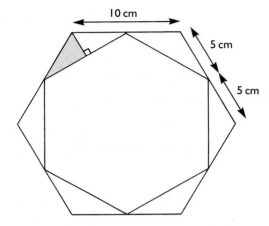

The shaded triangle has been redrawn on a larger scale in figure 96.

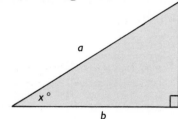

Figure 96

(a) State the size of the angle marked x.

(b) State the value of a.

(c) Find the length of the side marked b.

(d) Find the length of one of the sides of the inner hexagon.

8 Lemonade cans have the shape of a cylinder with radius 3 cm and height 15 cm. The cans are packed upright in a rectangular box with base 36 cm by 48 cm and height 15 cm.

(a) The cans are arranged in rows so that there is the same number of cans in each row. Calculate the greatest number of cans which can be fitted into the box in this way.

(b) It is proposed to arrange the cans in the box so that the centres of their bases are at the vertices of equilateral triangles of side 6 cm, as illustrated in figure 97.

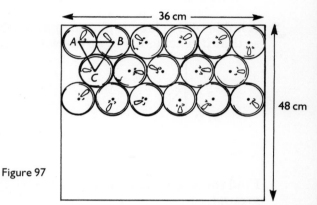

Figure 97

(i) Show that the height of the equilateral triangle ABC (shown in figure 97) is a little less than 5.2 cm.
(ii) Calculate the greatest number of rows of cans which will fit into the 48 cm long box in this way and the corresponding total number of cans.

MEG June 1986, Paper 6

9 CONTAINERS

In any kitchen, bathroom or garden shed you can find a large number of containers of many different shapes and sizes. It might help you to do this introductory task if you collect together a wide variety of containers.

● Describe the different shapes of containers

   Examples: cornflakes packets are cuboids.
              tins of paint are cylinders.

● Describe the different materials used for containers. Try to decide how the containers have been made and why particular materials were used.

   Example: cornflakes packets are made of cardboard.
              Packets are cut out of flat sheets and folded up. Cardboard is easy to cut and fold, and cornflakes are light so they won't split the cardboard.

● Make a list showing what units different items are usually sold in. You could consider some of the items in the list shown below.

   Examples: baked beans are sold in grams.
              lemonade is sold in litres.
              toothpaste is sold in millilitres.

Try to discover which types of items are sold in which units. Some items might be sold in more than one unit.

> Common units and abbreviations are listed on page 246.

adhesive tape	drawing/writing paper	nails	spinach
aubergines	dress material	parsley	string
baked beans	fertiliser	pepper	toilet paper
bananas	flour	perfume	tomatoes
bean sprouts	garlic	petrol	washing up liquid
carpet	garam masala	potatoes	yams
cauliflower	guavas	rice	wallpaper
celery	knitting wool	salt	wine
cheese	lentils	sand	wood for shelves
chilli powder	lychees	sausages	wrapping paper
coriander	milk	seeds	
cornflakes	noodles	soap powder	
disinfectant	orange juice	spaghetti	

SECTION A

1   If someone buys potatoes at a greengrocer's which of the following amounts are they most likely to ask for:

(a) 5 oz?   (b) 5 lb?   (c) 5 l?

Look at your answer. If you asked for that amount of potatoes how many potatoes of average size might you expect to get?

2   Which of the following amounts is a bag of sugar most likely to contain:

(a) 1 oz?   (b) 1 kg?   (c) 1 g?   (d) 1 l?

3   You are on holiday in France and your parents send you to buy 5 lb of potatoes. The shopkeeper only has 2 kg and 4 kg bags. How many bags of which size would you get?

4   A can of drink contains 440 ml. Roughly how much is this in pints?

5   The petrol tank of a car holds about 40 l of petrol. Roughly how much is this in gallons?

6   Which would you expect to cost more:

(a) 1 l of car oil or 1 pint of car oil?

(b) 1 lb of onions or 1 kg of onions?

(c) 1 oz of dried parsley or 10 g of dried parsley?

(d) 1 kg of bananas or 4 bananas?

(e) 1 kg of strawberries or a punnet of strawberries?

(f) 250 g of butter or half a pound of butter?

(g) half a litre of wine or 70 cl of wine?

7   When an item is sold in a container the amount of the item in the container is usually written on the outside of the container. Here are some examples:

290 g on a can of soup
1 litre on a carton of orange juice
55 ml on a tube of toothpaste
2 lb on a can of golden syrup
1.5 kg on a packet of flour
14 g on a drum of dried thyme
125 g on a carton of yogurt
1 pint on a milk bottle
10 fl oz on a carton of whipping cream
113 g on a jar of Marmite
71 g on a packet of stock cubes
3.85 kg on a packet of soap powder
284 ml on a jar of sauce

(a) Make a list of the items above which are sold by weight. Arrange the items in order by weight, starting with the heaviest.

(b) Make a list of the items above which are sold by volume. Arrange the items in order by volume, starting with the largest volume.

(c) What kinds of items are sold by weight? Are there any exceptions?

(d) What kinds of items are sold by volume? Are there any exceptions?

8   Some containers are made of metal, some of glass, some of plastic and some of cardboard.

(a) What is the usual shape of containers made of metal? Can you think of any exceptions?

(b) What is the usual shape of containers made of cardboard? Can you think of any exceptions?

(c) What are the usual shapes of containers made of plastic?

(d) What are the usual shapes of containers made of glass?

SECTION B

In this section give all your answers as sensible approximations of your calculated answers. If you want help with giving sensible approximations then look at the section called *'Approximating'* on page 249.

 To find the **circumference** of a circle you multiply the **diameter** of the circle by 3-and-a-bit. The number you multiply by is called π. You may have a π button on your calculator. If not, assume that π is 3.1.

1   The diameter of a jam jar is 7 cm. Find the circumference of the lid of the jar.

2   The diameter of a tin of baked beans is 8.6 cm.

(a) Find how far it is round the rim of the tin.

The height of the tin is 11.4 cm. Here is a picture of the tin's label.

(b) What are the dimensions (length and height) of the label?

(c) What is the area of the label?

3   The diameter of a tin of pineapple titbits is 8.5 cm. The height of the tin is 5 cm. There is a label on the tin which completely covers the side of the tin.

Find the area of the label.

 The **radius** of a circle is *half* the *diameter*.

To find the **area** of a circle you multiply the **radius** by itself and then multiply by π.

To find the **volume** of a **cylinder** you multiply the **area of the base** of the cylinder by the **height** of the cylinder.

4   Find the area of the jam jar lid of question 1.

5   (a) Find the area of the base of the baked bean tin of question 2.

(b) Find the capacity (volume) of the baked bean tin.

6 The diameter of a tin of spinach is 10 cm and its height is 11.5 cm. There is a label on the tin which completely covers the side of the tin.

Find

(a) The area of the label;

(b) the surface area of the tin (including the top and bottom of the tin);

(c) the capacity of the tin.

7 A box of E10 Persil holds 3.5 kg of soap powder. The cup used to measure the Persil holds about 150 g of soap powder.

If a family does 3 washes a week and each wash needs 2 cupfuls of soap powder how long will one E10 box last?

8 A paint can and a paint 'match pot' are both cylinders. The height of the paint can is 18 cm and its diameter is 15 cm. The height of the 'match pot' is 6 cm and its diameter is 5 cm.

How many match pots could be filled from the can?

Is the match pot the same shape as the can? Give reasons for your answer?

> For the following questions you will need the weight of water. You can find this on page 246.

9 The shape of a golden syrup tin is a cylinder. The tin holds 2 lb or 907 g of syrup. The diameter of the tin is 9 cm and the height of the tin is 10.5 cm.

Find the capacity of the tin.

Find also the weight of water which would fill the tin.

Is golden syrup heavier or lighter than water? How many times heavier or lighter?

10 The shape of a custard powder drum is a cylinder.

The drum has a diameter of 8 cm and a height of 9 cm and contains 300 g of custard powder.

What weight of water would fill the drum? Is custard powder heavier or lighter than water? How many times heavier or lighter?

11 The wholewheat flakes packet shown contains 500 g of flakes.

The dimensions of the flakes packet are 65 mm by 267 mm by 210 mm. Does this suggest that wheat flakes are lighter or heavier than water? How many times lighter or heavier?

12 A container holds 750 g of table salt. The container is more or less cylindrical.

The container is shown in the photo.

Find the capacity of the container by approximating the container to a cylinder of a suitable height. Is salt heavier or lighter than water? How many times heavier or lighter?

13 A box of chicken stock cubes is in the shape of a cuboid. The base of the box is a square with sides of length 4 cm.

The box contains 12 stock cubes. Given that the height of the box is less than 10 cm, how high is the box?

The total weight of the stock cubes is 71 g. What is the weight and volume of one stock cube? Are stock cubes heavier or lighter than water?

14 The can of paint shown contains 3.1 litres of paint. The directions on the can say that there is enough paint to paint 31 m² of wall with one coat of paint.

What is the thickness of paint in the recommended coat?

15 The following table contains information about some containers.

Show these results on a scattergram. Use a horizontal scale of 1 cm to represent 100 ml and a vertical scale of 1 cm to represent 100 g.

	Capacity of container (ml)	Weight of contents (g)
Large custard	900	623
Baked beans	540	538
Jam	280	340
Soup	430	425
Lemon curd	350	411
Cocoa	480	226

Now mark on your graph the containers described in questions 9, 10, 12 and 13.

Join some of the points representing containers to the origin. Comment on what you notice.

Which is the heaviest commodity shown on your graph? Which of the commodities shown on your graph are lighter than water?

> You will find formulae for the surface areas and volumes of various shapes such as a sphere, a prism and a cone on page 248.

16 The shape of a grapefruit is approximately a sphere. The diameter of the grapefruit is about 90 mm.

(a) Find the volume of the grapefruit.

(b) If the thickness of its skin is about 8 mm find the volume of the skin.

17 The photo shows the net of a box of Toblerone. The shape of the box is a triangular prism.

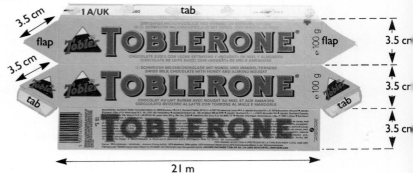

(a) Find the surface area of the box.

(b) Find the capacity of the box.

18 The photo shows the net for a box of Terry's Neapolitans. The shape of the box is a prism whose cross-section is a trapezium.

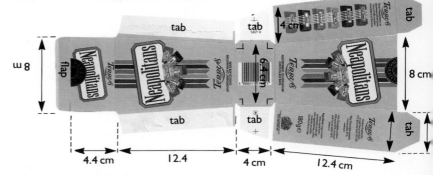

(a) Find the surface area of the box.

(b) Find the capacity of the box. (Make a suitable approximation.)

19 The chip cone shown in the picture below is made by rolling a sector of a circle as shown in figure 1.

(a) Find the length of the arc of the sector (ignore the tab).

(b) Find the area of the sector.

The sector is rolled up to make the chip cone.

(c) What is the surface area of the chip cone?

(d) What is the circumference of the top of the cone?

(e) What is the radius of the top of the cone?

(f) What is the height of the cone?

(g) What is the capacity of the cone?

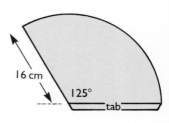

Figure I

20 A metal waste paper bin is the shape of a truncated cone.

The height of the bin is 270 mm, the diameter of the top of the bin is 300 mm and the diameter of the bottom of the bin is 230 mm.

A truncated cone is a cone with its top chopped off.

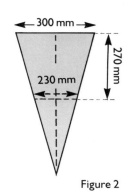

Figure 2 shows a section of the whole cone of which the bin is part.

Figure 2

(*a*) What is the height of the whole cone? (*Hint*: one of the triangles shown in figure 2 is an enlargement of the other. What is the scale factor?)

(*b*) Find the volume of the whole cone.

(*c*) Find the approximate capacity of the bin.

SECTION C

1 A can of shoe polish says it contains 25% extra. Previously it contained 200 ml. What does it contain now?

2 A drink can label says

> **NEW SIZE**
> **20% BIGGER**

The previous size was 275 ml. What is the new size?

3 A tube of toothpaste offers 15% free. Previously the tube contained 50 ml. What does it contain now?

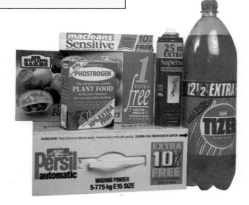

4 A shop was selling a 100 g jar of Nescafe for £1.69 and a 200 g jar for £3.19.

Which size of jar is the best value for money? Why might someone buy the size which is not the best value?

5 A shop was selling the 330 ml can of coke shown for 22 p and the 1.5 l bottle of coke shown for 69 p.

Which is the best buy? Why might it not be the best buy for you?

6 A particular make of baked beans is sold in three sizes. A supermarket was selling a 150 g tin for 17p, a 225 g tin for 20 p and a 450 g tin for 29 p. Which size was the best value for money? Why might some people buy a size which is not the best value for money?

Sometimes you know the amount *after* a percentage has been added to or taken from the original amount.

Suppose, for example, that after adding 25% to the size of a tin it now contains 200 ml. There are several methods that can be used to find how much the tin contained originally. Here are two.

First method

25% has been added. Thus

> 125% is 200 ml
> 25% is 200 ÷ 5 = 40 ml
> 100% is 40 × 4 = 160 ml

Thus the tin originally contained 160 ml.

Second method

Trial and improvement can be used. This is a quick method when a calculator is used.

Your first guess for the answer might be 150 ml.

Adding 25% to 150 gives 187.5, which is a little too low. Sooner or later you will discover that adding 25% to 160 gives 200.

Thus the tin originally contained 160 ml.

---

7 A bottle of car shampoo contains 600 ml, which is 20% extra free.

What did it contain before the free offer?

The label on the bottle says

How many washes were in the previous bottle?

> **24 WASHES IN THIS BOTTLE**

> **30% EXTRA FREE**

8 The label on a bottle of lemon juice says

The bottle now contains 325 ml.
What did it contain before the free offer?

> **13% EXTRA FREE**

9 A drink can offers

The volume of drink in the can is 500 ml. What was the volume of drink in cans before the free offer?

> **50% FREE**
> 284 ml for the price of 184 ml

10 The label on a jar of barbecue sauce says

How accurate is the percentage given on the label? Do you think the label is misleading?

11 A litre carton of pure orange juice says that it contains the juice of 13 oranges. How much juice is there in one orange on average?

This side of the carton has the nutritional information opposite.

> Each 100 ml contains 0.4 g protein and 10.0 g carbohydrate.

How much protein and how much carbohydrate is contained in each orange on average?

12 A wholewheat flakes packet contains 500 g of flakes. It says on the packet

> Contains approximately 17 servings

What quantity of flakes make up one serving?

The nutritional information is given on the packet.

Does anything lead you to suspect that the information provided is not as accurate as it appears to be?

According to the information provided, how many calories (1 calorie is the same as 1 kcal) are there in one serving? How much salt is there in one serving?

> **Each 100 g contains:**
> 1526 kJ/364 kcal,
> fat 2.0 g
> protein 12.0 g
> carbohydrate 78.0 g
> fibre 12.0 g
> added salt 1.0 g
> added sugars 2.4 g

13 A flour packet contains 500 g of flour. The nutritional information is provided on the packet.

> **Each 100 g contains:**
> 1390 kJ/332 kcal
> fat 1.5 g
> protein 9.0 g
> carbohydrate 75.0 g
> fibre 3.7 g

This flour and the wheat flakes in question 13 are both made from wheat. Therefore you would expect the dietary information to be similar for both products Write a short report comparing the information provided for each product.

14 A carton of fresh whipping cream contains 10 fl oz or 284 ml. 100 ml of cream contains 1560 kJ. How many calories are there in 100 ml of whipping cream? (You will need to use the information in question 13).

How many calories are there in a pint of whipping cream?

FURTHER
COURSEWORK TASKS

1〉 Collect empty containers and weigh them . Compare the weight of the container with the weight of its contents. You could draw a graph to help present and explain your results. What proportion of the weight of a typical weekly shop is packaging?

2〉 Collect some empty containers. Conduct a survey of how good people are at estimating the capacity of containers of different shapes. You can use your survey to find out when predictions are most accurate.

Which shape of container gives the best predictions?

Do people overestimate capacity more than they underestimate it?

Do people who shop regularly predict better than people who don't?

Do older people predict better than younger people?

3〉 Make containers of several different shapes, all of which have a capacity of 1 litre.

Which commodities would each shape of container be suitable for? Why?

4〉 Visit a supermarket. Here are some possible ideas to investigate.

Find out about the prices of various products. For example, concentrate on a particular commodity, such as baked beans, and look at the prices of different brands.

Look at the price of different sizes of the same brand.

Compare the nutritional information for different brands.

Find as many different shapes of containers as possible in the supermarket. What are the containers made of?

5〉 Use the information given on the sides of containers to compare the nutritional content of different foods. Suitable graphs of various types (for example, bar chart, pie chart, scattergram) may help to make comparisons clear. Here are some possible ideas.

Draw pie charts to show the fat, carbohydrate and protein in different foods (one chart for each food).

Draw a bar chart of energy in different foods.

Draw a scattergraph of carbohydrate against fat for several foods.

Explain your findings.

6〉 Collect the prices of as many different liquids as you can. You will need, not only the price, but also the volume of liquid you can get for that price.

Compare the prices of the liquids. For example, is milk cheaper or more expensive than petrol?

7〉 Make a collection of cylindrical containers. Some containers are tall and narrow, some are short and wide. Coke tins of different sizes often have the same diameter but different heights. For other products, such as golden syrup, a larger tin is both taller and wider than a smaller tin.

Draw a graph of height against diameter for the containers you collect. Comment on interesting features.

10 TILTED SQUARES

Here is a square drawn on square dotty paper.

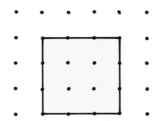

Here is another square. Notice that this square is 'tilted'.

● Draw several squares of different sizes on your dotty paper. Make sure that some of the squares you draw are 'tilted'.

 The area of the square at the top of the page is 9. The area of the second square is harder to find. There are several methods that could be used to find its area. Two of them are shown below.

The area of this triangle is 1 because it is half a 2 by 1 rectangle

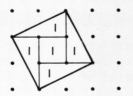

Area = 1 + 1 + 1 + 1 + 1
    = 5

Area = 9 − 1 − 1 − 1 − 1
    = 5

● Now find the areas of the squares *you* have drawn.

● Try to find out which numbers are possible areas of squares and which are not.

SECTION A

If you are going to compare your results with those of your neighbour you need to be able to decide whether you are both talking about the same square.

The squares below can be described as a $\begin{pmatrix} 2 \\ 1 \end{pmatrix}$ square and a $\begin{pmatrix} 3 \\ 0 \end{pmatrix}$ square.

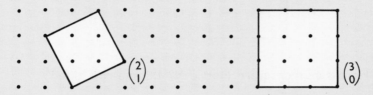

1   Label each of the squares you drew for the previous task with a pair of numbers.

2   Make a list of the squares you have drawn and the areas of these squares like this:

$\begin{pmatrix} 2 \\ 1 \end{pmatrix}$ Area = 5 $\begin{pmatrix} 3 \\ 0 \end{pmatrix}$ Area = 9 $\begin{pmatrix} 2 \\ 2 \end{pmatrix}$ Area = 8

Try to discover a rule which tells you what the area is when you know the two numbers. To help you to discover the rule, add to your list several squares where one of the numbers is zero.

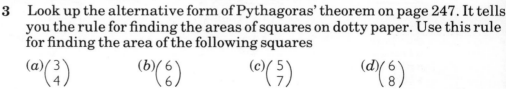

The rule connecting these numbers is called **Pythagoras' theorem.**

3   Look up the alternative form of Pythagoras' theorem on page 247. It tells you the rule for finding the areas of squares on dotty paper. Use this rule for finding the area of the following squares

(a) $\begin{pmatrix} 3 \\ 4 \end{pmatrix}$ (b) $\begin{pmatrix} 6 \\ 6 \end{pmatrix}$ (c) $\begin{pmatrix} 5 \\ 7 \end{pmatrix}$ (d) $\begin{pmatrix} 6 \\ 8 \end{pmatrix}$

(e) $\begin{pmatrix} 5 \\ 12 \end{pmatrix}$ (f) $\begin{pmatrix} 7 \\ 24 \end{pmatrix}$ (g) $\begin{pmatrix} 17 \\ 23 \end{pmatrix}$ (h) $\begin{pmatrix} 124 \\ 177 \end{pmatrix}$

4   (a) Can you construct a square of area 11 on dotty paper by joining the dots? Explain.

   (b) For each number between 1 and 20 try to draw a square on dotty paper whose area is that number. Make a list of the numbers which are possible and the numbers which are not possible.

5   Which prime numbers can be the areas of squares drawn on dotty paper? Try to find a rule which will help you to decide whether you can draw a square of area 1993 on a large enough piece of dotty paper.

SECTION B

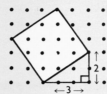

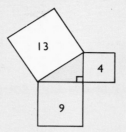

Look at the $\binom{3}{2}$ square shown in the drawing above.

The area of the square is $3^2 + 2^2 = 13$. The triangle that has been drawn under the square has a right angle. The length of one side of the triangle is 3 and the length of another side is 2.

The same square and triangle are shown above. This time the dotty paper has been left out and two more squares have been added. The areas of the three squares have been marked inside the squares.

You can see from this drawing that you get the area of the largest square by adding together the areas of the other two squares.

The largest square is always the one which is *not* next to the right angle.

This is another way of describing Pythagoras' theorem. Once you know this version of Pythagoras' theorem you can use it even when you don't have dotty paper.

1 For each of the following find the missing area. Each time decide carefully which square has the largest area. Then you will know whether to add or subtract.

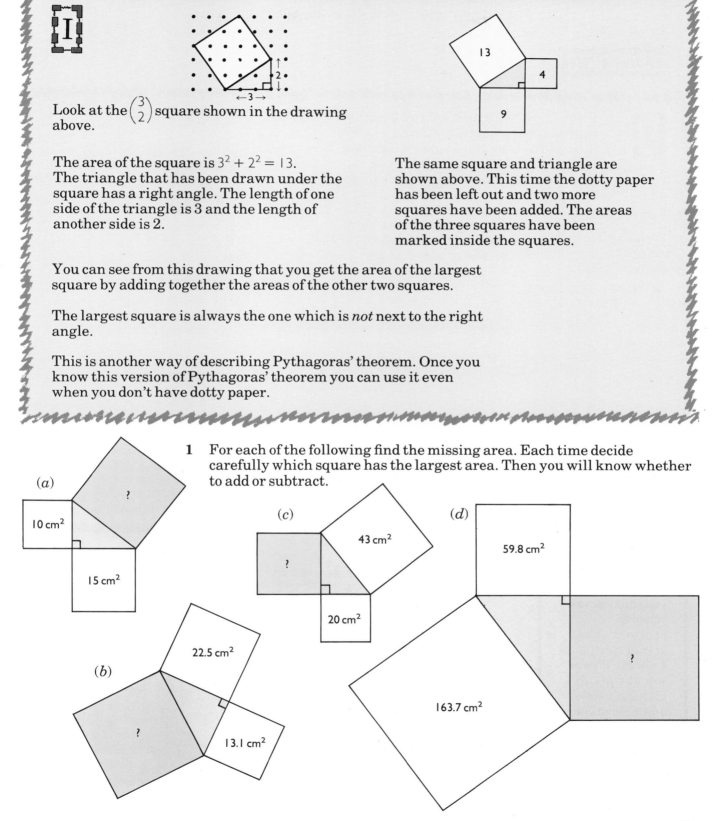

(a) 10 cm² · 15 cm² · ?

(b) 22.5 cm² · 13.1 cm² · ?

(c) 43 cm² · 20 cm² · ?

(d) 59.8 cm² · 163.7 cm² · ?

2 For this question you need the resource sheet called *'Proving Pythagoras' theorem'*.

Follow the instructions. When you have done this write an account explaining the proof to someone else.

SECTION C

I If you know the lengths of two sides of a right-angled triangle and want to know the length of the third side you can use Pythagoras' theorem. Suppose you know that the lengths of two sides are 6 cm and 8 cm.

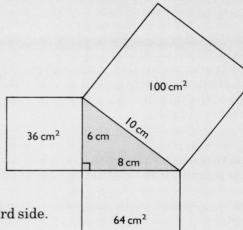

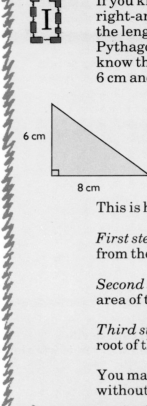

To find the length of the third side draw squares on the three sides of the triangle.

This is how you can find the length of the third side.

First step. Work out the areas of two of the squares from the lengths of their sides.

Second step. Add or subtract (use Pythagoras' theorem) to find the area of the third square.

Third step. Find the length of the third side by taking the square root of the area.

You may find that you can calculate the length of the third side without actually drawing the squares.

In all the questions in this section give your answers as sensible approximations of your calculated answers. If you want help with giving sensible approximations then look at the section called *'Approximating'* on page 249.

1 Find the lengths of the sides marked *x*.

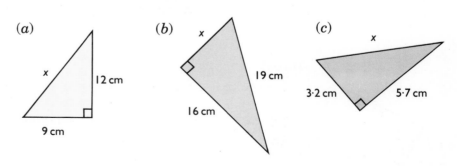

2 What is the length of a diagonal of a rectangle which measures 9 cm by 4 cm?

3 Find the lengths of the sides marked y.

(a)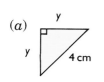

(b)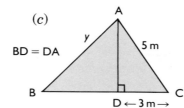

(c)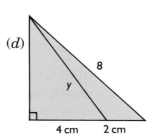

BD = DA

(d)

4 The diagonals of a square are 15 cm long. Find the perimeter of the square.

5 The lengths of the sides of an isosceles triangle are 6 cm, 6 cm and 5 cm. Calculate the area of the triangle.

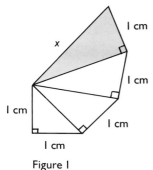

Figure 1

6 Find the length of the side marked x in figure 1.

7 In figure 2, BC is twice as long as AB and D is the midpoint of BC.

Prove that $2AD^2 + DC^2 = AC^2$.

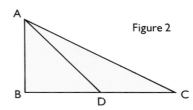

Figure 2

8 Is Pythagoras' theorem still true if the triangle is not right-angled? Give a reason for your answer.

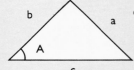

If a triangle is not right-angled there is an equation connecting the three sides of the triangle if one of the angles is used.

$$a^2 = b^2 + c^2 - 2bc \cos A$$

This is known as the **cosine rule**.

9 Use the cosine rule to find the side labelled x in figure 3.

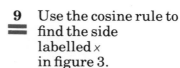

Figure 3

10 Now use the cosine formula to find the connection between p, q and r in figure 4.

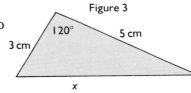

Figure 4

11 Each of the pairs of integers below give the lengths of two of the sides of a triangle containing an angle of 120°. The third length is also an integer. Find it. It is not always the length of the longest side which is missing.

(a) 7, 8   (b) 15, 21   (c) 16, 19   (d) 11, 24   (e) 24, 39

You might need to use 'trial and improvement' to find some of the third sides.

SECTION D

You will need squared paper or square dot paper for some of the questions in this section.

1 Use Pythagoras' theorem to find the length of the vector $\begin{pmatrix} 3 \\ 2 \end{pmatrix}$.

2 The sides of a triangle can be described by the vectors $\begin{pmatrix} 2 \\ -3 \end{pmatrix}$, $\begin{pmatrix} 4 \\ -1 \end{pmatrix}$ and $\begin{pmatrix} -2 \\ -2 \end{pmatrix}$

(a) Draw the triangle.

(b) Which vector describes the longest side of the triangle?

3 Two of the sides of a parallelogram can be described by the vectors $\begin{pmatrix} 7 \\ 1 \end{pmatrix}$ and $\begin{pmatrix} 5 \\ 5 \end{pmatrix}$.

(a) Draw the parallelogram.

(b) Prove that it is a rhombus.

4 Two of the sides of a parallelogram can be described by the vectors $\begin{pmatrix} -3 \\ 4 \end{pmatrix}$ and $\begin{pmatrix} 4 \\ 1 \end{pmatrix}$.

(a) Find vectors which can be used to describe its diagonals.

(b) Find the lengths of the diagonals of the parallelogram.

5 Two sides of a kite can be described by the vectors $\begin{pmatrix} 5 \\ 0 \end{pmatrix}$ and $\begin{pmatrix} 1 \\ 3 \end{pmatrix}$.

Draw such a kite and write down vectors which can be used to describe its other two sides.

SECTION E

When you were drawing your squares on dotty paper you probably noticed that squares of different sizes were tilted at different angles on the page.

It is not true that squares of different sizes are always tilted at different angles. A square with area 2 is tilted the same amount as a square of area 8, and a square of area 5 is tilted the same amount as a square of area 20. Why is this?

It is possible to use the two numbers which describe the square to determine how much the square is tilted.

A $\begin{pmatrix} 2 \\ 1 \end{pmatrix}$ square has the same slope as a $\begin{pmatrix} 4 \\ 2 \end{pmatrix}$ square because $\frac{1}{2} = \frac{2}{4} = 0.5$.

The drawing on the right might help to explain why.

The number 0.5 which you get for both squares not only tells you that both squares are tilted by the same amount, but can also be used to find the angle of tilt, A. To find A put the number 0.5 in your calculator and then press [invtan] (or [tan^{-1}]). You should find that angle A is about 27°.

Alternatively, you could find the angle B which another side of the square of area 5 makes with the horizontal. To do this you use $\frac{2}{1} = 2$.

Put 2 in your calculator and then press [invtan] (or [tan^{-1}]). You should find that the angle is about 63°.

1 Find the two angles which the sides of the following squares make to the horizontal:

(a) a square with area 10   (b) a square with area 8

(c) a square with area 13   (d) a square with area 50

2 What is the relationship between the two angles you obtain for each square? Explain this relationship; figure 5 might help.

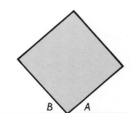

Figure 5

If instead of starting with the ratio of two sides you start with the angle you can use the $\boxed{\tan}$ button on your calculator to find the ratio. Look at the triangle shown in the diagram below.

To find the value of $\frac{y}{x}$ you put the angle 68.2° into your calculator and then press the $\boxed{\tan}$ button. The answer should be about 2.5.

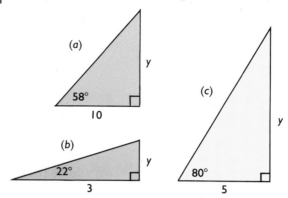

This means that y is 2.5 times as long as x. So, for example, if x is 4 then y is 10; if x is 7 then y is 17.5.

3 Find y in each of the triangles below

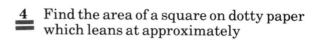

4 Find the area of a square on dotty paper which leans at approximately

(a) 14°   (b) 21.8°   (c) 81.9°

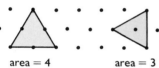

FURTHER COURSEWORK TASKS

1〉 For this task you will need some isometric dotty paper.

Figure 6 shows two triangles you can draw on this paper.

The areas of these triangles are shown. The unit of area used is the smallest equilateral triangle you can draw.

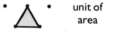
unit of area

Draw several equilateral triangles, and investigate which numbers are areas you can draw and which are not.

area = 4   area = 3

Figure 6

Count the number of dots on the perimeter of each triangle and the number of dots inside each triangle. Look for connections between the numbers of dots and the area of the triangle.

2〉 Squares can be made on a pegboard instead of a pinboard. Figure 7 shows a square made from 13 pegs.

Make some other pegboard squares. Investigate which numbers of pegs can be used to make pegboard squares.

3〉 Instead of drawing squares on the sides of a right-angled triangle draw other shapes. If equilateral triangles are drawn on the three sides of a right-angled triangle what is the connection between their areas?

Try the same thing with other shapes.

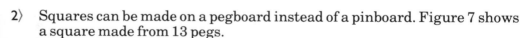

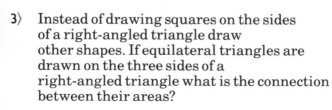

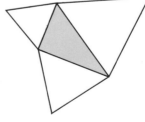

Figure 7

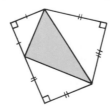

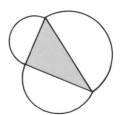

4) Write a computer program or a program for a programmable calculator to help you find a large number of Pythagorean triangles.

It will probably help you to know that the formulae

$$x^2 - y^2, \quad 2xy, \quad x^2 + y^2$$

give the sides of a Pythagorean triangle whenever x and y are positive integers. Can you explain why?

Investigate special types of Pythagorean triangles: for example,

(a) where the two longest sides differ by 1

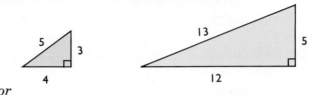

or

(b) where the two shortest sides differ by 1

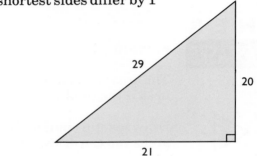

5) There are many different proofs of Pythagoras' theorem. Look up some proofs and write about them.

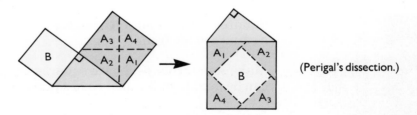

(Perigal's dissection.)

6) Investigate the volumes of cubes which can be made on 'three-dimensional dotty paper'.

WOULD YOU BELIEVE IT?

It's safer by air than by sea.

Pisceans are dreamers.

A high cholesterol diet causes heart trouble and a low cholesterol diet causes cancer.

Apply to Partnerline now and you will be married in six months.

Our biscuits help you to slim.

Our investment plan will help you double your money.

Cigarettes won't really do you any harm.

People are always keen to offer you advice. Sometimes you are wise to listen to that advice. Sometimes you are wise to ignore it. Sometimes it is difficult to know what to do.

When mathematicians explore situations they often make guesses about facts or about mathematical patterns. Sometimes these guesses are true. Sometimes they are not.

Often mathematicians go through three stages.

(1) They discover something.

(2) They make sure that it is true.

(3) They try to convince others that it is true.

Sometimes, when trying to convince others they decide that it is not true after all.

- Here are some statements. For each statement, try to decide if it is *always* true, *sometimes* true or *never* true. Find some good reasons for your decision. Then try to convince someone else.

  (1) A person has 8 great-grandparents.

  (2) When a baby is born it has two living parents.

  (3) A 14-year-old girl is taller than a 10-year-old girl.

  (4) If you buy something this year and sell it in five years time you will sell it for less than you paid for it.

  (5) If someone has three sisters, then each of those sisters will also have three sisters.

  (6) No matter how old a girl is, she was once exactly half as old as she is now.

  (7) No matter how old a boy is, he was once exactly five years younger than he is now.

  (8) If a girl has a younger brother then there was a time when she was more than twice his age.

  (9) If a boy wakes up early enough he can experience more hours of daylight on the 1st May than he can on 1st February.

  (10) If you spin a coin 50 times you will get 25 heads.

- Now make up some statements of your own. Give them to someone else to decide whether they are always true, sometimes true or never true. Try to think of some statements which are difficult to decide about.

SECTION A

Decide whether each of these statements is *always* true, *sometimes* true, or *never* true. Write down reasons you would use to convince someone else that what you say is correct.

1 When you add an odd number to an odd number the answer is an even number. For example, $19 + 35 = 54$, which is even.

2 You can multiply a number by 4 by doubling it twice. For example, double 12 is 24 and double 24 is 48. So $4 \times 12 = 48$.

3 When you multiply a number by 5 the answer ends in a 5. For example $5 \times 17 = 85$ which ends in a 5.

4 When you multiply an even number by 6 its last digit does not change. For example, $6 \times 18 = 108$.

5 When you multiply an odd number by an odd number the answer is an even number. For example, $7 \times 9 = 72$.

6 When you add 18 to a number it reverses its digits. For example, $24 + 18 = 42$.

7 This is how you can multiply a whole number by 5.

> *First* put a nought on the end of the number.
> *Then* halve the number you get.

For example to multiply 46 by 5: *first* put a nought on the end, to get 460: *then* halve it to get 230. So $5 \times 46 = 230$.

8 To multiply a 2-digit number by 11

> *First* write out the number with a gap in the middle.
> *Then* put into the gap the sum of the digits of the starting number.

For example if you start with 23 first write 2☐3 and then put 5 in the middle to give 253. So $11 \times 23 = 253$.

9 There are more digits in the square of a number than there are for the number itself.

For example $5^2 = 25$, and $1.2^2 = 1.44$.

10 When you square a number it gets bigger.

For example $7^2 = 49$, and 49 is bigger than 7.

11 Every number has two square roots.

For example, the square roots of 36 are 6 and -6.

12 If you double a square number you get another square number.

13 To square a number ending in 5.

> *First* knock off the 5.
> *Next* multiply what you get by the number which is one more than what you get.
> *Lastly* put 25 on the end.

For example, to square 65. First knock off the 5, giving 6. Then multiply 6 by 7 giving 42. Lastly put 25 on the end, giving 4225. So $65^2 = 4225$.

SECTION B

Decide whether each of these statements is *always* true, *sometimes* true, or *never* true. You will probably want to use drawings to convince yourself, and other people, that what you say is correct.

1 A parallelogram has two diagonals.

2 A pentagon has five diagonals.

3 A triangle has three acute angles.

4 A triangle has two obtuse angles.

5 None of the angles of a triangle is bigger than 50 degrees.

6 Four of the angles of a hexagon are right-angles.

7   Four of the angles of a pentagon are right-angles.

8   The four angles of a quadrilateral are right-angles.

9   A quadrilateral has exactly two lines of symmetry.

10 A hexagon has exactly two lines of symmetry.

11 A pentagon has exactly two lines of symmetry.

12 A quadrilateral has rotation symmetry but no reflection symmetry.

13 The largest angle of a triangle is opposite the longest side.

14 The longest side of a pentagon is opposite the largest angle.

15 The angles at opposite corners of a parallelogram are equal.

16 The diagonals of a rectangle are of equal length.

17 The diagonals of a kite meet at right-angles.

18 A quadrilateral with two diagonals of equal length is a rectangle.

19 The area of a rectangle whose perimeter is 16 cm is 12 cm^2.

20 The perimeter of a rectangle whose area is 16 cm^2 is 12 cm.

SECTION C

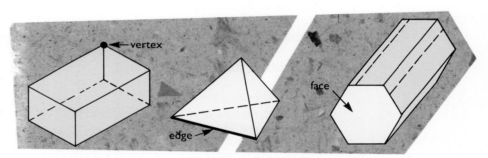

Decide whether each of these statements about polyhedra is *always* true, *sometimes* true, or *never* true. A polyhedron is a three-dimensional shape with flat faces. Three polyhdra are shown above. You will need to imagine other polyhedra when thinking about the statements below.

1   A polyhedron has an even number of faces.

2   A polyhedron has an odd number of edges.

3   Each vertex of a polyhedron has at least three edges meeting at it.

4   A polyhedron has two triangular faces and three quadrilateral faces.

5   A polyhedron has one quadrilateral face and four triangular faces.

6   A polyhedron has two pentagonal faces and ten triangular faces.

7   A polyhedron has five triangular faces and six quadrilateral faces.

SECTION D

 When more than two numbers are involved in a calculation multiplication or division is done *before* addition or subtraction.

For example:

$$2 + 3 \times 4 \text{ means } 2 + 12 = 14 \quad (\text{not } 5 \times 4 = 20)$$
$$12 - 6 \div 3 \text{ means } 12 - 2 = 10 \quad (\text{not } 6 \div 3 = 2)$$

If you want to show that addition or subtraction is to be done first, use brackets.

For example:

$$(12 - 3) \times 2 \text{ means } 9 \times 2 = 18$$
$$(5 + 7) \div 4 \text{ means } 12 \div 4 = 3$$

Add signs, $+ - \times$ or $\div$, to make each of the following statements true.
You might need to use brackets in some statements.

For example: given the statement $\qquad$ 8 2 5 = 21

you can make it true like this $\qquad$ $8 \times 2 + 5 = 21$

1 6   5 = 30

2 6   15   11   20 = 30

3 5   4   3 = 12

4 5   4   3 = 23

5 5   4   3 = 60

6 5   4   3 = 35

7 5   4   3 = 27

8 5   4   3 = 3

9 5   4   3 = 4

10 5   4   3 = 5

11 17.3   2.6 = 44.98

12 10.726   0.062 = 173

13 273.4   210.6   233.4 = 14657.52

14 52.6   89.3   172 = 101.31243

15 8   6   12   9   16   14 = 15

SECTION E

In the following statements N stands for a whole number between 1 and 20 (including 1 and 20). For each statement say whether it is (*a*) *always true* (*b*) *sometimes* true (*c*) *never* true. If it is sometimes true say what number or numbers N can be to make it true.

1 $4 + N = 10$

2 $2N = 20$

3 $6N = 0$

4 $2N + 5 = 37$

5 $N + 8 = 5 + N + 3$

6 $4N + 3 = 2N + 15$

7 $6N = 20$

8 $N \div 3 = 6$

9 $3N + 4 = 2N + 4 + N$

10 $20 + N = N + 16$

11 $20 - N = N - 16$

12 $4(N + 2) = 4N + 8$

13 $3(N - 3) = 3N - 6$

14 $2(N + 5) = 5N + 1$

< means 'is less than'. For example, 5 < 9.
> means 'is greater than'. For example, 9 > 5.

15 $N + 5 > 18$ **18** $N < 100$

16 $N + 5 > N - 7$ **19** $N < 3N$

17 $N - 6 > 32 - N$

SECTION F

The following statements refer to models made of interlocking cubes. Say whether each statement is (*a*) *always* true, (*b*) *never* true or (*c*) *sometimes* true for a model of any size.

A square of interlocking cubes means a model like this. The square can be of any size.

A stick means a model like this. It can be of any length.

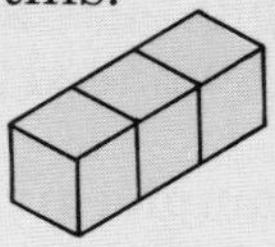

It should be clear what a cube model and cuboid model mean.

A rectangle of interlocking cubes means a model like this. The two sides of the rectangle can be of any length.

This is a single cube.

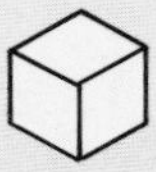

Figure I

1 Two squares of interlocking cubes fit together to make a rectangle (figure 1).

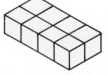

2 Two rectangles of interlocking cubes fit together to make a bigger rectangle (figure 2).

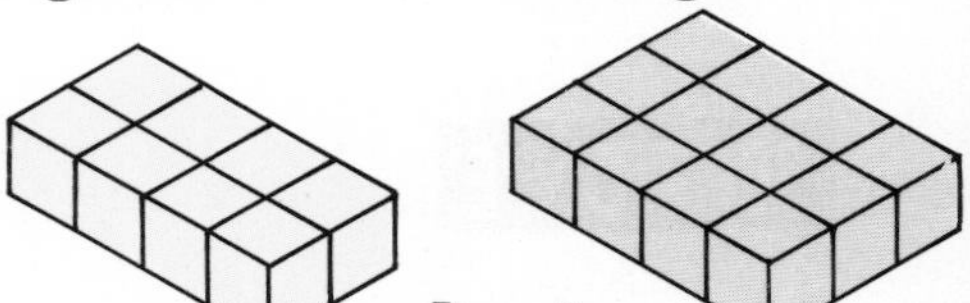

Figure 2

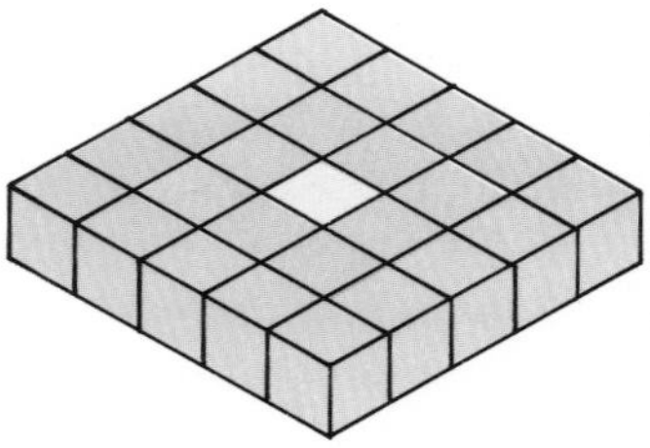

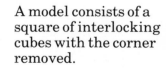

Figure 3

3 For any size square of interlocking cubes the colours can be chosen so that there are rings of colour around a single central cube (figure 3).

4 A model consists of a square of interlocking cubes with the corner removed.

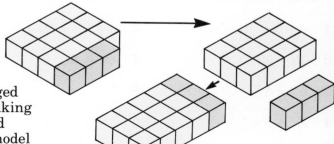

The model can be changed into a rectangle by breaking a stick off the model and putting it back on the model in a different place (see figure 4).

Figure 4

5 A model consists of a rectangle, with one side twice as long as the other, and with two corners removed.

The single cubes in the model can be rearranged to make a square (see figure 5).

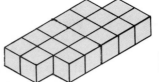
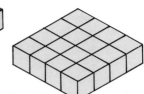

Figure 5

6 A model consists of a square with a square removed from its corner.

By breaking a rectangle off the model and putting it back on the model in a new position the model can be changed into a rectangle (see figure 6).

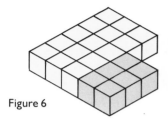
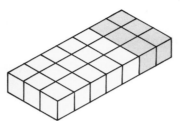

Figure 6

7 A square, two identical sticks and a single cube can be joined to make a square (see figure 7).

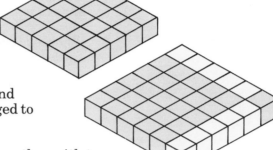

8 A square, five identical sticks and six single cubes can be rearranged to make a rectangle.

9 Two squares of different sizes, together with two identical rectangles, can be made into a bigger square.

Figure 7

10 Two staircases can be fitted together to make a rectangle (see figure 8).

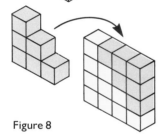

11 A model consists of a cube with one corner removed.

By breaking off a rectangle and a stick, the model can be changed into a cuboid together with a stick of the same height as the cuboid (figure 9).

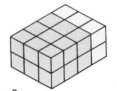

Figure 9

Figure 8

Look at question 2. You can show when the statement is true by using letters.

The picture shows the number of single cubes in each of the models.

You can do the same thing for question 4.

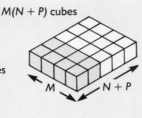

$M(N + P)$ cubes

MN cubes MP cubes

So $MN + MP = M(N+P)$

$(N - 1)(N + 1)$ cubes

$N^2 - 1$ cubes

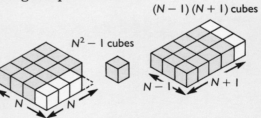

So $N^2 - 1 = (N - 1)(N + 1)$

---

12 Use letters in the way described in the box above for the models in questions 6, 7, 8, 9 and 11.

163

SECTION G

In the following statements N stands for a number, but not necessarily a positive number or a whole number. For each statement say whether it is (a) *always* true (b) *sometimes* true (c) *never* true.

If it is sometimes true say what number or numbers N can be used to make it true.

1 When a number is multiplied by 5 the answer is 100.

2 When a number is divided by 6 the answer is 13.

3 When a number is multiplied by 8 the answer is 50.

4 When a number is multiplied by itself the answer is 400.

5 When two consecutive whole numbers are multiplied together the answer is 132.

6 When two consecutive whole numbers are multiplied together the answer is 2256.

7 $7N = 343$	**12** $N^2 = 0$	**17** $N^2 - 3N = 1720$
8 $N \div 13 = 377$	**13** $N^2 = 30$	**18** $(N + 2)(N - 2) = N^2 - 4$
9 $8N = 30$	**14** $N^3 = 50$	**19** $N^2 < 100$
10 $N + 23 = 5$	**15** $N^2 - N = 72$	**20** $N^2 < N$
11 $7N + 33 = 33N + 7$	**16** $N^2 + 2N = 195$	

SECTION H

In the following pairs of statements M and N stand for numbers. *One* of the following pairs of statements is *never* true for the same values of N and M. *All* the rest are *sometimes* true.

Say which pair of statements is never true. If a pair of statements is sometimes true, state what numbers M and N make it true.

Here is an example.

$2N + M = 19$
and $M = 4N + 1$

One way to investigate this is to make a table and try different values of M and N

M	N	2N + M	4N + 1
9	5	19	21
11	4	19	17
13	3	19	13

So when $M = 13$ and $N = 3$ both statements are true. Consequently this pair of statements is *sometimes* true.

This method of making a table and using trial and improvement is usually a quick one when a calculator or a spreadsheet is used.

Remember that M and N might be negative and might not be whole numbers.

1 $M + 3N = 10$ and $M + N = 4$

2 $2M + 5N = 47$ and $M = 2N + 1$

3 $2M + 3N = 7$ and $M = 4 - N$

4 $2M + 3N = 22$ and $4M + 5N = 40$

5 $2M + N = 6$ and $2N = 9 - 4M$

6 $5N + 2M = 11$ and $3N - 4M = 4$

7 $2M + 2N = 25$ and $M + 4N = 5$

SECTION I

In the following statements M and N both stand for numbers. For each statement say whether it is (a) *always* true (b) *sometimes* true (c) *never* true.

1 $M + N = N + M$

2 $M + 2N = N + 2M$

3 $3(M + N) = 3M + 3N$

4 $4(2M - 3N) = 8M - 12N$

5 $(M - N)(M + N) = M^2 - N^2$

6 $(M + N)(M + N) = M^2 + 2MN + N^2$

7 $6(M - 2N) = 6M - 2N$

8 $(M + 2)(N + 3) = MN + 3M + 2N + 5$

9 $M^2N = MN^2$

SECTION J

Imagine two sticks attached to a grid of squares.

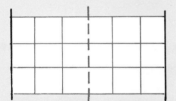

The grid can be stretched by pulling the sticks apart.

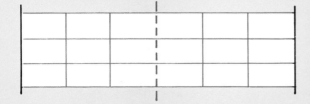

In the picture, points on the dotted line stay in the same place. All the other points on the grid end up twice (two times) as far from the dotted line as they were to start with. So this stretch has stretch factor 2.

Any shape drawn on the grid gets stretched too

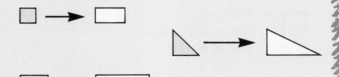

A stretch does not have to have a stretch factor of 2. Different stretch factors can be used.

Decide whether each of the following statements about stretching shapes is *always* true, *sometimes* true, or *never* true. You will find it helpful to try things out by drawing on squared paper.

1 When a triangle is stretched the shape obtained is a triangle.

2 When a quadrilateral is stretched the shape obtained is a quadrilateral.

3 When a square is stretched the shape obtained is a rhombus.

4 When a rectangle is stretched the shape obtained is a square.

5 When a regular hexagon is stretched the result is a hexagon whose opposite sides are parallel.

6 When a triangle is stretched, with stretch factor 2, its area is doubled.

7 When a rectangle is stretched, with stretch factor 3, its area becomes 3 times bigger.

8 When any shape is stretched, with stretch factor 2, its area is doubled.

9 When any shape is stretched, with stretch factor N, its area becomes N times as big.

10 When a shape with half-turn symmetry (rotational symmetry of order 2) is stretched the result is another shape with half-turn symmetry.

11 When a shape with bilateral symmetry, which has its line of symmetry drawn on it, is stretched the result is another shape with bilateral symmetry which has its line of symmetry drawn on it.

SECTION K

 Imagine two sticks attached to a grid of squares.

The grid can be sheared by keeping one stick fixed and moving the other so that it moves parallel to the fixed stick.

In the picture, points on the fixed stick stay in the same place. All the other points on the grid move parallel to the stick. The further a point is from the fixed stick the further it moves.

Any shape drawn on the grid gets sheared too.

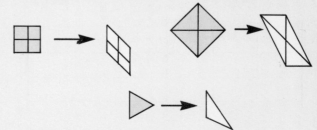

Decide whether each of the following statements about shearing shapes is *always* true, *sometimes* true, or *never* true. You will find it helpful to try things out by drawing on squared paper.

1 When a triangle is sheared the shape obtained is a triangle.

2 When a quadrilateral is sheared the shape obtained is a quadrilateral.

3 When a rectangle is sheared the shape obtained is a square.

4 When a square is sheared the shape obtained is a parallelogram.

5 When a regular hexagon is sheared the result is a hexagon whose opposite sides are parallel.

6 When a rectangle is sheared its area does not change.

7 When a triangle is sheared, its area does not change.

8 When any shape is sheared its area does not change.

9 When a shape with half-turn symmetry is sheared the result is another shape with half-turn symmetry.

10 The midpoints of the sides of a quadrilateral are joined. When this is sheared the result is another quadrilateral with the midpoints of its sides joined.

FURTHER COURSEWORK TASKS

1⟩ For this task you will need a number of identical cards or small pieces of paper.

Number some cards with numbers from 1 to 8 and arrange them on a three-by-three grid as shown in figure 10.

Figure 10

A move consists of sliding a card into the vacant space next to it. You can slide a card up, down, left or right, but not diagonally.

Figure 11

Figure 11 shows what the cards look like after moving the cards 6, 5, 8, 7, 4, 8, 2, 1, 8.

Is it possible to reverse the cards, so that they look like this?

How many moves does it take?

Is it *always*, *never* or *sometimes* possible to reverse the cards when the boards are rectangles or squares of other sizes?

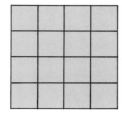

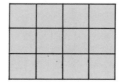

2〉 Place three coins in a row so that three heads are showing.

 Turn any two of the coins over.

Now turn any two of the coins over again.  How many goes does it take you to get three tails showing? Is it possible?

Now place five coins with their heads showing.

Turn any three of the coins over.

Now turn three of them over again. How many goes does it take to get five tails showing? Is it possible?

Try the same idea with different numbers of coins. You could also vary the number of coins you are allowed to turn over at each go.

When is it possible to get all tails showing?

3〉 In this version of *Frogs* the frogs have numbers on them.

You can move a frog into the square next to it if the square is vacant. Or you can hop a frog over one other frog into an adjacent square.

The task is to reverse the order of the frogs.

'The smallest number of moves is a triangular number.'

Is this true? Try a different number of frogs.

12 PLANNING A JOURNEY

- Describe your journey to school. Do you walk or cycle? Or do you travel by bus or train or coach? How long does each stage of your journey take? Do you travel a different way depending on the weather?

  (If your journey to school is entirely by bike it only has one stage. If you first walk and then catch a bus your journey has two stages.)

- How far is it from your home to school?

- Draw a picture, or rough map, showing your route to school.

- How fast do you travel (on average) on each stage of your journey?

  If your journey to school is very straightforward you might like to describe a journey you often do to somewhere else (e.g. to town) instead.

SECTION A

1   Someone walks to school. Which of the following is most likely to be the distance from their home to the school.

(a) 10 metres?   (b) 400 metres?   (c) 4 kilometres?

(d) 10 kilometres?   (e) 100 kilometres?

2   Someone else catches a train to school. Which of the following is most likely to be the distance from their home to school?

(a) 10 yards?   (b) 400 yards?   (c) 4 miles?

(d) 10 miles?   (e) 100 miles?

3   If you walk 1 mile, which of the following times is it most likely to take you:

(a) 1 minute?   (b) 5 minutes?   (c) 20 minutes?

(d) 2 hours?

4   (a) If someone can walk 1 mile in 15 minutes roughly how long will it take them to walk

(i) 3 miles?   (ii) 5 miles?   (iii) $\frac{1}{2}$ mile?

(b) If someone can cycle 12 miles in an hour

(i) roughly how far can they cycle in 20 minutes?
(ii) roughly how long will it take them to cycle 9 miles?

5   The table shown in figure 1 gives the distances between towns in Britain.

(a) Assuming that you can drive at an average speed of about 40 m.p.h. roughly how long will it take you to drive

(i) from Glasgow to Aberdeen?
(ii) from Aberystwyth to Exeter?
(iii) from Brighton to Holyhead?

(b) What is silly about the following statement.

'Travelling at about 40 m.p.h. it will take 3 hours 19.5 minutes to drive from Guildford to Hereford.'

Aberdeen	1																			
468	Aberystwyth	2																		
609	227	Barnstaple	3																	
430	122	183	Birmingham	4																
611	286	205	185	Brighton	5															
514	132	104	88	166	Bristol	6														
471	218	273	101	121	172	Cambridge	7													
534	117	142	108	201	47	207	Cardiff	8												
232	235	376	198	378	282	260	302	Carlisle	9											
520	48	205	171	264	110	270	68	288	Carmarthen	10										
524	288	296	171	112	195	47	230	312	293	Colchester	11									
593	210	92	167	116	61	182	126	360	189	208	Dorchester	12								
630	322	278	205	78	206	122	241	398	304	113	206	Dover	13							
126	335	476	298	478	381	342	401	99	388	395	460	464	Edinburgh	14						
588	206	40	162	169	84	252	121	355	184	275	53	249	455	Exeter	15					
159	445	586	407	588	491	469	511	209	497	522	570	607	133	565	Fort William	16				
146	334	475	297	477	381	359	401	99	387	411	459	497	46	455	102	Glasgow	17			
480	110	130	54	157	36	124	66	247	129	172	114	197	347	110	457	347	Gloucester	18		
568	226	176	143	45	106	92	141	335	204	103	98	101	435	147	545	434	102	Guildford	19	
481	79	148	55	188	54	158	58	249	85	203	132	228	349	127	458	348	31	133	Hereford	20
461	106	331	153	333	237	249	205	229	154	319	315	353	328	310	438	328	202	290	158	Holyhead	21

Figure 1

6   The timetable in figure 2 gives the times of trains between Leicester and London.

(a) Explain what the symbol sx means.

(b) There are three symbols on the timetable next to the 0704 from Leicester to London. What do these symbols mean?

(c) On which trains from Leicester to London on Monday morning can SAVER tickets **not** be used?

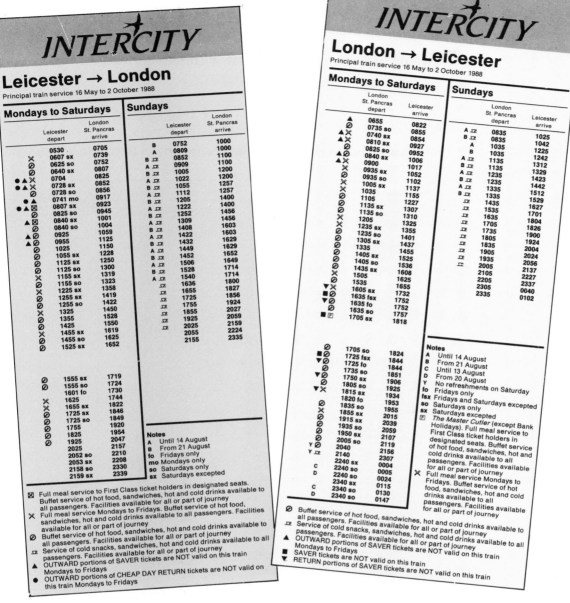

Figure 2

7 For this question you will need to refer to figure 2.

(a) Someone living in Leicester wants to get to London on a Wednesday by 10 a.m. What train should she catch?

(b) Someone else who lives near Leicester has an important meeting to attend on Monday in West London. The meeting starts at 11 a.m. She needs to allow 40 minutes for the underground journey from St Pancras and a quarter of an hour for the walk from the underground to the meeting. What train should she catch from Leicester?

(c) Someone wants to spend about four hours in London on a Tuesday, but he wants to travel on a SAVER ticket. He is going out in the evening and wants to get back to Leicester by 6 p.m. at the latest. But he does not want to get up any earlier than he needs to.

Which train should he catch to London and on which train should he return to Leicester?

(*d*) A railway enthusiast wants to travel from Leicester to London on a train which leaves Leicester before 9 a.m. on a Thursday.

He would like to travel on the train with the shortest journey time.

Which train should he catch?

How long does the train take?

The distance between Leicester and London is 110 miles. What is the average speed of this train?

Figure 3

14 Birmingham — Stoke — Crewe — Liverpool — Manchester

Mondays to Saturdays

	⊘g	A⊘		⊘				⊘	⊘
Birmingham International	—	0708	—	—	0805	0026c	—	0927c	0957
Birmingham New St (arrive)	—	0720	—	0753d	0821	0839	—	0942	1011
Birmingham New St (depart)	0609	0725	0735	0756	0823	0842	0913	0951	1015
Sandwell & Dudley	0618	0733	0743	—	0832	—	0921	0959	—
Wolverhampton	0629	0744	0754	0814	0844	0901	0933	1010	1032
Stafford	0647	0801	0811	0831	0901	0918	—	1027	—
Stoke-on-Trent	—	0833	—	—	0947	—	1050	—	
Macclesfield	—	0852	—	—	1007	—	1110	—	
Crewe	0710	0824	—	0855	0925	—	1010	—	1111
Hartford	—	0909	—	—	1048	—			
Runcorn	0801	—	0919	1005	—	1101	—		
Liverpool Lime Street	0828	—	0940	1026	—	1126	—		
Wilmslow	0757h	0905	—	1022	—	—	1222		
Stockport		0915	0908	—	1022	—	1124	—	
Manchester Piccadilly		0926	0917	—	1032	—	1135	—	

Mondays to Saturdays

	⊘	⊘		B	A⊘		A⊘	⊘
Birmingham International	—	1026c	—	1125c	1137c	—	1256c	
Birmingham New St (arrive)	—	1042	1129d	1142	1150	1210d	—	1311 1354d
Birmingham New St (depart)	1029	1050	1142	1155	1158	1220	1311	1326 1412
Sandwell & Dudley	—	1059	—	—	—	—	1319	
Wolverhampton	1048	1111	1203	1215	1215	1236	1332	1343 1432
Stafford	1104	—	—	1231	1231	1254	1348	
Stoke-on-Trent	—	1149	—	1252	1252	—	1409	
Macclesfield	—	1210	—	1312	1312	—		
Crewe	—	—	1246	—	—	1322	—	1432 1514
Hartford	1138	—	—	—	1338	—	1548	
Runcorn	1148	—	—	—	1348	—	1601	
Liverpool Lime Street	1209	—	—	—	1408	—	1626	
Wilmslow	—	—	—	1422	—	1505	—	
Stockport	—	1226	—	1327	1327	1433	1440 1516	
Manchester Piccadilly	—	1236	—	1337	1337	1445	1450 1526	

Mondays to Saturdays

	⊘	A⊘			⊘	A⊘	B	⊘
Birmingham International	1400	1426c	1458	—	1638	1655	—	1727c 1807
Birmingham New St (arrive)	1412	1442	1512	1556d	1651	1711	—	1742 1822
Birmingham New St (depart)	1420	1458	1514	1804	1655	1715	1715	1756 1826
Sandwell & Dudley	—	1507	—	1614	—	—	—	
Wolverhampton	1438	1518	1532	1625	1713	1737	1737	1815 1843
Stafford	—	1534	—	1641	—	1753	1753	1859
Stoke-on-Trent	1513	1618	—	1707	—	1816	1816	1920
Macclesfield	1533	1648	—	1726	—	1836	1836	1939
Crewe	—	1600	1614	—	1754	—	—	1855
Hartford	—	1616	1653	—	1812	—		
Runcorn	—	1625	1706	—	1822	—		
Liverpool Lime Street	—	1646	1733	—	1842	—		
Wilmslow	—	—	1637	—	1847k	—		
Stockport	1547	—	1647	1742	—	1854	1854	1954
Manchester Piccadilly	1557	—	1656	1755	—	1904	1904	2003

Mondays to Saturdays

	⊘	⊘			B	A		
Birmingham International	1821	1856c	2012	2033c	2057c	—	2130c	
Birmingham New St (arrive)	—	1911	2026	2046	2112	—	2144	
Birmingham New St (depart)	1855	1925	2029	2105	2125	2132	2159	
Sandwell & Dudley	—	—	—	2135	2140	2208		
Wolverhampton	1912	1943	2047	2125	2149	2154	2221	
Stafford	1928	2001	2103	2142	2207	2213	2239	
Stoke-on-Trent	—	2024	2204	—	—	2235	2316	
Macclesfield	—	2045	2233	—	—	2254		
Crewe	2001	—	2127	2210	2237	—	2304	
Hartford	2017	—	2209	—	2257	—		
Runcorn	2027	—	—	2233	2310	—	2331	
Liverpool Lime Street	2047	—	—	2258	2333	—	2354	
Wilmslow	2107	—	2147	—	2327	—		
Stockport	—	2101	2157	—	—	2309		
Manchester Piccadilly	—	2111	2207	—	—	2320		

Notes for this and opposite page:
A   Mondays to Fridays.
B   Saturdays only.
c   From The South, see Table 16.
d   From The Southwest, see Table 17.
g   ⊘ Mondays to Fridays.
h   0752 Saturdays.
k   1907 Saturdays.
n   Special bus service.

Light printed timings indicate connecting service.

14 Manchester — Liverpool — Crewe — Stoke — Birmingham

Mondays to Saturdays

	A	C	D	B			⊘	⊘n
Manchester Piccadilly	0510	—	—	—	0654	0718	—	0808 0918
Stockport	0519	—	—	—	0703	0726	—	0818 0926
Wilmslow	—	—	—	—	—	0734	0805	
Liverpool Lime Street	—	—	0603	—	—	—	0808	
Runcorn	—	—	0620	—	—	—	0825	
Hartford	—	—	—	—	—	—	0836	
Crewe	0550	—	0647	0651	—	0801	0853	
Macclesfield	—	—	—	—	0717	—	—	0833 0938
Stoke-on-Trent	—	—	—	—	0737	—	—	0855 0958
Stafford	0619	—	0710	0714	—	0822	—	0919 1019
Wolverhampton	0641	0641	0728	0732	0811	0841	0928	0939 1038
Sandwell & Dudley	0653	0653	0740	0742	—	—	0940	— 1053
Birmingham New St (arrive)	0703	0703	0753	0753	0835	0902	0951	1002 1103
Birmingham New St (depart)	0706	0706	0801	0801	0840	0906	—	1006 1115g
Birmingham International	0717d	0717d	0812d	0812d	0851d	0917d	—	1017d 1128h

Mondays to Saturdays

	⊘	⊘				⊘	⊘	⊘
Manchester Piccadilly	1010	—	1030	1118	—	1218	1320	— 1330
Stockport	1018	—	1041	1126	—	1226	1328	— 1341
Wilmslow	0952	1018h	1052	—	1152	—	—	1352
Liverpool Lime Street	—	1021	—	—	—	—	—	1325
Runcorn	—	1038	—	—	—	—	—	1342
Hartford	—	1049	—	—	—	—	—	1353
Crewe	1052	1104	1152	—	1248	—	—	1412 1448
Macclesfield	—	—	—	1138	—	1238	1340	
Stoke-on-Trent	—	—	—	1158	—	1258	1400	
Stafford	—	1130	—	1219	—	1319	1424 1435	
Wolverhampton	1130	1150	1232	1238	1330	1337	1442 1453 1528	
Sandwell & Dudley	—	—	—	1252	—	1351	—	
Birmingham New St (arrive)	1151	1208	1251	1305	1348	1403	1505 1512 1548	
Birmingham New St (depart)	—	1212g	1305	1311	1358g	1406	1511h 1530g 1611	
Birmingham International	—	1228h	1318d	1321	—	1417	1521h — 1623d	

Mondays to Saturdays

	⊘	⊘R	B⊘		C⊘	B⊘	⊘
Manchester Piccadilly	1418	—	1520	—	1605	1620	1714
Stockport	1426	—	1528	—	1614	1628	1722
Wilmslow	—	—	1536	—	—	—	— 1722m 1752k
Liverpool Lime Street	—	—	1512	1530	—	—	1728
Runcorn	—	—	1529	1548	—	—	1745
Hartford	—	—	—	1600	—	—	1758
Crewe	—	1537	1607	1620	—	—	1815 1839
Macclesfield	1438	—	—	1513	1627	1640	1734
Stoke-on-Trent	1458	—	—	1541	1646	1700	1759
Stafford	1519	—	—	1648	1708	1721	1820 1835
Wolverhampton	1537	1616	1643	1709	1728	1739	1838 1857 1919
Sandwell & Dudley	1551	—	—	1721	1737	1751	1850
Birmingham New St (arrive)	1603	1636	1706	1736	1749	1805	1902 1918 1939
Birmingham New St (depart)	1606	1648g	1711	1741	1758g	1815g	1906 1936 1948
Birmingham International	1616	1658	1726	1745d	—	—	1916 1947d 2002

Mondays to Saturdays

	C⊘	B⊘		⊘	⊘n	⊘n
Manchester Piccadilly	1840	1840	—	—	—	2030
Stockport	1848	1848	—	—	—	2041
Wilmslow	—	—	1852	—	—	2052
Liverpool Lime Street	—	—	—	1915	—	2022
Runcorn	—	—	—	1932	—	2039
Hartford	—	—	—	1919	—	2050
Crewe	—	—	1945	1958	2001	2140
Macclesfield	1900	1900	—	—	—	
Stoke-on-Trent	1920	1920	—	—	—	
Stafford	1941	1941	2009	2024	—	2201
Wolverhampton	2000	2000	2028	2043	2038	2219
Sandwell & Dudley	—	—	—	2048	—	2231
Birmingham New St (arrive)	2020	2020	2048	2103	2100	2242
Birmingham New St (depart)	—	—	2031	2057p	—	
Birmingham International	—	—	2042	2108q	—	

Notes for this and opposite page:
A   Mondays only.
B   Mondays to Fridays.
C   Tuesdays to Saturdays.
D   Saturdays only.
d   To The South, see Table 16.
g   To The Southwest, see Table 17.
h   Mondays to Fridays.
k   Saturdays only.
n   ⊘ Mondays to Fridays.
p   2052 Saturdays.
q   2103 Saturdays.
r   Special bus service.

Light printed timings indicate connecting service.

8 Look at figure 3. Someone has a day off work on a Monday and wants to travel from Wolverhampton to Crewe to spend the day with a friend, and then to return to Wolverhampton on the Monday night. She does not want to catch a train before 7 a.m. but she does want to spend as long as possible with her friend.

How long can she spend in Crewe?

9 The distance between Paris and the South of France is approximately 600 km.

Roughly how long would it take to drive from Paris to the South of France at an average speed of 40 miles per hour?

(1 mile = 1.6 km approximately)

10 Ann Davidson set sail from Portsmouth and arrived in Dominica 65 days later on 20th November 1952.

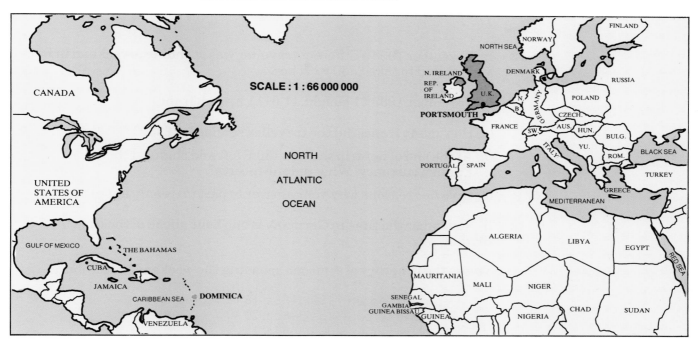

(*a*) On what date did she leave Portsmouth?

(*b*) Estimate from the map the distance she sailed.

(*c*) What was her average speed?

11 David Scott Cowper left Plymouth on 22 September 1981 to sail round the world single-handed. His journey took him 221 sailing days and he arrived back in England on 17 May 1982.

(*a*) On how many days did he not sail?

(*b*) Assuming that on sailing days he sailed all day and all night, what was his average speed? (It is about 25 000 miles all the way around the world.)

12 The hotel bills on a trip to Hamburg had been paid in advance, but the traveller needed to take some spending money in Deutschemarks.

In November 1988 £1 bought 3.2365 DM.

(*a*) The traveller decided to take £100 spending money. How many Deutschemarks would this buy?

(*b*) How many Deutschemarks would £165 buy?

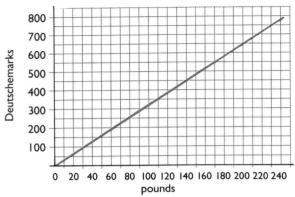

Figure 4

If you did not have your calculator handy you could use a conversion graph to help with calculations such as these.

(c) Use the conversion graph shown in figure 4 to check your answer to (b).

(d) At the end of the trip the traveller had 90 DM left and changed these back into English pounds. Using the conversion graph, find out how much money she received.

13 In November 1988 a different traveller was spending a weekend in Paris and wanted to take £350 with her.

In November 1988 £1 bought 11.0111 French francs.

(a) How many francs did the traveller receive for £350?

(b) At the end of her trip she had 130 F left and changed this back into English currency. What did she receive?

(c) Give *two* reasons why your answer to part (b) is only approximate.

14 In November the time in Germany is one hour ahead of the time in Britain.

This is the itinerary of someone spending the weekend in Hamburg

Depart Birmingham	18–11–88 at 18.15
Arrive Hamburg	18–11–88 at 20.40
Depart Hamburg	20–11–88 at 15.05
Arrive Birmingham	20–11–88 at 16.25

(All times shown are local times)

(a) The return flight took longer than the outward flight. How much longer did it take?

(b) How many hours were spent in Hamburg?

Figure 5

15 For this question you need the resource sheet '*Distance map of England*'. Figure 5 shows some rail fare increases at the start of 1989.

(a) Calculate the cost per mile of travelling to London from each of the towns shown.

(b) From which town is the cost per mile the greatest?

(c) Suppose that the new fares from Birmingham had been fixed so that the percentage increase was the same as the percentage increase from Salisbury. What would the new fares for a 7-day season ticket and an annual season ticket from Birmingham have been?

| STANDARD CLASS SEASON FARES TO LONDON ||||
From		Old rate	New rate	Increase (%)
Birmingham	7-day	£75.00	£90.60	20.80
	annual	£2,620	£3,168	20.92
Bournemouth	7-day	£50.50	£57.20	13.20
	annual	£2,020	£2,288	13.20
Bristol	7-day	£72.50	£87.60	20.80
	annual	£2,900	£3,504	20.80
Cardiff	7-day	£81.50	£98.50	20.80
	annual	£3,260	£3,940	20.80
Salisbury	7-day	£43.50	£48.20	10.80
	annual	£1,740	£1,928	10.80
Swindon	7-day	£54.00	£65.20	20.70
	annual	£2,160	£2,608	20.70

(d) Give evidence for and against the following statement

The percentage increase in fares was greatest for those towns farthest away from London.

(e) Why do you think it costs different amounts per mile to travel from different towns to London?

SECTION B

1 Figure 6 describes what the weather was in a number of places at midday on a day in January.

WORLD WEATHER

YESTERDAY, MIDDAY: c,cloud; f,fair; fg,fog; r,rain; sn,snow; s,sunny

	C	F			C	F			C	F			C	F
Aberdeen	s	12 54	Cardiff	c	10 50	Kingston*	s	29 84	Paris	c	9 48
Aberdovey	c	9 48	Carlisle*	c	8 46	Kuala Lumpur	f	33 91	Peking	f	0 32
Accra*	s	25 77	Casablanca	s	18 64	Las Palmas	c	21 70	Perth	r	20 68
Ajaccio	s	15 59	Chicago	c	14 58	Lerwick	f	8 46	Plymouth	c	11 52
Akrotiri	r	13 55	Christchurch	r	18 64	Lima	f	25 77	Port Stanley*	c	9 48
Alexandria	s	15 59	Cologne	c	10 50	Lisbon	f	13 55	Prague	c	4 39
Algiers	s	17 63	Copenhagen	r	3 37	Liverpool	c	10 50	Reykjavik	c	1 34
Amsterdam	c	10 50	Corfu	f	12 54	Lizard	c	11 52	Rhodes	f	9 48
Anchorage*	c	-8 18	Dakar*	s	23 73	Locarno	s	5 41	Rio de Janeiro	c	34 93
Anglesey	c	10 50	Darwin	th	32 90	London	c	11 52	Riyadh	s	18 64
Athens	f	8 46	Dover	r	8 46	Los Angeles	f	12 54	Rome	f	7 45
Auckland	r	20 68	Dublin	c	12 54	Luxembourg	r	7 45	Ronaldsway	c	11 52
Ayr	c	11 52	Dubrovnik	s	10 50	Madrid	f	11 52	Salzburg	r	4 39
Bahrain	f	18 64	Edinburgh	c	11 52	Majorca	s	16 61	San Francisco	c	10 51
Bangkok	f	33 91	Faro	c	15 59	Malaga	s	17 63	San Juan	f	28 82
Barbados	f	29 84	Florence	c	5 41	Malta	s	15 59	Santiago	f	26 79
Barcelona	s	11 52	Frankfurt	c	7 45	Manchester	c	10 50	Seoul	f	7 45
Beirut	f	15 59	Funchal	f	15 59	Manila	f	34 93	Singapore	f	32 90
Belfast	r	10 50	Geneva	c	6 43	Mecca	c	28 82	Southampton	r	10 50
Belgrade	c	2 36	Gibraltar	s	16 61	Melbourne	s	27 81	Southend	r	9 48
Berlin	r	5 41	Glasgow	r	11 52	Mexico City	f	24 75	Stockholm	c	5 41
Bermuda	f	21 71	Guernsey	c	9 48	Miami	f	25 76	Stornoway	s	9 48
Berwick	f	10 50	Harare	f	27 81	Milan	fg	0 32	Strasbourg	c	7 45
Biarritz	c	8 46	Havana	f	28 83	Mombasa	f	31 88	Sydney	c	25 77
Birmingham	c	10 50	Helsinki	c	1 34	Montevideo*	f	31 87	T'aipei	c	24 75
Blackpool	c	9 48	Hong Kong	f	22 72	Montreal*	f	-17 1	Tel Aviv	c	16 61
Bogota	f	19 66	Honolulu	c	28 82	Moscow	c	0 32	Tenerife	f	18 64
Bombay	f	25 77	Inverness	s	10 50	Munich	r	4 39	Tiree	s	9 48
Bordeaux	c	9 48	Ipswich	c	10 50	Nairobi	f	25 77	Tokyo	c	10 50
Bournemouth	c	10 50	Islamabad	f	16 60	Nassau	r	28 82	Toronto*	sn	-6 21
Brighton	c	9 48	Isles of Scilly	r	10 50	Newcastle	r	11 52	Tunis	c	15 59
Brisbane	s	29 84	Istanbul	c	3 37	New Delhi	f	15 59	Valencia	s	14 57
Bristol	r	10 50	Jakarta	c	31 88	Newquay	r	10 50	Vancouver*	c	5 41
Brussels	r	11 52	Jeddah	f	25 77	New York	c	1 34	Venice	fg	-1 30
Budapest	f	5 41	Jersey	c	10 50	Nice	s	13 55	Vienna	c	3 37
Buenos Aires	r	36 96	Jerusalem	c	10 50	Nicosia	f	16 61	Warsaw	sn	1 34
Cairo	c	16 61	Johannesburg	c	23 73	Norwich	c	10 50	Washington*	r	2 36
Calgary*	sn	-5 23	Karachi	s	19 66	Nottingham	c	10 50	Wellington	c	21 70
Cape Town	s	28 82	Kathmandu	f	9 48	Oslo	c	0 32	York	c	11 52
Caracas	c	24 75	Kiev	c	0 32	Oxford	r	10 50	Zurich	r	6 43

*Latest available figure.

Figure 6

(a) In which of the following British towns was it sunny: Blackpool, Aberdeen, Birmingham, Inverness, Bournemouth?

(b) In which of the following European capitals was it warmest and in which was it coldest: Amsterdam, Copenhagen, Moscow, London, Madrid, Dublin, Belgrade?

(c) Which Italian town was warmer: Venice or Rome? How much warmer was it in degrees Celsius?

(d) Which Canadian town was warmer: Toronto or Montreal? How much warmer was it in degrees Celsius?

(e) Describe what you might have worn if you had gone out for a walk in each of the following places:

(i) Belfast?   (ii) Brussels?
(iii) Anchorage?   (iv) Kingston?
(v) Nassau?

2 Temperatures can be measured in either degrees Fahrenheit or degrees Celsius. One way of converting a temperature measured in one unit to the corresponding temperature measured in the other unit is to use a conversion graph, such as the one shown in figure 7.

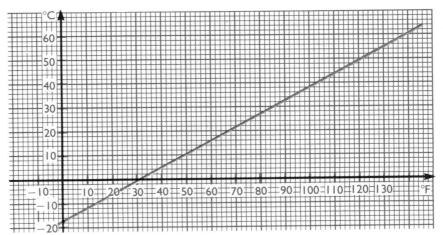

Figure 7

(a) Use the graph to convert the following temperatures to degrees Celsius:

(i) 45°F,   (ii) 79°F,   (iii) 25°F.

(b) Use the graph to convert the following temperature to degrees Farenheit:

(i) 20°C,   (ii) 40°C,   (iii) 55°C,   (iv) −20°C.

3 Figure 8 shows the main railway routes in Britain.

(a) If someone is travelling by train from Plymouth to Birmingham which of the following stations are they likely to pass through

(i) Bristol?   (ii) Bath?   (iii) Watford?
(iv) Cheltenham Spa?

(b) Which London terminus will you arrive at if you travel by train to London from

(i) Norwich?   (ii) Sheffield?   (iii) Bournemouth?
(iv) Dover?   (v) Aberdeen?

Figure 8

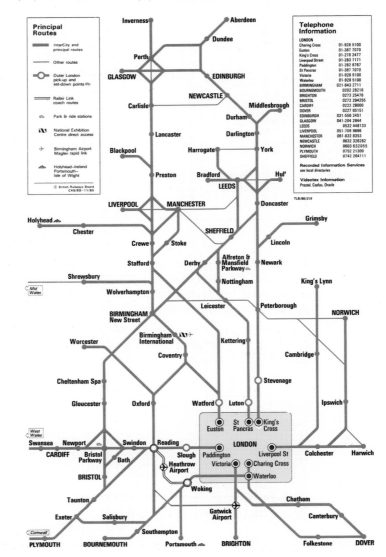

London Transport Underground Map.
Registered User Number 91/1224

Figure 9

4   Using the underground map shown in figure 9, explain how to get

(a) from Victoria to Liverpool Street

(b) from Victoria to Euston

(c) from Waterloo to King's Cross

(d) from Ealing Broadway to Harrow-on-the-Hill

5   When full the petrol tank of a particular car holds 45 litres.
The needle on the fuel
gauge is as shown below

The driver stops at a filling station and fills the tank. Roughly how much
petrol can she put in?

If petrol costs 37 p per litre, roughly how much will she pay for this petrol?

6   The petrol tank of a particular car holds 55 litres. On average the car goes
6 miles per litre of petrol. The driver of the car looks at the fuel gauge
which reads as shown below.

The driver is 250 miles from home. Will he need to stop for petrol before
he gets home?

7   On average the owner of a particular car drives approximately 350 miles
a week. The car needs servicing every five thousand miles.

On 10th February the driver notices that
the mileometer reads as follows:

Approximately when will the car be ready for its next service?

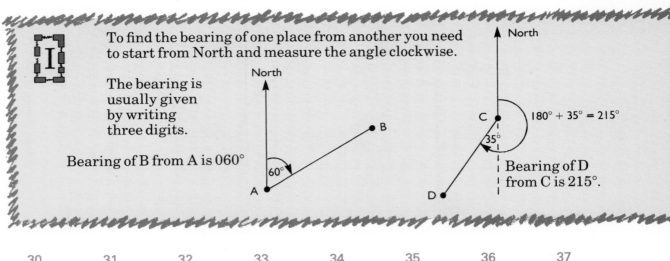

To find the bearing of one place from another you need to start from North and measure the angle clockwise.

The bearing is usually given by writing three digits.

Bearing of B from A is 060°

North

60°

A

B

North

C

$180° + 35° = 215°$

35°

D

Bearing of D from C is 215°.

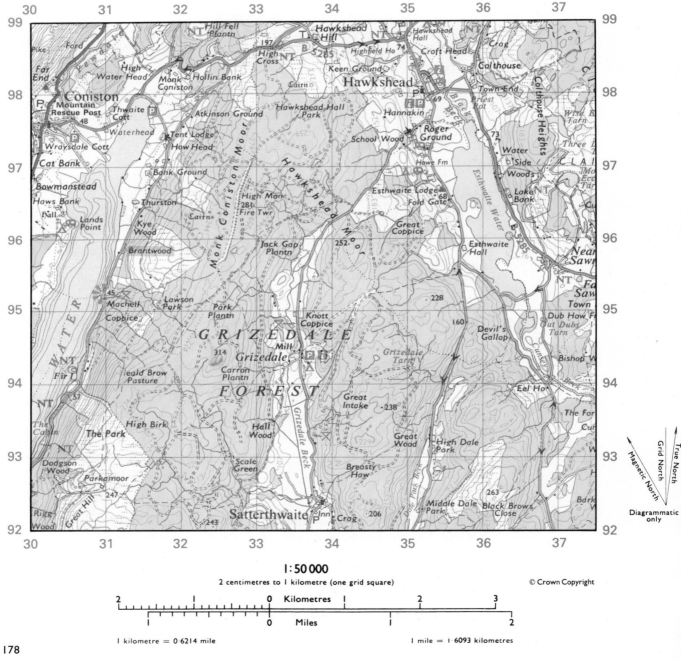

1:50 000

2 centimetres to 1 kilometre (one grid square)

© Crown Copyright

Kilometres

Miles

1 kilometre = 0·6214 mile

1 mile = 1·6093 kilometres

8 (a) What is the scale of this map?

(b) What does 1 cm represent

   (i) in centimetres?
   (ii) in metres?
   (iii) in kilometres?

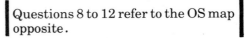

Questions 8 to 12 refer to the OS map opposite.

9 Hawkshead Church is at grid reference 352 980.

(a) Draw the symbol used on the map to represent Hawkshead Church.

(b) What does the 2 mean in the grid reference for Hawkshead Church?

(c) Give the grid reference for Satterthwaite Church.

10 At grid reference 369 941 on the map there is a bridge.

(a) Draw a picture to show how a bridge is represented.

(b) Give the grid reference of another bridge.

11 (a) How far is it from Coniston Church to Hawkshead Church 'as the crow flies'?

(b) How far is it from Coniston Church to Hawkshead Church by road?

(c) What is the bearing of Hawkshead Church from Coniston Church?

(d) What is the bearing of Coniston Church from Satterthwaite Church?

(e) What is the bearing of the caravan site at Lands Point on Coniston Water from Hawkshead Church?

12 How many copies of the map would you need to completely cover the ground which the map represents?

13 Road gradients are marked in one of two different ways. For example, a very steep hill might be marked in either of the following ways

  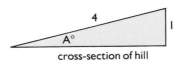

cross-section of hill

(a) What is the alternative way of marking roads with the following gradients:

   (i) 1:10?
   (ii) 20%?
   (iii) 12%?

(b) Calculate the angle marked A on the drawing above.

(c) If a 25% hill is one mile long, as measured along the road, calculate the horizontal distance from one end of the hill to the other.

(d) If the apparent length of a 10% hill read from a map is 800 m, calculate the length of the hill measured along the road.

SECTION C

1 To get to school someone walks to the bus stop and then catches the school bus. Figure 10 shows her journey.

(*a*) How far is it from home to school?

(*b*) How long does the journey take altogether?

(*c*) How long is she on the bus?

(*d*) After leaving her bus stop how many times does the bus stop before reaching the school?

(*e*) At what speed does she walk to the bus stop?

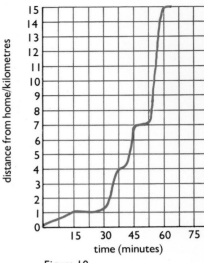

Figure 10

2 Two friends like to walk to school together. They live at different places but they meet up on the way to school.

Figure 11 shows their journeys to school on one particular morning.

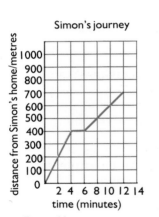

Figure 11

(*a*) Which person has the longer distance to walk to school?

(*b*) How long did Jasbir's journey to school take altogether?

(*c*) When one of the boys arrived at the meeting place he had to wait for the other boy to come. How long did he have to wait?

(*d*) When the other boy saw his friend at the meeting place he ran to him. How fast did he run?

(*e*) Which of the boys walked faster at the start of his journey? How fast did this boy walk?

3 Ann cycles to school but often sees her friend Carol on the way. Carol walks to school and when Ann sees Carol she slows down to Carol's speed.

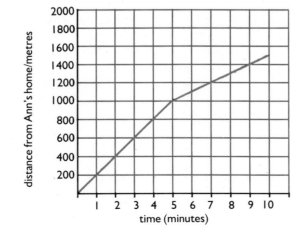

Figure 12

Figure 12 shows Ann's journey to school on one Tuesday morning.

(*a*) How far is it from Ann's home to school?

(*b*) How far did Ann and Carol travel together?

(*c*) How long would Ann's journey to school have taken if she had not met Carol?

4 Two girls are youth hostelling. To travel from one youth hostel to another they climb up one side of a mountain and down the other side. Figure 13 shows their journey.

(a) How long did the whole journey take?

(b) How long do you think it took the girls to climb to the top of the mountain?

(c) How much further did they walk going up the mountain than they walked coming down it?

(d) How long did they stop on the top of the mountain?

(e) How long did they stop for lunch?

(f) How fast did they travel up the steepest part of the mountain?

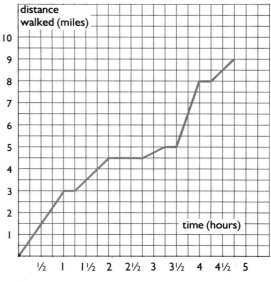

Figure 13

5 Find the graph for question 5 on the resource sheet called 'Planning a journey 1'.

A brother and sister who live in a village decide to go to the nearest town and go round the shops together. The brother decides to walk and the sister decides to cycle by the same route. The brother leaves home first. The graph shows his journey.

(a) The sister leaves home 20 minutes after her brother and cycles at 10 miles per hour. Add to the graph a line showing the sister's journey to the town.

(b) How far from home does the sister pass her brother?

(c) How long does she have to wait in town for her brother to arrive?

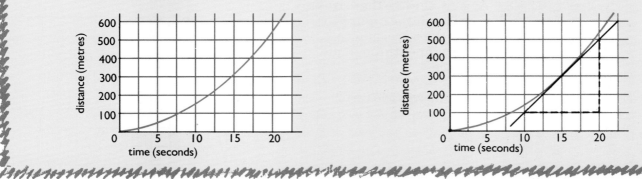

The graph below shows the motion of a plane down a runway before taking off. Because the plane is accelerating the speed is increasing.

To find the speed at any moment, say after the first 15 seconds, you need to know the gradient of the graph. So you draw a tangent to the graph.

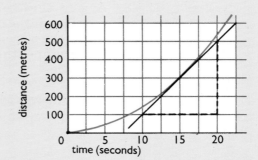

6 Find the graph for question 6 on the resource sheet called '*Planning a journey 1*'.

The graph shows the movement of a car after leaving some traffic lights.

(*a*) By drawing tangents to the graph, find the speed of the car after
   (i) 6 seconds
   (ii) 14 seconds

(*b*) How far does the car travel during the first 10 seconds? What is its average speed?

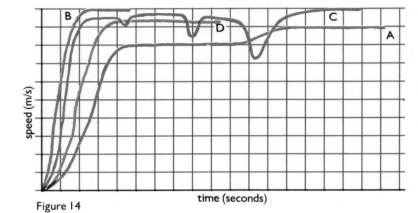

Figure 14

7 An athletics meeting included events for the 100 m, the 200 m, the 400 m and 4 by 100 m relay.

The speed–time graphs in figure 14, marked A, B, C and D, show the performance of the winners of these four events.

Say which graph represents which event.

The graph below shows someone travelling at a constant speed of 40 m/s.

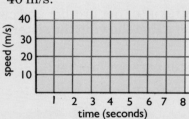

If she travels for 8 seconds the distance she travels is 320 metres. The area of the rectangle under the graph shows this distance.

The second graph shows a stone dropping. If it drops for 4 seconds you can work out the distance it drops by finding the area of the triangle under the graph. It drops a distance of 80 m.

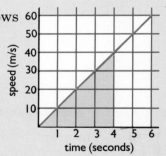

---

8 At a village fete there was a race for adults. Figure 15 shows the performance of the winner throughout this race.

How long was the race?

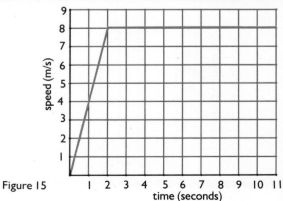

Figure 15

9 A jogger goes out for a run. Her run is shown on the speed–time graph in figure 16.

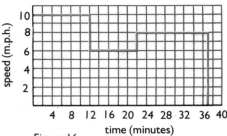

How far did the jogger run?

Figure 16

10 Figure 17 shows a train's journey between two stations.

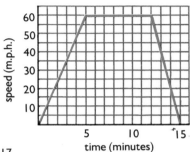

Figure 17

How far is it between the two stations?

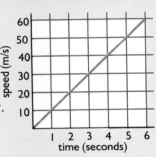

The graph shows a stone dropping.

The gradient of the graph is $40 \div 4 = 10$.

This tells you that the stone is accelerating at 10 m/s^2. This means that in every second the velocity of the stone increases by 10 m/s.

11 (a) What was the acceleration of the winner at the beginning of the race described in question 8?

(b) What was the acceleration of the train in question 10?

(c) What was the deceleration of the train in question 10?

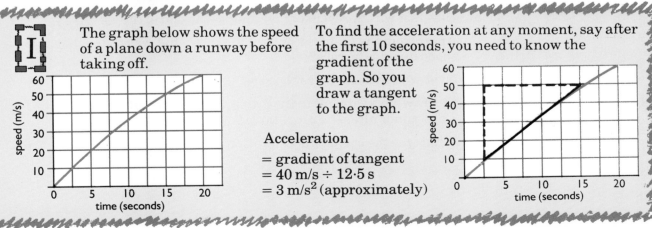

The graph below shows the speed of a plane down a runway before taking off.

To find the acceleration at any moment, say after the first 10 seconds, you need to know the gradient of the graph. So you draw a tangent to the graph.

Acceleration
= gradient of tangent
= $40 \text{ m/s} \div 12 \cdot 5 \text{ s}$
= 3 m/s^2 (approximately)

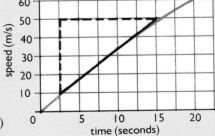

12 Find the graph for questions 12 and 13 on the resource sheet called 'Planning a journey 2'. The graph shows the movement of a bus after leaving a bus stop.

(a) What was the acceleration of the bus after 5 seconds?

(b) What was the acceleration of the bus after 10 seconds?

If the speed–time graph is a curve the area under it still represents the distance travelled. You can find this area approximately by dividing it up into trapezia, as shown in the diagrams below.

Page 247 explains how to find the area of a trapezium.

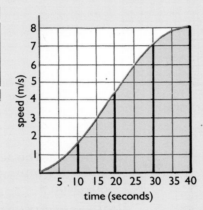

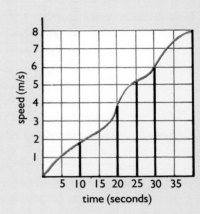

13 You will need the graph for the bus.

(a) Find how far the bus travels during the first 10 seconds.

(b) What is the average speed of the bus during the first 12 seconds?

14 Find the graph for question 14 on the resource sheet called 'Planning a journey 2'.

The graph shows the performance of the winner of a cycle sprint race.

(a) How fast was the cyclist travelling at the end of the race?

(b) Apart from the first 5 seconds of the race what was the cyclist's slowest speed during the race?

(c) Over what distance was the race?

(d) By drawing a tangent to the graph, find the cyclist's acceleration 130 seconds after the race started.

(e) What was the cyclist's deceleration 60 seconds after the race started?

15 A woman goes to the local swimming bath for a swim. Figure 18 shows the start of her swim.

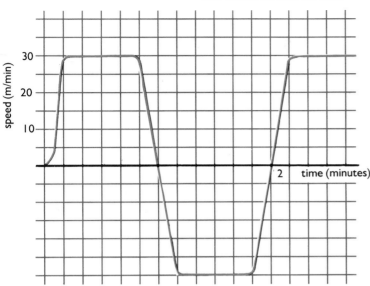

(*a*) Approximately what is the length of the swimming bath?

(*b*) Why is part of the graph drawn below the horizontal axis?

(*c*) The woman swims 30 lengths at the same speed. How far does she swim altogether? What is her average speed?

Figure 18

FURTHER COURSEWORK TASKS

1⟩ Plan a package holiday. To do this you will need brochures from a travel agent. Who is going on the holiday? What type of holiday do they want (for example, beach, sight-seeing, sports)?

Decide where to go and for how long, how much spending money to take, and in which foreign currency. Consider passports and insurance. What will the weather be like? What clothes will you want to take?

How will you get to and from the airport, harbour or coach terminus?

2〉 Plan your own holiday. You will need to consider many of the issues suggested for the package holiday.

You will also need to consider some other issues. What kind of accommodation you are going to have: hotel, cottage, tent, youth hostel, caravan? Are you going to cater for yourself? If so, plan menus and costs. Decide how you will get to where you are going to stay and how much it will cost.

3〉 Plan an expedition or trip. This could be a fishing, sailing, canal boat, skiing, pony trekking or cycling trip. You may be going to play or watch a sport. You may be playing in or watching a concert.

You will need to consider some of the issues suggested for planning holidays.

4〉 Plan a walk. This could be over some hills, for example. Use a large scale (1:50000 or 1:25000) Ordnance Survey or similar map. Plan the route in detail. Bear in mind who is going, how easy or hard the walk should be. How long will the walk take? What clothing and equipment will be required? What food will you need? What about first aid and safety? How will you get between home, or where you are staying, and the start and finish of the walk?

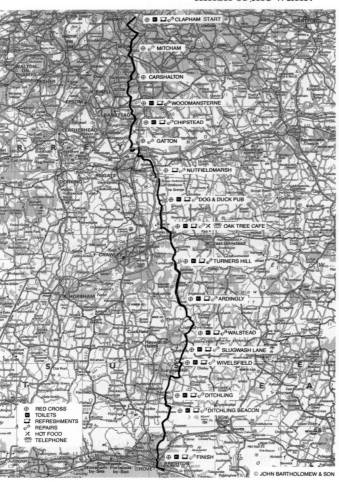

5〉 Plan a marathon, sponsored walk, or cycle road race or time trials.

Work out exact routes from suitable maps. Provide precise instructions for marshalls and timekeepers. Consider the need to consult with the police.

6〉 Plan the best route for someone doing a paper round or a similar round near to where you live.

One type of problem is where the round needs to visit nearly every house. A second type of problem is where the round visits a few houses over a wider area.

7〉 Write about the migration of mammals, birds or fish.

Do not just copy information from books. Use maps. Calculate speeds. Consider migration dates, and the influence of the weather. What happens if animals or birds stray off route? Have human beings disrupted or changed migration patterns?

13 INFINITY

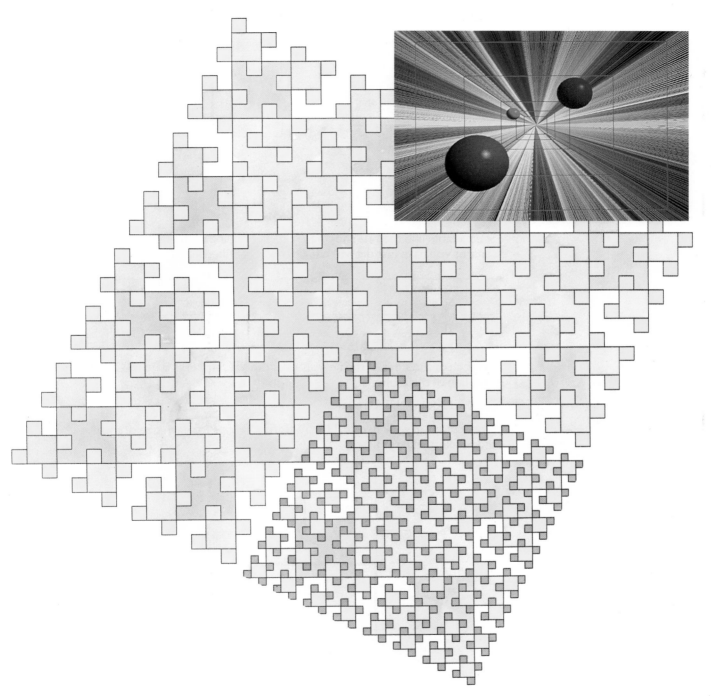

This chapter is about things that go on for ever. It begins with a paragraph describing the chapter. This is what the paragraph says. This chapter is about things that go on for ever. It begins with a paragraph describing the chapter. This is what the paragraph says. This chapter . . .

It was decided not to print the whole of the previous paragraph.

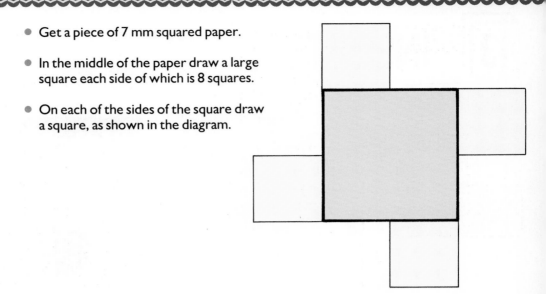

- Get a piece of 7 mm squared paper.

- In the middle of the paper draw a large square each side of which is 8 squares.

- On each of the sides of the square draw a square, as shown in the diagram.

- Start a table like the one shown here. The first line of the table (for the four squares you have just drawn) has already been filled in.

Size of square	Number of squares drawn	Area of each square	Total area of squares
4 by 4	4	16	64

- On each of the sides of the new squares draw a square, as before. Complete the next line of the table.

- Continue doing this for ever.

- Now colour in your design. Use a different colour for each size of square. Colour the smallest squares first.

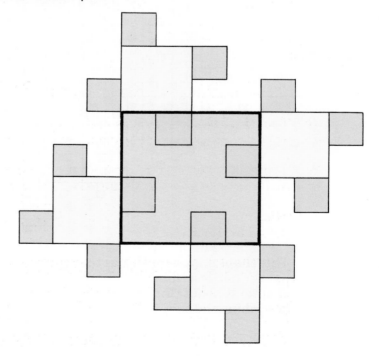

SECTION A

1   Write down the next two lines of your table without drawing any more of the pattern.

2   (*a*) What area of the original square was covered by smaller squares after the stage when you added

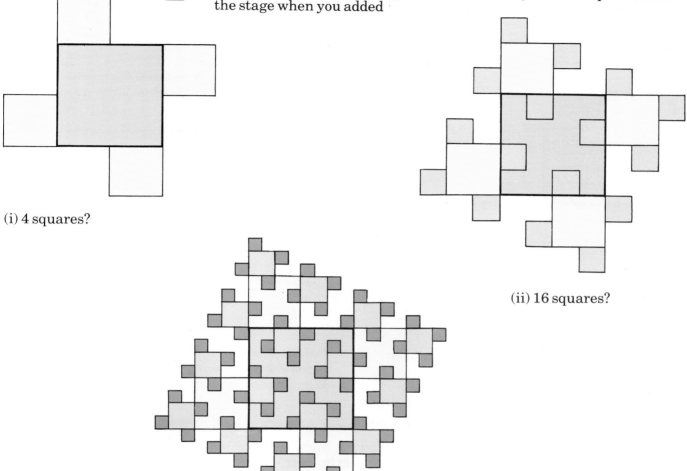

(i) 4 squares?

(ii) 16 squares?

(iii) 64 squares?

(*b*) How does this pattern continue?

3   If you did carry on adding squares for ever what fraction of the original square would be covered by smaller squares?

4   If you did carry on adding squares for ever, estimate how large the total shaded area would be, compared to the area of the original square.

(*Hint*: the work you did at the beginning of the chapter on tilted squares should help with this.)

SECTION B

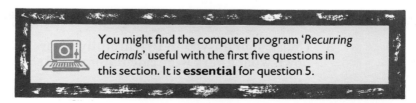

You might find the computer program '*Recurring decimals*' useful with the first five questions in this section. It is **essential** for question 5.

If you want to work out $\frac{3}{8}$ as a decimal you can press the following keys on your calculator:

The answer will probably be shown as

0.375

If you want to work out $\frac{1}{3}$ as a decimal you can press the following keys on your calculator:

The answer will probably look something like this:

0.333333333

If your calculator was a lot wider the answer might look like this:

0.3333333333333333333333

What would the answer look like if your calculator was infinitely wide?

As it is impossible to write down an infinite

number of 3s people often write this number as

$0.\dot{3}$

The dot over the 3 tells you that there are really an infinite number of 3s.

If you work out $\frac{2}{3}$ as a decimal *some* calculators give something like this as an answer:

0.66666666

and *other* calculators give you something like this:

0.66666667

Explain why *both* these answers are reasonable answers for a calculator to give.

Use a calculator to check the following.

$$\frac{1}{6} = 0.1\dot{6} \qquad \frac{2}{11} = 0.\dot{1}\dot{8} \qquad \frac{4}{27} = 0.\dot{1}4\dot{8}$$

Putting the dots above the numbers as shown is one way of showing which numbers repeat. What is the rule for where you put the dots?

1   Work out the following fractions as decimals. Use dots over the numbers for decimals that go on for ever.

$(a)\frac{1}{2}$

$(b)\frac{1}{3},\frac{2}{3}$

$(c)\frac{1}{4},\frac{2}{4},\frac{3}{4}$

$(d)\frac{1}{5},\frac{2}{5},\frac{3}{5},\frac{4}{5}$

$(e)\frac{1}{6},\frac{2}{6},\frac{3}{6},\frac{4}{6},\frac{5}{6}$

$(f)\frac{1}{7},\frac{2}{7},\frac{3}{7},\frac{4}{7},\frac{5}{7},\frac{6}{7}$

$(g)\frac{1}{8},\frac{2}{8},\frac{3}{8},\frac{4}{8},\frac{5}{8},\frac{6}{8},\frac{7}{8}$

$(h)\frac{1}{9},\frac{2}{9},\frac{3}{9},\frac{4}{9},\frac{5}{9},\frac{6}{9},\frac{7}{9},\frac{8}{9}$

$(i)\frac{1}{10},\frac{2}{10},\frac{3}{10},\frac{4}{10},\frac{5}{10},\frac{6}{10},\frac{7}{10},\frac{8}{10},\frac{9}{10}$

2   Some answers to question 1 occurred more than once. Write down the different fractions which give the same answer.

3   Check your answer to 1(*f*) carefully. Share answers with friends. Write down what a very wide calculator would show for $\frac{3}{7}$ if it showed $\frac{1}{3}$ as

0.33333333333333333333333

In question 1 you will have found that

$$\frac{4}{7} = 0.\overset{.}{5}7142\overset{.}{8}$$

Another way of showing $\frac{4}{7}$ is to use a wheel.

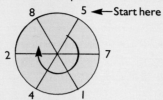

It is interesting that the same wheel also shows

$$\frac{1}{7}, \frac{2}{7}, \frac{3}{7}, \frac{5}{7} \text{ and } \frac{6}{7}$$

depending on where you start on the wheel.

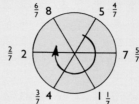

4 (a) Work out the following fractions as decimals.

$$\frac{1}{13}, \frac{2}{13}, \frac{3}{13}, \frac{4}{13}, \frac{5}{13}, \frac{6}{13}, \frac{7}{13}, \frac{8}{13}, \frac{9}{13}, \frac{10}{13}, \frac{11}{13}, \frac{12}{13}$$

(b) Two wheels are needed if you want to show all the decimals in part (a).

Draw these wheels.

5 Use the computer program '*Recurring decimals*' to work out $\frac{5}{29}$ and $\frac{24}{29}$ as decimals.

What is the connection between the patterns of numbers in the two decimals?

It is easy to write $\frac{1}{10}$ as a decimal, because $\frac{1}{10}$, is 0.1. It is fairly easy to write $\frac{1}{8}$ as a decimal. $\frac{1}{8}$ is an exact number of thousandths and so it can be written with just three digits after the decimal point. $\frac{1}{8} = 0.125$. It is not so easy to write $\frac{1}{3}$ as a decimal. If you try to work it out on paper

$$\begin{array}{r} 0.\ 3\ 3---\\ 3\overline{)1.^10^10---} \end{array}$$

you will find that after the first digit you are back where you started. So $\frac{1}{3}$ when written as a decimal goes on producing this digit for ever. It is even harder for $\frac{1}{7}$. If you work it out on paper it only repeats itself after six digits

$$\begin{array}{r} 0\ 1\ 4\ 2\ 8\ 5\ 7\ 1--\\ 7\overline{)1.^10^30^20^60^40^50^10--} \end{array}$$

but then goes on producing these six digits for ever. Because there are six digits the decimal for $\frac{1}{7}$ is harder to remember than the decimal for $\frac{1}{3}$. Some people use mnemonics to help them remember numbers. Here is a mnemonic for $\frac{1}{7}$.

A week of horrible windy weather (142857)

Each word stands for a digit. The digit it stands for is the number of letters in the word.

To get $\frac{1}{7}$ you have to repeat these six digits for ever: an eternity of horrible windy weather. Week after week after week of it!

All fractions can be turned into decimals which repeat themselves eventually. Some fractions only repeat after a large number of digits (see question 5).

Box continued overleaf

But there are other numbers such as $\sqrt{2}$, which are even more difficult to write as decimals. $\sqrt{2} = 1.41421356...$

Even if you have a sentence to remember the digits shown above for $\sqrt{2}$ you will still only know how to write the first nine digits of $\sqrt{2}$, because the decimal for $\sqrt{2}$ *never* repeats itself. It goes on changing for ever. This is because $\sqrt{2}$ is *not* a fraction like $\frac{1}{7}$ is.

Numbers which can be written as fractions are called **rational** numbers. All rational numbers can be written as decimals which either end or repeat themselves. (Rational numbers can be positive or negative, and zero is a rational number.) Numbers, like $\sqrt{2}$, which cannot be written as fractions, are called **irrational** numbers. If you write irrational numbers as decimals the digits go on changing for ever.

π is another example of a number which is not a fraction. π is the number which is obtained by dividing the circumference of a circle by its diameter.

If you measure the circumference and diameter of a circle you will only get an approximate value of π. You might discover if you are *very* accurate that π is about 3.14. For practical purposes 3.142 is probably as accurate a value of π as you will ever need. But mathematicians are fascinated by the *exact* value of π and have discovered methods of working it out (*not* by drawing very accurate circles!) They have discovered that, like the decimal for $\sqrt{2}$, the decimal for π *never* repeats itself.

People have invented mnemonics for π. Here are two mnemonics.

> May I have a large container of coffee

> How I want a drink, alcoholic of course, after the heavy chapters involving quantum mechanics

But, however long the mnemonic is, it will not be long enough to know all about π, because the digits of π *never* repeat.

6 Use the longer mnemonic for π to write out as many digits for the decimal for π as you can.

Use your calculator to check as many digits as possible.

7 Why are *ratio*nal numbers so called? You may be able to guess the answer to this question.

8 (a) Explain how you can tell from figure 1, without measuring, that π is bigger than 3.

(b) Explain how you can tell from figure 2, without measuring that π is less than 4.

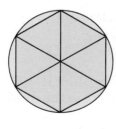

Figure 1

Figure 2

9 One of these numbers is irrational. Which one?

(a) $\frac{3}{4}$　(b) 1.6754327　(c) $-\frac{3}{17}$　(d) $\sqrt{81}$　(e) $\sqrt{10}$　(f) $6\frac{1}{8}$

10 One of the numbers marked x in the diagrams below is irrational. Which one?

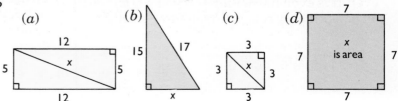

11 Invent mnemonics for $\frac{2}{13}$ and $\frac{1}{13}$.

You will need to think how to code the digit zero. You could, for example, use a word of ten letters, or a piece of punctuation.

12 $\frac{1}{9}$ is $0.\dot{1}$. If you multiply this by 9 you get $0.\dot{9}$. So $\frac{9}{9} = 0.\dot{9}$. but $\frac{9}{9} = 1$. Explain.

SECTION C

"Tell me the weight of a snowflake," a coalmouse asked a wild dove. "Nothing more than nothing," was the answer. "In that case I must tell you a marvellous story," the coalmouse said.

"I sat on the branch of a fir, close to its trunk, when it began to snow – not heavily, not in a raging blizzard: no, just like a dream, without a sound and without any violence. Since I did not have anything better to do, I counted the snowflakes settling on the twigs and needles of my branch. Their number was exactly 3,741,952. When the 3,741,953rd dropped onto the branch – nothing more than nothing as you say – the branch broke off." Having said that the coalmouse flew away.

The dove, since Adam's time an authority on the matter, thought about the story for a while, and finally said to herself: "Perhaps there is only one more person's voice lacking for peace to come to the world."

(New Fables, *Thus spoke the Marabou* by Kurt Kauter)

If you describe the number of cubes, or the surface area, or the number of edges, of a model you have made with interlocking cubes you are likely to use whole numbers which are not very big (say between 1 and 1000). But because the universe is very big, and because the particles in the universe are very small, some things need very big numbers or very small numbers to describe them.

When calculators deal with very *big* numbers they often display them like this:

$$\boxed{2.4476 \quad 12}$$

The 12 means 'multiply by 10 twelve times'.

So the number shown above would be 2 447 600 000 000. The number is not very easy to read in this form, because you have to count how many digits there are. To make it easier to read you can write it more like the calculator displays it. You can write it as

$$2.4476 \times 10^{12}$$

People call this way of writing a number **standard form**.

When calculators deal with very *small* numbers they often display them like this:

$$\boxed{1.44 \quad -07}$$

The -07 means 'divide by 10 seven times'.

So the number shown above is 0.000000144. But it can also be written, in *standard form*, as

$$1.44 \times 10^{-7}$$

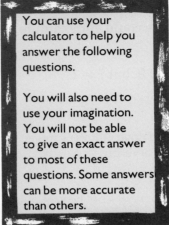

You can use your calculator to help you answer the following questions.

You will also need to use your imagination. You will not be able to give an exact answer to most of these questions. Some answers can be more accurate than others.

1 How many seconds have you been alive?

2 How much liquid do you drink in a year?

3 What is the thickness of a page in this book?

4 The average Briton throws away about ten times his or her own body weight in household refuse every year. The population of Britain is about 50 million.

What weight, in tonnes, of household refuse is thrown away in Britain in a week?

(Assume that an average person's weight is about 70 kg. 1 tonne = 1000 kg)

5 The Moon is about 400 000 kilometres from the Earth. Placed end to end, the drink cans thrown away in Britain in a year would reach from the Earth to the Moon.

How many drink cans are thrown away in a year?

(The height of a standard drink can is 140 mm.)

6 Start with a square whose sides are 8 cm.

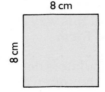

Keep joining the midpoints of the sides.

After how many stages will the square not be visible to the naked eye?

7 In 1952, using a computer, Lehmer showed that the number $2^{251} - 1$ is a prime number.

(i) Write this number in standard form, correct to two significant figures.
(ii) Is this number larger or smaller than the number of particles in the universe, which is about 10^{85}?

SECTION D

1 (a) Copy this rectangle on squared paper.

(b) Shade $\frac{1}{2}$ of the rectangle.
(c) Now shade another $\frac{1}{4}$ of the rectangle.

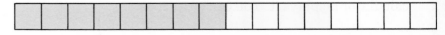

What fraction of the rectangle is now shaded?

(d) Now shade another $\frac{1}{8}$ of the rectangle. What fraction of the rectangle is now shaded?

(e) What fraction of the rectangle would be shaded after the next step?

(f) And the next?

(g) What fraction would be shaded if you continued for ever?

2 (a) Draw a rectangle on squared paper which is 18 squares long and 1 square wide.

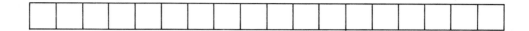

(b) Shade $\frac{1}{3}$ of the rectangle.

(c) Now shade another $\frac{1}{9}$ of the rectangle. What fraction of the rectangle is shaded altogether?

(d) What fraction of a rectangle would be shaded after the next stage?

(e) And the next?

(f) What fraction of the rectangle would be shaded if you continued for ever?

3 Try doing the following by *imagining* the process instead of drawing.

(a) Shade $\frac{1}{4}$ of a rectangle.

(b) Now shade another $\frac{1}{16}$ of the rectangle. What fraction of the rectangle is now shaded?

(c) Now shade another $\frac{1}{64}$ of the rectangle. What fraction of the rectangle is now shaded?

(d) What fraction is shaded after the next stage?

(e) And the next?

(f) What fraction would be shaded if you went on for ever?

4 (a) Look at your answers to questions 1, 2 and 3. Predict what would happen eventually if you started by shading in $\frac{1}{5}$.

(b) What would happen eventually if you started by shading in $\frac{1}{N}$?

5 (a) Shade $\frac{1}{3}$ of a rectangle.

(b) Now shade $\frac{1}{3}$ of what is left unshaded. What fraction is now shaded?

(c) Now shade $\frac{1}{3}$ of what is left unshaded. What fraction is now shaded?

(d) What fraction is shaded after the next stage?

(e) What fraction would be shaded if you went on for ever?

6 Make up rules of your own for shading rectangles and discover what happens when you follow them.

SECTION E

1   The instructions to the right describe the path of a point moving on a piece of squared paper.

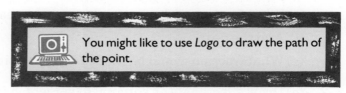

You might like to use *Logo* to draw the path of the point.

(a) On squared paper draw as much of the path as you can.

(b) Write down the coordinates of each corner of the path.

(c) Predict what the coordinates of the next few corners will be.

(d) Where do you think the point would end up eventually?

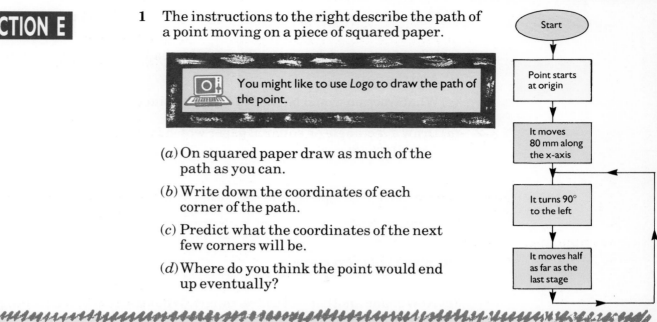

Start

Point starts at origin

It moves 80 mm along the x-axis

It turns 90° to the left

It moves half as far as the last stage

A point moves along a line. Its distance from a fixed point on the line after n moves is x_n. It moves according to the following rule:

$$x_n = \frac{x_{n-1} + 8}{2}$$

This means that the next position is obtained from the current position by adding 8 and dividing by 2.

Suppose the moving point starts 64 units from the fixed point. So $x_0 = 64$.

Hence the next position is

$$x_1 = (64 + 8) \div 2 = 36.$$

In the same way you can calculate that the next three positions are

$$x_2 = (36 + 8) \div 2 = 22$$
$$x_3 = (22 + 8) \div 2 = 15$$
$$x_4 = (15 + 8) \div 2 = 11.5$$

These first four stages are shown in the diagram below.

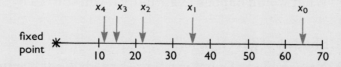

2   A point moves along a line. Its distance from a fixed point on the line after n moves is x_n. It moves according to the following rule:

$$x_n = \frac{x_{n-1} + 10}{2} \text{ and } x_0 = 100$$

(a) Calculate x_1, x_2 and x_3.

(b) How far is the point from the fixed point after 7 moves?

(c) If the point continues to move for ever how far do you think it will be from the fixed point at the finish?

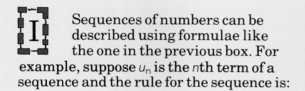

Sequences of numbers can be described using formulae like the one in the previous box. For example, suppose u_n is the nth term of a sequence and the rule for the sequence is:

$$u_{n+1} = 5u_n + 4$$

This means that each term is obtained from the previous term by multiplying by 5 and adding 4.

So if
$u_1 = 7$
then $u_2 = 5 \times 7 + 4 = 39$
then $u_3 = 5 \times 39 + 4 = 199$

3 u_n is the nth term of a sequence. Each term is obtained from the previous term using this rule:

$$u_{n+1} = 3u_n - 4$$

The fourth term, u_4, is 20.

(a) What are u_5, u_6 and u_7?

(b) What are u_3 and u_2?

(c) If the sequence is continued for ever what happens to the numbers in the sequence?

4 A sequence whose nth term is a_n is defined by the following rule:

$$a_{n+1} = \frac{-a_n}{1 + a_n} \quad and \quad a_{20} \text{ is } 4$$

(a) What are a_{21}, a_{22} and a_{23}?

(b) What is a_1?

5 A sequence whose nth term is x_n is defined as follows:

$$x_n = \frac{x_{n-1} + x_{n-2}}{2} \quad and \quad x_1 = 0 \text{ and } x_2 = 100$$

(a) What are x_3, x_4 and x_5?

(b) If the sequence is continued for ever what do you think will happen to the numbers in the sequence?

6 If you want to find the square root of 12 but do not have a square root button on your calculator you can use the following method.

(A) Guess the square root of 12. (Perhaps you guess 3.)

(B) Divide 12 by your guess. (If the guess was 3 the answer will be 4.

(C) If your guess really was the square root of 12 it should be the same as the number you obtained in (B). But it probably is not. So find the average of the guess and the number you obtained in (B). (If these were 3 and 4 the average is 3.5.)

(D) Use this average as your new guess and go back to (B).

If you do this for ever you will end up with the square root of 12.

Use this method to find the square root of 12 correct to 3 decimal places.

7 Use the method of question 6 to find the square root of 13 correct to 3 decimal places.

The method of question 6 can be adapted to find the solutions of equations.

Suppose you want to find a solution of the equation

$$x^2 - 2x - 5 = 0 \qquad (A)$$

This equation can be rearranged as follows:

$$x^2 = 2x + 5$$

Therefore

$$x = \frac{2x + 5}{x} \qquad (B)$$

Suppose you *guess* a solution to the equation labelled (A). If the solution was *correct* the left hand side of the equation labelled (B) would be equal to the right hand side.

It probably is *not correct*. But if you put your guess into the right hand side of equation (B) you obtain a new guess which is closer to one of the solutions of the equation.

So you can write the rule for obtaining a new guess as

$$x_{new} = \frac{2x + 5}{x}$$

To find a solution to the equation you need to guess a solution. Suppose you guess 3. Then the new guess is

$$x_{new} = (2 \times 3 + 5) \div 3 = 3.66667$$

and the next new guess is

$$(2 \times 3.66667 + 5) \div 3 = 3.363636$$

The numbers get closer and closer to the solution of the equation, which is 3.45, correct to 2 decimal places.

8 (*a*) Show that the equation

$$x^2 - 3x + 1 = 0$$

can be rearranged to give

$$x = \frac{3x - 1}{x}$$

(*b*) You can use the rearrangement as a rule for finding a new guess.

$$x_{new} = \frac{3x - 1}{x}$$

If the first guess is 2 use the rule to find the next two guesses.

(*c*) Find a solution of the equation

$$x^2 - 3x + 1 = 0$$

correct to 2 decimal places.

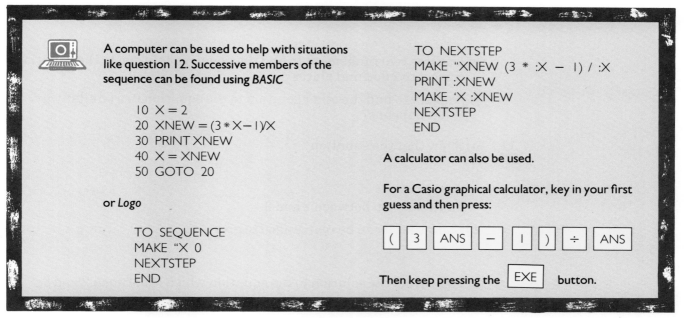

A computer can be used to help with situations like question 12. Successive members of the sequence can be found using *BASIC*

```
10 X = 2
20 XNEW = (3 * X − 1)/X
30 PRINT XNEW
40 X = XNEW
50 GOTO 20
```

or *Logo*

```
TO SEQUENCE
MAKE "X 0
NEXTSTEP
END
```

```
TO NEXTSTEP
MAKE "XNEW (3 * :X − 1) / :X
PRINT :XNEW
MAKE 'X :XNEW
NEXTSTEP
END
```

A calculator can also be used.

For a Casio graphical calculator, key in your first guess and then press:

(3 ANS − 1) ÷ ANS

Then keep pressing the EXE button.

9 (*a*) Show that the equation

$$2x^2 - 5x - 4 = 0$$

can be rearranged to give

$$x = \frac{5x + 4}{2x}$$

(*b*) Choose your own first guess and find a solution of the equation

$$2x^2 - 5x - 4 = 0$$

correct to 2 decimal places.

10 (*a*) Draw a graph of $y = x^2 + 3x - 7$. You might want to use a graphical calculator or a graph-plotting program on a computer.

(*b*) What is the value of $x^2 + 3x - 7$ when

(i) $x = 1$?
(ii) $x = 2$?
(iii) $x = -4$?
(iv) $x = -5$?

(c) Explain why there must be a solution to the equation

$$x^2 + 3x - 7 = 0$$

between 1 and 2 and another solution between -5 and -4.

(d) Show that the equation

$$x^2 + 3x - 7 = 0$$

can be rearranged to give

$$x = \frac{7 - 3x}{x}$$

(e) Use this rearrangement to find the negative solution to the equation, correct to 2 decimal places.

(f) Now try to find the other solution to the equation in a similar way. What happens?

11 (a) Show that the equation

$$x^3 - x = 10$$

has a solution between 2 and 3.

(b) Show that it can be rearranged to give

$$x = \sqrt[3]{10 + x}$$

(c) Hence find the solution to the equation which is between 2 and 3, correct to 2 decimal places.

1) Draw some fractals. Here are some ideas.

- On each side of a triangle draw a triangle. And on each side of these triangles draw a triangle. And on each side . . .

- In a triangle draw and shade in another triangle by joining the midpoints of the sides. In each of the unshaded triangles draw and shade in another triangle by joining the midpoints of the sides. In each of the unshaded triangles . . .

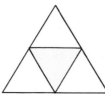 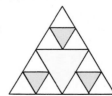 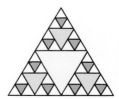

You might want to write *Basic* or *Logo* programs to make some of your drawings. You could also use a graphical calculator.

• In a pentagon draw all the diagonals and shade in the acute-angled triangles. Inside the new pentagon draw all the diagonals and shade in the acute-angled triangles. Inside the new pentagon . . .

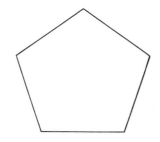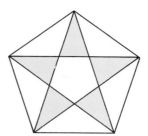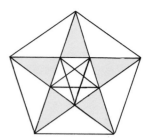

• In an octagon . . .

You might want to shade or colour some of your drawings in different ways.

Try answering questions similar to those you answered about the fractal pattern at the beginning of this chapter.

You might also want to make up some fractal rules of your own.

2〉 Figure 3 shows the wheel which represents the way sevenths are written as decimals.

The wheel was explained in *Section B* of this chapter.

To represent $\frac{1}{13}, \frac{2}{13}, \frac{3}{13}, \frac{4}{13}, \frac{5}{13}, \ldots, \frac{12}{13}$ you need two wheels.

To represent $\frac{1}{17}, \frac{2}{17}, \frac{3}{17}, \ldots, \frac{16}{17}$ you need one wheel with 16 points marked on it.

To represent $\frac{1}{41}, \frac{2}{41}, \frac{3}{41}, \ldots, \frac{40}{41}$ you need several wheels.

Draw wheels for different families of decimals and write about the patterns you notice.

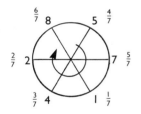

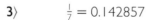

Figure 3

3〉 $\frac{1}{7} = 0.142857$

so there are 6 digits that keep repeating in the decimal for $\frac{1}{7}$. $\frac{1}{7}$ has *period* 6.

Find the periods of fractions such as $\frac{1}{3}, \frac{1}{7}, \frac{1}{11}, \frac{1}{13}, \frac{1}{17} \ldots$ which are 1 divided by a prime number.

Find the periods of fractions such as $\frac{1}{6}, \frac{1}{14}, \frac{1}{22}, \ldots$ which are 1 divided by double a prime number.

Find the periods of fractions such as $\frac{1}{11}, \frac{1}{111}, \frac{1}{1111}$ and so on.

Find the periods of fractions such as $\frac{1}{14}, \frac{2}{14}, \frac{3}{14}, \frac{4}{14}$ and so on.

Write about the patterns you find.

Choose other sets of fractions to look at.

o use the program, 'Recurring decimals' to help you with this task.

4) World resources are not infinite. Choose a world resource such as energy.

Consider some of the ways in which this resource is being used up, perhaps by people in this country.

Think of policies which will help to make savings, so that the resource is not used up so quickly.

Give estimates of the amount of savings your policies would produce.

Do not spend too long on these tasks. Even infinity has to come to an end.

▓▓ REVIEW EXERCISES B

EXERCISE 15   Measures

1 Which of the following estimates are good and which are bad? (Write 'good' or 'bad' for each.)

(*a*) A new-born baby weighs 100 g.

(*b*) A new-born baby is 50 cm long.

(*c*) A house is 8 m high.

(*d*) A bus is 20 m high.

(*e*) A full kettle contains 20 ml.

(*f*) An egg weighs 1 kg.

(*g*) The population of a large English city is 200 000.

(*h*) A piece of paper is 0.001 m thick.

(*h*) The temperature on a Summer day in England is about 65°C.

(*j*) A girl of 13 is 152 cm tall.

2 Estimate the height of the 'statue' shown in the photograph.

3 A bag of apples weighs approximately 2 kilograms. The average weight of an apple is 205 grams. Estimate the number of apples in this bag.

SEG A Summer 1988, Paper 1

4 Figure 1 shows a 5 litre can of oil. 1 litre is about 1¾ pints.

(*a*) Write 1¾ as a decimal.

(*b*) Find the number of pints of oil in the 5 litre can.

Figure 1

MEG SMP, May 1988, Paper 1

5 A piece of uniform piping weighs 1.8 kg. It is cut into two pieces, one of which is twice as long as the other. What does the longer piece weigh?

6 A recipe for blackcurrant ice cream to serve 4 people is

> 400 g blackcurrants
> 160 g sugar
> 140 ml cream
> 90 ml water

Write down the amounts that you would require to make a similar ice cream to serve 6 people.

MEG May 1988, Paper 1

7 If the ingredients opposite are mixed together, there will be enough dough to make eight pizzas.

> **PIZZA RECIPE**
> (*makes eight*)
> 16 ounces of flour
> 4 ounces of butter
> 3 eggs
> ¼ pint of milk
> 1 ounce of yeast

(*a*) How much flour is needed to make one pizza?

(*b*) How much butter would be needed for six pizzas?

(*c*) Ahmed makes twelve pizzas to store in his freezer. What is the total weight in pounds and ounces of all the ingredients, excluding milk and eggs? (16 ounces = 1 pound).

NEA Syllabuses A and B, May 1988, Paper 2

8   In 1990 Monday May 28th was a bank holiday.

(*a*) What day of the week was 6th June?

(*b*) On the third Saturday in June Frances started her holiday. What date was that?

9   The Post Office empties this post box at various times during the day.

Collection Times
1. 08.15
2. 12.30
3. 17.45

POST OFFICE

(*a*) Winston posts a letter at 10.45 in the morning. How many hours and minutes will it be before the letter is collected?

(*b*) Wayne posts his letter at 10.45 in the evening. How long will it be before this letter is collected?

NEA Syllabuses A and B, Paper 2

10 (*a*) At 6.45 p.m. Alan discovered that the next train he could catch to Sheffield left at 2035. How long did he have to wait?

(*b*) Jim and Doreen Smith hope to catch the ferry to the Continent which leaves at 1610. It is a quarter to nine in the morning and the journey to the ferry usually takes about eight hours. Do you think they will catch the ferry?

11 Naresh sets his video recorder to record 'The Saturday Feature' film. The time at which the film begins is 2140 and it ends at 2325.

(*a*) How long will the film last?

(*b*) Naresh uses a new 180 minute tape. How many minutes recording time will he have left on his tape?

MEG SMP, May 1988, Paper 2

12 John, Mary and Majid charge for baby-sitting. Their charges are given in the table.

For each hour (or part of an hour) before midnight	For each hour (or part of an hour) after midnight
£0.75	£1.05

Work out the amount earned when

(*a*) John sat for 3 hours before midnight.

(*b*) Mary sat from 9 o'clock at night until 1 o'clock the following morning.

(*c*) Majid sat from 1800 to 2120.

LEAG SMP, May 1988, Paper 1

13 The table shown below gives the times of high and low tides displayed on a particular Tuesday in Cromer.

HIGH TIDES	11 30	23 50
LOW TIDES	05 20	17 40

(*a*) How long is it between the two high tides?

(*b*) If the same pattern of time difference between the tides continued what notice would be displayed in Cromer on

(i) the Wednesday of the same week,
(ii) the Thursday of the same week?

14 Figure 2 is a simplified version of how the world is divided into international time zones.

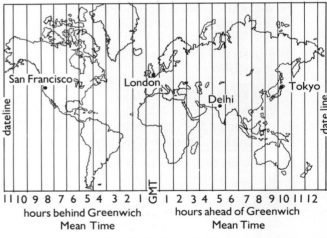

11 10 9 8 7 6 5 4 3 2 1 GMT 1 2 3 4 5 6 7 8 9 10 11 12
hours behind Greenwich Mean Time   hours ahead of Greenwich Mean Time

Figure 2   *NEA Syllabus C, May 1988, Paper 2*

(*a*) When it is 5 p.m. GMT in London, what time is it in San Francisco?

(*b*) The Tokyo Stock Exchange closes at 3.30 p.m. Japanese time. When the London Stock Exchange opens at 9.00 a.m. GMT, for how long has the Toyko Stock Exchange been closed?

(c) Mr. Surajah is to return to Delhi on a flight lasting 8½ hours, leaving London Heathrow at 0215 hours GMT. What time will it be in Delhi when he arrives?

15 A storage unit for records is ⅓ m wide. An average LP record is 4 mm thick. Approximately how many LP records can be stored in the unit?

16 A 5 litre can of emulsion paint can cover 70 square metres of wall.

A room is 6.7 m long, 5.8 m wide and 2.4 m high. It has two windows each of which is 3.4 m long and 1.1 m high, and two doors, each of which is 1.9 m high and 0.8 m wide.

How many cans of this paint would be needed to give two coats to the walls of this room?

17 An aircraft leaves London at 1400 and arrives in Toronto, Canada at 1730 local time.

The return flight, which has the same flight time, leaves Toronto at 1645 local time and arrives in London at 1015 the following morning.

What is the time difference between London and Toronto?

18 The instructions on a bottle of dried milk read as follows:

'To make one pint of fresh milk add 5 tablespoons of dried milk powder to one pint of cold water and stir thoroughly. Each bottle makes 5 pints of fresh milk.'

David uses the dried milk powder in the following ways:

Use	Amount
Fresh milk	5 tablespoons per pint
Tea	1 teaspoon per cup
Coffee	2 teaspoons per cup

On average David makes one pint of fresh milk per week and drinks two cups of tea and two cups of coffee a day. How long, on average, will a bottle of dried milk last David?
(1 tablespoon = 5 teaspoons.)

NEA Syllabus C, May 1988, Paper 3

EXERCISE 16 Percentages

1 When Sue did a part-time job she agreed to pay her parents 25% of her wages towards her keep.

In the first week Sue earned £12. How much did she pay her parents?

2 A newspaper reported a survey which found that 1 in 4 people said their favourite colour was red, 30% said it was yellow and 15% said it was blue.

(a) Was red more popular than yellow? Explain your answer.

(b) What percentage chose a colour other than red, yellow or blue?

3 A pair of trousers normally costs £25. There is a reduction of 20% in a sale. What is the sale price of the trousers?

4 A hockey team has 20 practice sessions between Christmas and Easter. Chris attends 17 of them.

What percentage of sessions did Chris miss?

5 The floor area of a living room is 45 square metres. 80% of the floor is covered by a carpet.

What is the area of the floor which is not covered by a carpet?

6 Brian Finch gets commission from a mail order firm on orders he gets from his neighbours which he can take either as cash or in goods. The commission is 8% in cash or 12½% as goods.

One month he gets orders worth £80. How much commission does he receive if he takes it

(a) in cash?

(b) as goods?

7 If income tax is 25% of income, how much tax would you pay when you earned £240?

205

8 (a) How much deposit is required for the Hire Purchase agreement?

Cash price £275
or   Hire Purchase 20% deposit of cash price followed by 24 equal monthly instalments of £13
or   £7.50 per month rental.

22 inch colour TV
Full guarantee on parts and labour for 4 years

(b) What is the total cost of buying the television on Hire Purchase?

(c) How much is required for 6 months rental?

(d) What is the total cost of renting the television for 4 complete years?

SEGA Summer 1988, Paper 1

9 The chart shows the number of staff employed by a County Council.

Staff Employed			
The Council is the largest employer in the County.			
Number of Staff Employed (Full-time equivalent)			
		Change since last year	
Type of Employee	**Last Year**	**Number**	**%**
Teachers and Lecturers	6678	+103	+ 2
Schools Support Staff	1386	+ 95	+ 7
School Meals Staff	861	− 21	− 2
Other Education Staff	1365	+330	+24
Social Services Staff	2708	+271	+ B
Police Officers	1152	0	0
Fireman	269	0	0
Roadmen	232	+ 7	+ 3
Library Staff	260	− 2	− 1
Other Service Staff	1713	+ 41	+ 2
Total	A	+824	

Find

(a) the total number of staff employed last year, indicated by the letter A.

(b) the percentage change since last year in Social Services Staff, indicated by the letter B. Give your answer to the nearest whole number.

MEG November 1987, Paper 4

10 The price list shows the cost of Wire 'O' Bound and Loose Leaf folders.

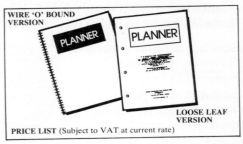

PRICE LIST (Subject to VAT at current rate)

Number of copies	Wire 'O' Bound price each £	Loose Leaf price each £	Post and packing £
Single	5.15	4.70	1.80
2–5	4.95	4.50	3.00
6–10	4.75	4.30	4.20
11–20	4.60	4.15	6.90
21–35	4.45	4.00	9.90
36–50	4.30	3.85	11.40
51–65	4.15	3.70	13.00
66–85	4.05	3.60	14.50
85 Plus	3.95	3.50	15.50

(a) Write down the price of one Loose Leaf folder.

(b) You buy 12 Loose Leaf folders. Write down the price of each folder.

(c) You buy 40 Wire 'O' Bound folders.

(i) Find the cost of the 40 folders.
(ii) Write down the cost of post and packing for the 40 folders.
(iii) To the total cost of the 40 folders, including post and packing, 15% VAT is added. Calculate the full cost of buying the 40 Wire 'O' Bound folders.

LEAG Specimen 1991, Paper 2

11 John Starling earns £850 each month. He pays 6% of this towards his pension. He pays £120 each month for National Insurance. After deducting the pension payment and National Insurance payment he pays income tax on what is left at the rate of 25%.

(a) What is his pension payment?

(b) How much does he take home?

(c) What percentage of his total pay does he take home?

12 The repayment table below shows you how much your monthly repayments would be on any bank loan from £200 to £5000, over a period of between 1 and 3 years.

Amount of loan £	200	500	1000	2000	5000
Repayment term 12 months at 11% p.a. flat					
Total payable £	222.00	555.00	1110.00	2220.00	5550.00
Monthly repayment £	18.50	46.25	92.50	185.00	462.50
Repayment term 24 months at 11% p.a. flat					
Total payable £	244.08	610.08	1219.92	2440.08	6100.08
Monthly repayment £	10.17	25.42	50.83	101.67	254.17
Repayment term 36 months at 11% p.a. flat					
Total payable £	266.04	664.92	1329.84	2660.04	6649.92
Monthly repayment £	7.39	18.47	36.94	73.89	184.72

(a) What would be the total payable on a bank loan of £1500 over 12 months?

(b) Mrs. Weller has made 5 monthly payments of £92.50 off a bank loan of £1000. How much has she yet to pay?

(c) Vijay wants to borrow £2000 for a motor bike and can only afford to pay off the bank loan at a maximum of £80 per month. What is the total payable on this loan?

(d) Instead of borrowing money from the bank, Vijay could afford a 10% deposit and 36 payments of £75 on Hire Purchase. How much more would it cost him?

NEA Syllabus C, May 1988, Paper 2

13 Pat bought a bike for £20, smartened it up and sold it for £27.50. What was her percentage profit?

14 Before her 7.5% pay rise Fiona earned £1220. How much did she earn after her pay rise?

15 A dealer bought a car for £2200. When she sold it she made a profit of 15%. What was the selling price?

16 A garage bill for servicing comes to £48.60, to which 15% VAT is added.

What was the total garage bill?

17 (a) At the start of 1990 Samantha Berry's mileometer read 36542. At the end of the year it read 49823. How many miles did she travel in 1990?

(b) In 1989 she travelled 11892 miles. What was the percentage increase in her mileage from 1989 to 1990? Give your answer to the nearest whole number.

18 A supermarket sells packets of breakfast cereal for 78 p. A Cash and Carry sells the same packets of breakfast cereal at 8 packets for £5.50. What is the percentage saving on the breakfast cereal at the Cash and Carry? Give your answer correct to the nearest whole number.

19 In 1986 there were about 20.7 million households in the UK. 86% of them had washing machines.

Approximately how many households in the UK did not have washing machines in 1986?

20 Pauline and Karl each won £2000 in a competition. They looked in a Building Society's window and saw two posters.

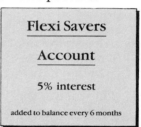

(a) Pauline buys two Super Saver Bonds. What is the total amount she can cash them in for after two years?

(b) Karl puts his £2000 into the Flexi Savers Account. How much will he have in the account after

(i) six months?
(ii) 1 year?
(iii) 2 years?

(c) State *one* advantage that the Flexi Savers Account has over buying Super Saver Bonds.

NEA Syllabus A, May 1988, Paper 3

21 In a certain area of Britain house prices in 1988 rose by 65% on average.

If a house was bought in that area at the beginning of 1988 for £47,500 how much could it have been expected to be worth at the end of 1988? Give your answer to a sensible degree of accuracy.

22 The following is an extract from a newspaper article at the end of May 1989.

> Just 0.9 mm of rain has fallen in London since the start of the month, compared to the average of 50.4 mm. The previous driest May this century was in 1919, when 3.5 mm was recorded. Rainfall in the Midlands was 58 per cent lower than normal.

According to this newspaper article, how much lower than normal was rain in London in May 1989? Give your answer as a percentage.

23 Margaret Jay sells her car for £3200. This means that Margaret made a loss of 60% on what she paid for it.

What did she pay for the car?

24 An item costing £2 includes VAT at 15%.

What is the cost of the item before adding VAT?

25 An employment agency charges its clients commission of 6% of what is earned or £48, whichever is the greater.

One month the amount James Sparrow earns means that both methods of working out commission give the same answer. How much does he earn?

26 According to the *Green Consumer Guide* 119 Mobil petrol stations in Britain were selling unleaded petrol in 1987. This was a higher proportion, 14.67%, than the petrol stations of any other petrol company.

How many Mobil stations were there in Britain?

27 The charge for rooms and meals on a hotel bill was £260. Before presenting the bill the hotel first added a 10% service charge and *then* 15% VAT. What was the total bill presented?

28 (a) Last year the insurance premium for Jill Smith's motor insurance was £360. However, a 40% discount was allowed.

How much did Jill pay?

(b) This year the premium has increased by 12% but Jill is now allowed a 60% discount.

How much does she pay this year?

(c) By what percentage has the payment decreased this year?

29 Given that $P = xy$

find the percentage increase in P when there is a 10% increase in both x and y.

MEG June 1986, Paper 3

30 The rule for converting a temperature in degrees Celsius (°C) to one in degrees Fahrenheit (°F) is as follows:

> Divide the temperature in degrees Celsius by 5, multiply by 9 and then add 32. This will give the temperature in degrees Fahrenheit.

(a) Convert a temperature of 52°C to degrees Fahrenheit.

(b) Convert a temperature of 70°F to degrees Celsius.

A rule for approximately converting °C to °F is as follows:

> Double the temperature in degrees Celsius and then add 30.

(c) Find the error, and express it as a percentage of the correct temperature, when using this rule to convert a temperature of

(i) 20°C   (ii) 50°C

(d) Find the temperature (in degrees Celsius) for which the approximation rule provides an exact conversion.

(e) Considering your answers to (c) and (d), comment on the accuracy of the approximation.

NEA Syllabus A, May 1988, Paper 4

EXERCISE 17   Reading for information

1 Study the information contained in the group of advertisements on the next page.

(a) How much is saved on the fare for a return flight to Sydney by booking with Trailfinders instead of the London Flight Centre?

(b) Which of these firms advertises the cheapest return flight to Hong Kong?

NEA Syllabus C, May 1988, Paper 1

OVERSEAS TRAVEL

IT'S ALL AT TRAILFINDERS

	Return
SYDNEY	£660
PERTH	£600
AUCKLAND	£748
BANGKOK	£338
SINGAPORE	£418
HONG KONG	£496
DELHI/BOMBAY	£385
COLUMBO	£418
NAIROBI	£369
JO'BURG	£426
LIMA	£495
LOS ANGELES	£296
NEW YORK	£198
WASHINGTON	£360
BOSTON	£298
HONOLULU	£457
GENEVA	£ 94

TRAILFINDERS

42-48 EARLS COURT ROAD
LONDON W8 6EJ
Europe/USA Flights 01-937 5400
Long Haul Flights 01-603 1515
and 01-937 9631
1st/Business Class 01-938 3444
Government Licensed/Bonded
ABTA   IATA   ATOL/1458

DISCOUNT FLIGHTS

	Return
Sydney	£764
Auckland	£775
Los Angeles	£340
Jo'burg	£485
Bangkok	£360
Rio	£504

LONDON FLIGHT CENTRE
01-370 6332

OVERSEAS TRAVEL

DISCOUNTED FARES

	Return		Return
Jo'burg/Har	£465	Douala	£420
Nairobi	£390	Sydney	£760
Cairo	£230	Auckland	£785
Lagos	£360	Hong Kong	£550
Del/Bombay	£350	Miami	£330
Bangkok	£350	And Many More	

AFRO ASIAN TRAVEL LTD
162/168 Regent St. W1
TEL.: 01-437 8255/6/7/8
Late & Group Bookings Welcome
AMEX/VISA   ACCESS/DINERS

LOWEST FARES

	Return		Return
Paris	£69	N YORK	£275
Frankfurt	£60	LA/SF	£355
Lagos	£320	Miami	£320
Nairobi	£325	Singapore	£420
Jo'burg	£460	Bangkok	£335
Cairo	£205	Katmandu	£440
Del/Bombay	£335	Rangoon	£350
Hong Kong	£510	Calcutta	£425

Huge Discountss Avail on 1st & Club Class

SUN & SAND
21 Swallow St. London W1
01-439 2100/437 0537

NEW LOW FARES WORLDWIDE

	Return		Return
AMMAN	£260	KARACHI	£270
BOMBAY	£325	LAGOS	£330
CAIRO	£210	MIAMI	£283
DELHI	£345	ROME	£105
FRANKFURT	£55	SEOUL	£605
HONG KONG	£495	SYD/MEL	£765
ISTANBUL	£180	TOKYO	£580

SKYLORD TRAVEL LTD
2 DENMAN STREET, LONDON W1
Tel: 01-439 3521/8007
AIRLINE BONDED

Sundays and Public Holidays (Bus 327)

Luton Bus Station ⇌	....	....	....	0650	50	
Lantern Fields Slip End Turn	....	....	....	0659	59	
Kingsbourne Green Harrow	....	....	....	0904	04	
Harpenden George ⇌	....	....	....	0910	10	Then
Sandridgebury Lane	....	....	....	0920	20	at
St. Albans Bus Garage (A)	....	....	....	0923	23	these
St. Albans St. Peters Street	....	....	....	0924	24	minutes	UNTIL
Chiswell Green Three Hammers	....	....	....	0933	33	past
Garston Watford Bus Garage	0720	0758 0641	0941	41	each
Watford Junction ⇌	....	0731 0609 0852	0952	52	hour
Watford Town Centre	....	0734 0612 0855	0955	55	
Croxley Green Station ⇌	....	.... 0819 0902	1002	02	
Croxley Green Manor Way	....	.... 0823 0906	1006	06	
Rickmansworth Station ○⇌	....	 0915	1015	15	

Luton Bus Station ⇌	....	1750	....	1850	....	....	....	....
Lantern Fields Slip End Turn	....	1759	....	1859	....	....	....	....
Kingsbourne Green Harrow	....	1804	....	1904	....	....	....	....
Harpenden George ⇌	....	1810	....	1910	....	....	....	....
Sandridgebury Lane	....	1820	....	1920	....	....	....	....
St. Albans Bus Garage (A)	....	1823	1917	1923	2023	2123	2217	2317
St. Albans St. Peters Street	....	1824	1918	1924	2024	2124	2218	2318
Chiswell Green Three Hammers	....	1833	1927	1933	2033	2133	2227	2327
Garston Watford Bus Garage	....	1841	1936	1941	2041	2141	2235	2335
Watford Junction ⇌	....	1852	....	1952	2052	2152	2246	....
Watford Town Centre	....	1855	....	1955	2055	2155	2249	....
Croxley Green Station ⇌	....	1902	....	2002	2102	2202	2256	....
Croxley Green Manor Way	....	1906	....	2006	2106	2206	2300	....
Rickmansworth Station ○⇌	....	1915	....	2015	2115	2215	....	....

2 The table above shows the times of the 327 bus on Sundays.

(a) What is the latest time you can catch a bus from Luton to Rickmansworth?

(b) How many minutes does the bus take to travel from St. Albans Bus Garage to Watford Junction?

(c) How many journeys are made by a 327 bus on Sundays from Luton to Rickmansworth?

SEG B Summer 1988, Paper 1

Europe

All-up rates

There is only one class of mail available for letters to Europe, i.e. 'All-up'. The rates charged are the same as those for surface letters outside Europe, but the items are sent by air whenever this will result in earlier postal delivery.

Air mail labels or envelopes with coloured borders should *not* be used.

EEC Concessionary Rate

Items not over 20 g sent to an EEC destination are charged at the inland class first weight step rate.   18p.

Letters and Postcards

Not over	£ p	Not over	£ p	Not over	£ p	Not over	£ p
20g	22	250g	1 06	500g	2 02	1750g	5 17
60g	37	300g	1 25	750g	2 77	2000g	5 72
100g	53	350g	1 44	1000g	3 52		
150g	70	400g	1 64	1250g	4 07		
200g	88	450g	1 83	1500g	4 62		

Classification of Europe

EEC destinations are marked with an asterisk

Albania	* Denmark	Iceland	* Poland
* Andorra	Faröe Is	* Ireland (Rep of)	Romania
Austria	Finland	* Italy	* San Marino
* Azores	* France	Liechtenstein	* Spain
* Balearic Is	German Dem Rep	* Luxembourg	Spitzbergen
* Belgium	* Germany	Madeira	Sweden
Bulgaria	(Fed Rep of)	Malta	Switzerland
* Canary Is	* Gibraltar	* Monaco	Turkey
Cape Verde Is	* Greece	* Netherlands	USSR
* Corsica	Greenland	Norway	* Vatican City
Cyprus	Hungary	Poland	State
Czechoslovakia			Yugoslavia

3 (a) Find the postage for a 15 g letter posted in England and addressed to:

(i) Belgium,
(ii) Hungary.

(b) Find the postage for a 420 g letter posted in England and addressed to Gibraltar.

NEA Syllabus C, May 1988, Paper 1

4 The table below gives a summary of the results for the Milford Hockey League half way through the season.

Team	Played	Won	Drawn	Lost
Arndale	6	5	0	1
Baildon	6	1	2	3
Chelmer	6	2	0	4
Dartford	6	2	2	2

(a) A team gets 2 points for a win, 1 point for a draw and 0 points for a loss.

(i) How many points has Arndale gained?
(ii) Which two teams have gained the same number of points?

When teams have the same number of points they are placed in order by goal difference (goals for, minus goals against). The greater the goal difference the higher the position of the team in the league.

(b) (i) Copy and complete the following table.

Team	Goals for	Goals against	Goal difference
Edmond	10	6	+4
Fritch	8	13	
Grantham	7	15	−8
Hinkley	12	9	

(ii) If all these teams had the same number of points, place them in order.

LEAG SMP May 1988, Paper 1

5

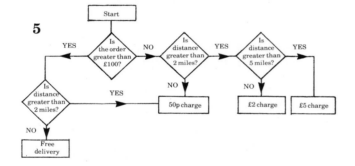

Abdul buys a ladder which costs £65 from a store 5 miles from his house. Use the flow chart to find the delivery charge.

SEG B, Summer 1988, Paper 1

6 The table gives monthly payments for loans of money from £1000 to £15000 over periods of time of 3, 5, 8 or 10 years.

Loan £	36 monthly payments	60 monthly payments	96 monthly payments	120 monthly payments
15000	527.23	364.64	277.79	251.12
12500	439.36	303.86	231.49	209.26
10000	351.48	243.10	185.20	167.42
9000	316.34	218.78	166.67	150.67
8000	281.19	194.47	148.15	133.93
7000	246.04	170.17	129.63	117.19
6000	210.89	145.86	111.12	100.45
5000	179.27	125.35	99.83	88.17
4500	161.34	112.81	89.85	79.36
4000	143.41	100.28	79.86	70.54
3500	125.49	87.74	69.88	61.72
3000	107.56	75.21	59.90	52.91
2500	89.63	62.67	49.92	44.09
2000	71.71	50.14	39.93	35.27
1500	53.78	37.61	29.95	26.46
1000	35.86	25.07	19.97	17.64

Use the table to answer the following questions:

(a) What is the monthly payment for a loan of £8000 over 5 years?

(b) What is the total amount of money paid for a loan of £4500 over 10 years?

NEA Syllabus A and B, May 1988, Paper 1

Bath Spa 134d	0053b	0353a	..	0607	..	....	0642	..	0707	..	..	0752	..	..	..	0822	..	0845	0857	...		
Chippenham .... d				0619	..	....	0654	....	0719	..	....	0804	..	....	0823	0834	....	0901	0909	...		
Swindon .... d		0432	0547	0635	..	0708	0710	0726	0735	..	0600	0821	0630	0637	0842a	0851	0905	0920a	..	..		
Didcot 116a		....	0609	0652	..	0717	0727	....	0752	....	....	....	....	0654	....	....	....	....	....	...		
Oxford 116a	..	..	0650	0714	..	..	0800	..	0818	..	..	..	..	0916	..	..	..	..	..	..		
Reading 116, 117a	0224	0515	0624	0706	..	0730	0740	0752	0806	....	0826	....	..	0908	....	..	....	..	0946	0955		
Gatwick Airport 124a		0723	0823	..	..	0953	..	..	..	..	1027	..	..	..	..	..	..	..	..	1124		
Heathrow Airport 405a		0640	0740	..	..	0840	....	0910	..	..	0940	....	..	1040	....	....	....	....	..	1110		
Slough 116, 117a		0631	0711	0746	..	0759	..	..	0838	..	..	..	..	0922s	..	..	..	..	..	..		
London Paddington .... ○116, 117a	0310	0605	0700	0735	..	0800	0810	0822	0835	....	0855	0910	0920	0940	..	0943	0956	..	1015	1024		

Reading 122d	0626	0650	..	0753	0855	..	0936	0955	..	1100	1107	..	1152	1155	..	1300	1310	..	1355	1500
Reading West 122d	0629	0653	...	0756	0858	....	0958	..	1110	..	1158	....	1313	....	1358	....				
Mortimer .... d	0638	0702	..	0805	0907	..	..	1007	..	..	1119	..	..	1207	..	1322	..	1407	..	
Bramley (Hants) .... d	0644	0704	..	0811	0913	..	..	1013	..	..	1125	..	..	1213	..	....	1328	..	1413	..
Basingstoke .... a	0652	0714	..	0819	0922	..	0955	1021	..	1123	1133	..	..	1222	..	1323	1336	..	1422	1524
Salisbury 145a	....	0826	..	0919	1034	..	....	1153	..	....	1234	....	....	1353	....	....	1434	....	1553	....
Winchester 158a	0715	0749	..	0849	0943	....	..	1049	..	1143	1207	..	..	1243	..	1349	1407	..	1443	1543
Southampton 158a	0746	0809	..	0909	1009f	..	1025	1109	..	1159	1233	..	..	1309f	..	1355	1433	..	1509	1559
Bournemouth 158a	0836	0851	..	0951	1051f	..	1057	1151f	..	1239	1313	..	..	1351f	..	1429	1513b	..	1551	1631
Poole 158a	....	0909	..	1031e	1108g	..	1108	1231e	..	1252	1331n	..	..	1431p	..	1442	1531n	..	1631	1644
Portsmouth & Southsea 156, 165a	....	0842b	..	0945b	1046	..	1135h	1144b	..	1242b	1339n	..	1318	1345	....	1442p	1535n	..	1544	1642
Portsmouth Harbour 156, 165a	....	0846b	..	0948b	1049	....	1142h	1148b	..	1246b	1344n	..	1322	1349	....	1446b	1540n	....	1548	1646

7 A man wishes to travel by train from Bath Spa to Basingstoke. He needs to travel first from Bath Spa to a second station. At this station he changes trains and takes another train to Basingstoke.

(*a*) Consult the two timetables on the previous page, and write down the name of the second station.

(*b*) What is the latest train he can catch from the second station if he is to arrive at Basingstoke before 0830?

(*c*) What is the latest train he can catch from Bath Spa if he is to make this connection?

SEG B Summer 1988, Paper 2

8

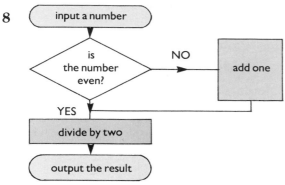

(*a*) What is the output when the input is 7?

(*b*) If the output is 3, what are the two possible inputs?

SEG B Summer 1988, Paper 2

9 The timetable for the evening trains between Birmingham New Street and London Euston is shown below.

Birmingham New Street	1818	1848	1953	2052	2153	2221
Birmingham International	1828	1858	2003	2103	2204	2237
Coventry	1840	1910	2015	2115	2216	2256
Watford Junction	1945	2008	2114	2213	2315	0037
London Euston	2006	2030	2136	2234	2340	0100

London Euston	1853	1910	1940	2030	2140	2315
Coventry	2003	2017	2052	2142	2247	0035
Birmingham International	2013	2028	2103	2154	2258	0048
Birmingham New Street	2029	2044	2119	2207	2315	0105

(*a*) Wendy wants to catch a train at Birmingham International and to get to Watford Junction by 9.30 p.m. What is the time of the latest train she should catch?

(*b*) Calculate the time, in hours and minutes, the 2221 train from Birmingham New Street takes to travel to London Euston.

(*c*) Walid catches the 1818 train from Birmingham New Street to go to London. He wants to be back at Birmingham New Street before midnight. What is the longest time he can spend in London?

(*d*) It is 18.5 km by rail from Birmingham International to Coventry. Calculate the average speed, in km/h correct to three significant figures, of the 2237 train between these two stations.

MEG, May 1988, Paper 5

10 The table shows the monthly payments to be made for a mortgage with a building society.

Amount of advance(£)	Monthly Payments(£)		
	25 year term	20 year term	15 year term
100	0.78	0.84	0.97
200	1.55	1.68	1.93
300	2.32	2.52	2.90
400	3.09	3.36	3.86
500	3.86	4.20	4.83
600	4.63	5.04	5.79
700	5.40	5.88	6.76
800	6.17	6.72	7.72
900	6.94	7.56	8.69
1000	7.71	8.40	9.65
2000	15.42	16.79	19.30
3000	23.13	25.18	28.95
4000	30.83	33.58	38.59
5000	38.54	41.97	48.24
6000	46.25	50.36	57.89
7000	53.95	58.76	67.53
8000	61.66	67.15	77.18
9000	69.37	75.54	86.83
10000	77.07	83.94	96.47
11000	84.78	92.33	106.12
12000	92.49	100.72	115.77
13000	100.19	109.12	125.41
14000	107.90	117.51	135.06
15000	115.61	125.90	144.71
16000	123.31	134.30	154.35
17000	131.02	142.69	164.00
18000	138.73	151.08	173.65
19000	146.43	159.48	183.29
20000	154.14	167.87	192.94
21000	161.85	176.26	202.59
22000	169.55	184.65	212.23
23000	177.26	193.05	221.88
24000	184.97	201.44	231.53
25000	192.67	209.83	241.18
26000	200.38	218.23	250.82
27000	208.09	226.62	260.47
28000	215.79	235.01	270.12
29000	223.50	243.41	279.76
30000	231.21	251.80	289.41

Alan Scott borrowed £8000 for a 20 year term.

(*a*) Write down the amount of his monthly payment.

Connie Brown's monthly payment is £158.

(*b*) Find the amount of her advance on a 25 year term.

The building society will normally lend up to three times a person's annual income. Harminder Singh earns £780 per month.

(*a*) Find the maximum amount of money he could borrow from the building society.

Harminder decides to buy a house costing £32 000.
The building society lends him 80% of the purchase price.

(*d*) Calculate the amount of money the building society lends to Harminder.

(*e*) Calculate his monthly payment on a 25 year term.

LEAG A June 1988, Paper 3

EXERCISE 18 Substituting in formulae

1 The number of units of electricity which are used up by an electrical appliance is given by the following formula.

> Number of units = time in hours × power in kilowatts

(*a*) How many units are used by a 3 kW fire if it is switched on at 7 p.m. and switched off at 9 p.m.?

(*b*) How many units would be used by a 100 watt bulb if it was left on day and night for a week? (100 watts is $\frac{1}{10}$ of a kilowatt.)

2 Some people use the following formula to estimate the length of the journey on the underground

> Time in minutes = 2 × (number of stations) + 5 × (number of interchanges) + 5

(*a*) Sam has to travel five stations on one line, then interchange and then travel six stations on another line.

Estimate the time of his journey.

(*b*) Maire is at Wimbledon and wants to catch a train to Birmingham in three quarters of an hour's time, after travelling to Euston station by underground.

She decides to travel eight stations on the District line to Earl's court, then travel five stations on the Bakerloo line to Green Park, and then travel three stations on the Victoria line to Euston.

Do you predict that she will catch her train?

3 A maintenance engineer makes a charge of £*C* for examining and repairing a washing machine. The charge depends on the time, *t* hours, the job takes.

The formula connecting *C* and *t* is

$$C = 9t + 15$$

Calculate the charge when the job takes

(*a*) 3 hours,   (*b*) 1½ hours.

MEG May 1989, Paper 4

4 The sum, *S*°, of the interior angles of a polygon with *n* sides is given by the following formula

$$S = 180n - 360$$

Find the sum of the interior angles of each of the following polygons.

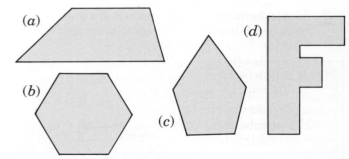

(*a*)

(*b*)

(*c*)

(*d*)

5 A temperature in degrees Fahrenheit (*F*) can be changed to a temperature in degrees Celsius (*C*) by using the formula

$$C = \frac{5(F - 32)}{9}$$

Use the formula to calculate the value of *C* when *F* = 77.

NEA Syllabuses A and B, May 1988, Paper 1

6 The number of seconds, t, a stone takes to fall down a well of depth d metres is given by the formula

$$t = 0.45\sqrt{d}$$

How long does it take a stone to fall down a well of depth 25 metres?

MEG May 1989, Paper 1

7 If a stone is thrown vertically upwards into the air with a speed of 30 m/s, its distance from the ground, s, in metres after t seconds is given by the following formula

$$s = 30t - 5t^2$$

(a) How high is the stone above the ground after 3 seconds?

(b) How high is the stone above the ground after 6 seconds?

8 Advertisements from private individuals can be placed in a local newspaper. The charge for n words is C pence, where C is given by the following formula.

$$C = 16n + 38$$

(a) What is the cost of the following advertisement?

> Congratulations Bob and Rita on your engagement. Love Nimal, Tracey, Shelley and Ian.

(b) What is the longest advertisement that can be placed, if you do not want to spend more than £5?

9 Charities frequently make money by selling sweatshirts carrying their own slogan or motif. The amount manufacturers charge charities depends on the number of sweatshirts bought.

One manufacturer charges £C for N sweatshirts, according to the following formula.

$$C = 4N + 30$$

(a) What does the manufacturer charge for 50 sweatshirts?

(b) The organisers of a particular charity promotion do not want the price per shirt to be greater than £4.25.

What is the smallest number of sweatshirts they can buy?

10 To hold a party at Bingham Manor, the charge is £8 for each person attending.

The manager of Bingham Manor estimates the cost of providing the party using the formula

estimated cost = £150 + (£2 per person)

(a) For a party of 60 people at Bingham Manor, what would be

(i) the charge for this party?
(ii) the estimated cost to the manager of Bingham Manor?
(iii) the profit made by Bingham Manor from the party?

(b) What is the least number of guests needed at a party so that Bingham Manor will make a profit?

NEA Syllabus A, May 1988, Paper 3

11 A rocket is fired vertically into the air. After t seconds its height, h metres, is given by

$$h = 50t - 5t^2$$

and its speed, v metres per second, is given by

$$v = 50 - 10t$$

(a) When $t = 6$, find the value of

(i) h,   (ii) v.

(b) Interpret, in words, your answers to (a) (i) and (ii).

MEG June 1987, Paper 2

12 Chris is ironing one evening and listening to the radio. The power used by each appliance is given by the following table.

Appliance	Power
Iron	1.2 kilowatts (kW)
Radio	40 watts
Light bulb	100 watts
Fire	2 kilowatts (kW)

The number of units of electricity used is given by the formula

Power in kW × time in hours = units used
(One kilowatt = 1000 watts.)

(a) Chris starts ironing at 8 p.m. with both the radio and light on. At 8.45 p.m. he feels cold and switches on a 2 kW electric fire. He finishes ironing at 9.30 p.m. and switches everything off.

How many units of electricity does Chris use between 8 p.m. and 9.30 p.m.?

(b) One unit of electricity costs 5.67 p. Find the cost of the electricity Chris has used, correct to the nearest penny.

NEA Syllabus C, May 1988, Paper 3

13 Heron's formula can be used to find the area of a triangle.

First find s using the formula

$$s = \tfrac{1}{2}(a + b + c)$$

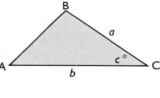

Then the area A is given by

$$A = \sqrt{s(s - a)(s - b)(s - c)}$$

(a) Find, correct to 2 significant figures, the area of a triangle with sides of length 3 cm, 5 cm and 6 cm.

(b) Find, correct to 2 significant figures the area of an equilateral triangle with a perimeter of 30 cm.

(c) (i) Find the area of a triangle with sides of length 16 m, 30 m and 34 m.
(ii) Use Pythagoras' theorem to show that this triangle is right-angled.
(iii) Use the result of (ii) to check your answer to (i).

14 The area of a triangle can be calculated if two sides and one angle of the triangle are known, provided that the angle is between the sides.

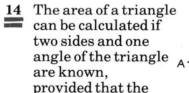

The area A is given by the formula

$$A = \tfrac{1}{2}\,ab\sin C$$

Figure 3

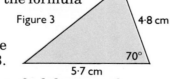

4·8 cm
70°
5·7 cm

(a) Find the area of the triangle in figure 3.

(b) (i) Use the formula to find the area of an equilateral triangle with perimeter 30 cm.
(ii) Check your answer by comparing it with the answer to question 13(b).

(c) Two sides of a parallelogram are of length 8 m. The other two sides are length 5 m. Find the angle between two adjacent sides if the area of the parallelogram is 24 m².

15 The period of a pendulum is the time it takes, starting at one end of its swing, to swing backwards and forwards to the same place as it started.

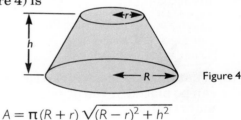

A simple pendulum is a weight swinging vertically on the end of a piece of string. If the string is L m long the period T secs of a simple pendulum is given by the following formula.

$$T = 2\pi \sqrt{\frac{L}{9.8}}$$

(a) Find the period of a pendulum if the length of the string is 0.85 m.

(b) A seconds pendulum is a pendulum whose period is 1 second. What is the length of string required for a seconds pendulum?

16 The formula for finding the area of the curved surface of a truncated cone (see figure 4) is

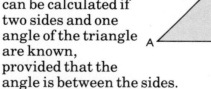

Figure 4

$$A = \pi(R + r)\sqrt{(R - r)^2 + h^2}$$

r is radius of top of truncated cone

h is height of truncated cone

R is radius of bottom of truncated cone.

(a) Find the total surface area of a waste paper bin if the diameter of the top of the bin is 300 mm, the diameter of the bottom of the bin is 230 mm and the height of the bin is 270 mm.

(b) (i) Find the area of the 'curved surface' when $R = 10$ cm, $r = 0$ and $h = 0$.
(ii) Describe the shape whose area you have just found.

(c) (i) Find the area of the curved surface when $R = 10$ m, $r = 10$ m and $h = 10$ m.
(ii) Describe the solid whose curved surface area you have just found.

EXERCISE 19 Conversions

1 Copy and complete the following statements.

(a) 3.48 kg =   g

(b) 706 mm=   cm

(c) 0.45 m =   mm

2 Jamie is going to cook bread and cakes for a party. He needs 5 kg of flour.

Flour is sold in bags of two sizes: 1.5 kg and 500 g. The larger bags are better value.

How many bags of each size should Jamie buy?

3 When Jason was born he was 20 inches long. On his second birthday his height was 2 feet 10 inches. How much more did he need to grow to be double his length at birth?

4 Mary loses 2 stone 5 lb whilst attending a Weight Watcher's course. Her weight is now 11 stone 12 lb. What was her original weight? (1 stone = 14 lb.)

NEA Syllabus C, May 1988, Paper 2

5

Heather wants to buy 3 metres of curtain material. The shop sells lengths measured in yards. She knows that 1 metre is approximately 1.1 yards.

(a) Using this approximation convert 3 metres into yards.

(b) The shop will only cut lengths to the nearest quarter of a yard.

What length should she ask for?

SEG B Summer 1988, Paper 2

6

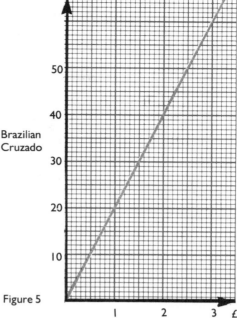

Figure 5

Figure 5 shows a graph to convert £ sterling to Brazilian Cruzados.

(a) Change £2.30 into Brazilian Cruzados.

(b) How many pounds and pence should you get for 37 Cruzados?

(c) Calculate the number of Cruzados you should get for £7.50.

SEG B Summer 1988, Paper 1

7 The graph in figure 6 can be used to convert French francs into English pounds.

Figure 6

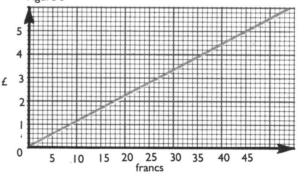

(a) How many French francs would you receive in exchange for £3?

(b) In France a magazine is priced at 15 francs. How much is this in English money?

(c) Use the graph to convert £400 into French francs.

NEA Syllabuses A and B, Paper 2

8 The table shows the rates of exchange between pounds and other currencies on a day in July 1989.

Answer the following questions with reference to these rates.

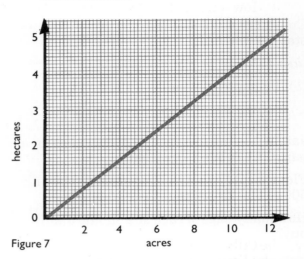

TOURIST RATES	
£1 buys	
Australian dollars	2.17
Austrian schillings	21.3
Belgian francs	64.0
Canadian dollars	1.94
Cyprus pounds	0.80
Danish kroner	11.90
Dutch guilders	3.44
Finnish marks	6.93
French francs	10.30
German marks	3.04
Greek drachmas	259
Hong Kong dollar	12.75
Irish punts	1.1425
Italian lire	2200
Japanese yen	229
Maltese pounds	0.5575
New Zealand dollars	2.77
Norwegian kroner	11.23
Portuguese escudos	256
Spanish pesetas	190
Swedish Kroner	10.54
Swiss francs	2.61
Turkish lire	3325
US dollars	1.645
Yugoslav dinars	25700

(*a*) Someone going on holiday to Germany changes £100 into marks for spending money. What does she receive in marks?

At the end of the holiday she changes 120 marks back into English currency. How much does she receive?

(*b*) Someone on holiday in New York (USA) bought a cheeseburger for $1.40. How much is this in pounds?

(*c*) Jan is on holiday in Italy and buys a bottle of wine for 3000 lira. Jan wonders whether it is cheaper than comparable wine in Britain, which she reckons would cost about £2.20.

According to Jan's reckoning, by what percentage is this wine cheaper in Italy?

9 When travelling abroad you might want to know whether what you are buying is good value. To do this you might do an approximate conversion into English currency without using a calculator.

Using the table in question 8, find the approximate equivalent in English money of the following prices, *without* using a calculator:

(*a*) 80 francs in France for a pair of sandals,

(*b*) 25 francs in Switzerland for scent,

(*c*) 10 pounds in Malta for a shirt,

(*d*) 150 000 dinars in Yugoslavia for a souvenir,

(*e*) 200 dollars in Hong Kong for a bathing costume,

(*f*) 600 yen in Japan for a camera.

10 Figure 7 shows a graph for converting acres into hectares.

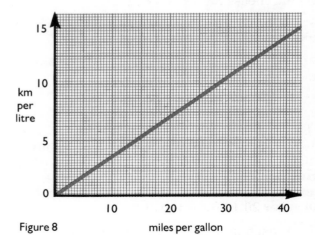

Figure 7   acres

(*a*) A market garden has an area of 6 acres. What is this area in hectares?

(*b*) A playing field has the shape of a rectangle 250 m by 128 m.

(i) What is the area of the field in square metres?
(ii) What is the area of the field in hectares?
(1 hectare = 10 000 m^2)
(iii) Use the graph to find the area of the field in acres.

MEG May 1989, Paper 1

Figure 8   miles per gallon

11 Figure 8 shows the relationship between 'petrol consumption in miles per gallon' and 'petrol consumption in kilometres per litre'.

(*a*) At a steady speed of 50 miles per hour, a British car travels 30 miles per gallon of petrol.

(i) Express the petrol consumption in kilometres per litre.
(ii) How much petrol, in gallons, will this car use if it is driven at 50 miles per hour for 1½ hours?

(b) A French car, driven at 100 kilometres per hour, has a petrol consumption of 10 kilometres per litre.

Express this petrol consumption in miles per gallon.

(c) Give a reason why it is not possible to say which of the two cars is more economical with petrol.

MEG May 1988, Paper 5

12 (a) The tallest block of flats in the world is Lake Point Towers in Chicago, USA. Its height is 645 ft.

What is its height in metres?
(1 metre is approximately 3.28 feet.)

(b) The average distance between the Earth and the Sun is approximately 93 000 000 miles.

What is this distance in kilometres?
(5 miles is approximately the same as 8 kilometres.)

13 Nick wanted to use 12 oz of a special sort of cream cheese for some cooking.

When he went to the shop he found that this cheese was sold only in 100 g packets.

How many packets did he need to buy for his cooking?
(1 ounce is approximately 28 grams)

14 Jane is going on holiday to France and needs to buy some films for her camera. If she buys them in England before she goes, they will cost her £2.25 each. If she waits until she gets to France and buys them there they will cost her 20.16 francs each.

If the exchange rate is £1 to 9.60 francs, find out how much, in English currency, she can save on each film by buying them in France.

MEG May 1988, Paper 3

15 On a certain day, £1 could be exchanged for 1.44 U.S. dollars ($).

(a) Using a scale of 2 cm to represent £2 on the x-axis and 2 cm to represent £2 on the y-axis, draw a straight line graph for converting pounds (£) into dollars ($). [Mark the x-axis from 0 to 12 and the y-axis from 0 to 18]

(b) Using your graph, or otherwise, find
(i) how many dollars could be obtained for £7,
(ii) how much English money has to be paid to obtain $8.

(c) The table below shows the prices of some American books and the amount being charged for them in an English bookshop.

Book	A	B	C	D
Price ($)	4.60	9.00	11.00	15.00
Charge (£)	3.00	5.20	8.50	12.00

(i) Plot points on your graph to represent this information and label them A, B, C, D, respectively.
(ii) Which one of these books represents the best exchange rate for the customer?

MEG June 1987, Paper 5

16 John is cycling at 10 metres per second.

Calculate his speed in kilometres per hour.

17 Sanjeev is considering buying a new car. Of two similar models, one is claimed to do 45 miles per gallon, whilst the manufacturers of the other model claim that it uses 6 litres per 100 km.

Compare the petrol consumption of the two cars and state which car has the better claimed petrol consumption.
(One mile = 1.609 km, One gallon = 4.54 litres.)

NEA Syllabus C, Paper 3

18 (a) Assuming that the exchange rate is 10.3 French francs to the £, which is better value, 1 lb of tomatoes bought in England for 90 p, or 1 kg of tomatoes bought in France for 19 francs?

(b) The French tomatoes are of better quality than the English tomatoes. How does this affect your answer to (a)?
(1 kg is approximately 2.2 lb)

19 The label on a jar of treacle indicates that 1 lb (1 pound) is the same as 454 g (454 grams). Given that there are 2240 lb in 1 ton and 1000 kg in 1 tonne calculate the ratio of 1 tonne to 1 ton in the form 1:k. Give k correct to 3 places of decimals.)

MEG SMP June 1988, Paper 4

EXERCISE 20   Speed and travel graphs

1 A car travels 100 miles in 2 hours. How far would it travel in 3 hours if it kept the same average speed?

2 Jean can walk to the station in 20 minutes. If she can run twice as fast as she can walk how long does it take her to run to the station?

3 Figure 9 shows the shortest distances between some towns in Britain in miles and in kilometres.

(a) How far is it in miles between London and Bristol?

(b) How far is it in kilometres between Edinburgh and Glasgow?

(c) A family living in Birmingham wants to go to the seaside for the weekend. Which is nearer: Bournemouth or Great Yarmouth?

(d) The family travels to and from the nearer seaside resort at an average speed of 40 miles per hour. How long does the travelling take them (there and back)?

(e) Their car does an average of 45 miles to the gallon. How much petrol do they use to get there and back?

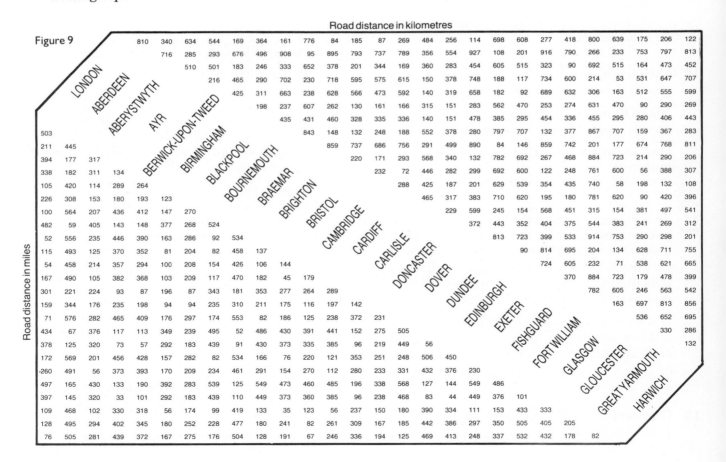

Figure 9. Road distance in kilometres (upper right), Road distance in miles (lower left).

Diagonal town labels: LONDON, ABERDEEN, ABERYSTWYTH, AYR, BERWICK-UPON-TWEED, BIRMINGHAM, BLACKPOOL, BOURNEMOUTH, BRAEMAR, BRIGHTON, BRISTOL, CAMBRIDGE, CARDIFF, CARLISLE, DONCASTER, DOVER, DUNDEE, EDINBURGH, EXETER, FISHGUARD, FORT WILLIAM, GLASGOW, GLOUCESTER, GREAT YARMOUTH, HARWICH.

Road distance in kilometres (upper-right triangle, by row):

810 340 634 544 169 364 161 776 84 185 87 269 484 256 114 698 608 277 418 800 639 175 206 122
716 285 293 676 496 908 95 895 793 737 789 356 554 927 108 201 916 790 266 233 753 797 813
510 501 183 246 333 652 378 201 344 169 360 283 454 605 515 323 90 692 515 164 473 452
216 465 290 702 230 718 595 575 615 150 378 748 188 117 734 600 214 53 531 647 707
425 311 663 238 628 566 473 592 140 319 658 182 92 689 632 306 163 512 555 599
198 237 607 262 130 161 166 315 151 283 562 470 253 274 631 470 90 290 269
435 431 460 328 335 336 140 151 478 385 295 454 336 455 295 280 406 443
843 148 132 248 188 552 378 280 797 707 132 377 867 707 159 367 283
859 737 686 756 291 499 890 84 146 859 742 201 177 674 768 811
220 171 293 568 340 132 782 692 267 468 884 723 214 290 206
232 72 446 282 299 692 600 122 248 761 600 56 388 307
288 425 187 201 629 539 354 435 740 58 198 132 108
465 317 383 710 620 195 180 781 620 90 420 396
229 599 245 154 568 451 315 154 381 497 541
372 443 352 404 375 544 383 241 269 312
813 723 399 533 914 753 290 298 201
90 814 695 204 134 628 711 755
724 605 232 71 538 621 665
370 884 723 179 478 399
782 605 246 563 542
163 697 813 856
536 652 695
330 286
132

Road distance in miles (lower-left triangle, by row):

503
211 445
394 177 317
338 182 311 134
105 420 114 289 264
226 308 153 180 193 123
100 564 207 436 412 147 270
482 59 405 143 148 377 268 524
52 556 235 446 390 163 286 92 534
115 493 125 370 352 81 204 82 458 137
54 458 214 357 294 100 208 154 426 106 144
167 490 105 382 368 103 209 117 470 182 45 179
301 221 224 93 87 196 87 343 181 353 277 264 289
159 344 176 235 198 94 94 235 310 211 175 116 197 142
71 576 282 465 409 176 297 174 553 82 186 125 238 372 231
434 67 376 117 113 349 239 495 52 486 430 391 441 152 275 505
378 125 320 73 57 292 183 439 91 430 373 335 385 96 219 449 56
172 569 201 456 428 157 282 82 534 166 76 220 121 353 251 248 506 450
260 491 56 373 393 170 209 234 461 291 154 270 112 280 233 331 432 376 230
497 165 430 133 190 392 283 539 125 549 473 460 485 196 338 568 127 144 549 486
397 145 320 33 101 292 183 439 110 449 373 360 385 96 238 468 83 44 449 376 101
109 468 102 330 318 56 174 99 419 133 35 123 56 237 150 180 390 334 111 153 433 333
128 495 294 402 345 180 252 228 477 180 241 82 261 309 167 185 442 386 297 350 505 405 205
76 505 281 439 372 167 275 176 504 128 191 67 246 336 194 125 469 413 248 337 532 432 178 82

4 A representative, who travels, has to keep a careful record of the time spent travelling and the distance travelled. The entry for 3 May is shown below.

Time	Mileometer reading	Comment
0730	36186	Leave home in Bristol
1030	36326	Call 1 at Brighton
1100	36326	Leave Brighton
1215	36396	Call 2 Bournemouth
1300	36396	Leave Bournemouth
1500	36501	Call 3 London
1600	36501	Leave London
1900	36621	Arrive home at Bristol

(a) For the journey from Bristol to Brighton

(i) how many miles did the representative travel?
(ii) how long did the journey take?
(iii) work out, to the nearest whole number, the representative's average speed.

(b) What was the total distance travelled by the representative on this day?

(c) For how long was the representative away from home on this day?

LEAG SMP May 1988, Paper 1

5 A girl cycles 6 kilometres in 20 minutes. What is her average speed in kilometres per hour?

6 A boy lives 2.4 miles from his school.

(a) Calculate the time, in minutes, that he takes to walk from his home to school, if he walks at an average speed of 3 m.p.h.

(b) If he arrives at the school at 8.35 a.m., at what time did he leave home?

MEG May 1988, Paper 1

British Airways
Winter Schedules – Effective 26 October 1986

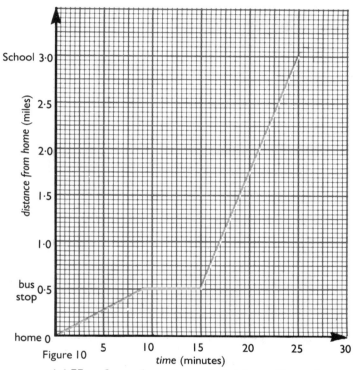

From LONDON HEATHROW to:—

	Dep.	Arr.	Days	Flight No.	Class
ABERDEEN	0720	0840	12345	BA 5604	M
	0915	1040	Daily	BA 5608	M
	1130	1255	12345	BA 5610	M
	1305	1430	Daily	BA 5612	M
	1525	1650	Daily	BA 5614	M
	1746	1905	12345 7	BA 5618	M
	2000	2120	Daily	BA 5620	M
ABU DHABI	1240	2325	4 7	BA 033	FJM
	1415	0100	3	BA 011	FJM
	1745	0430	5	BA 011	FJM
ADELAIDE	2030	0925	6	BA 011	FJM
	2130	0610	1	BA 011	FJM
	2130	1030	3	BA 009	FJM
AMMAN	1345	0035	4	BA 237	FJM
	1400	2105	7	BA 239	FJM
	2230	0720	5	BA 235	CM
AMSTERDAM	0800	1000	123456	BA 406	CML
	1000	1200	12345 7	BA 408	CML
	1200	1400	123456	BA 410	CML
	1500	1700	Daily	BA 414	CML
	1630	1830	12345 7	BA 416	CML
	1900	2100	12345 7	BA 418	CML
ANCHORAGE	1210	1210	Daily	BA 005	FJM

To LONDON HEATHROW from:—

	Dep.	Arr.	Days	Flight No.	Class
ABERDEEN	0700	0830	12345	BA 5601	M
	0800	0925	67	BA 5603	M
	0935	1100	12345	BA 5605	M
	1126	1250	Daily	BA 5609	M
	1400	1525	12345	BA 5611	M
	1515	1640	Daily	BA 5613	M
	1740	1905	Daily	BA 5615	M
	2000	2125	12345 7	BA 5619	M
ABU DHABI	0025	0540	1	BA 034	FJM
	0035	0540	3	BA 144	FJM
	0200	0540	2 6	BA 032	FJM
	0215	0555	5 7	BA 012	FJM
	1125	1630	4	BA 222	FJM
ADELAIDE	1300	0555	1	BA 010	FJM
	1300	0640	5	BA 010	FJM
	1645	0555	3	BA 012	FJM
AMMAN	0215	0555	5	BA 236	FJM
	0910	1440	6	BA 234	FJM
	2225	0555	7	BA 238	FJM
AMSTERDAM	0900	0900	123456	BA 401	CM
	1100	1100	Daily	BA 407	CM
	1300	1300	12345 7	BA 409	CM
	1500	1500	123456	BA 411	CM
	1800	1800	Daily	BA 415	CM
	1930	1930	12345 7	BA 417	CM

7 (a) (i) Find how long the 0700 flight from Aberdeen to London takes.
(ii) The distance from Aberdeen to London by air is 492 miles. What is the average speed in miles per hour of the 0700 flight from Aberdeen to London?

(b) The 1500 flight from London to Amsterdam arrives at 1700 whereas the 1500 flight from Amsterdam to London arrives at 1500. Explain this. How long does an actual flight take between London and Amsterdam?

NEA Syllabus C, May 1988, Paper 1

8 Figure 10 shows Anne's journey from home to school. She walks from home to a bus stop, waits, then catches the bus to school.

(a) How long does Anne take to walk to the bus stop?

(b) How long does she wait at the bus stop?

(c) How far from home is she after 20 minutes?

(d) How many miles is it from the bus stop to school?

(e) What is the average speed of the bus in miles per hour from Anne's bus stop to school?

SEG A Summer 1988, Paper 1

9

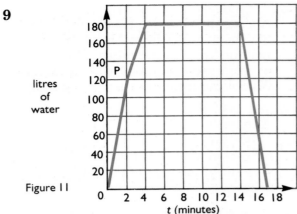

Figure 11

Figure 11 shows the number of litres of water, *l*, in the bath *t* minutes after the taps have been turned on.

(*a*) How much water is in the bath after 2 minutes?

(*b*) Suggest a reason for the change in the graph at the point P.

(*c*) How many minutes does it take to empty the bath?

MEG November 1986, Paper 1A

10 A car leaves Carlisle and travels to Birmingham at a speed of 70 m.p.h. At the same time a car leaves Birmingham and travels to Carlisle on the same route at a speed of 50 m.p.h. Copy figure 12.

On your diagram, draw the travel graph for the first car.

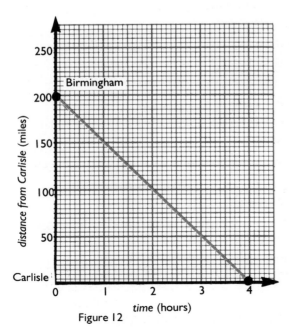

Figure 12

Clearly mark on your graph the point at which the two cars pass each other.

(*a*) At what distance from Carlisle does the diagram suggest that they will pass?

(*b*) How long have the cars been travelling when they pass each other? Give your answers in hours and minutes.

NEA Syllabus C, May 1988, Paper 2

11 John leaves his house at 1000. He cycles to his friend's house 20 km away, arriving at 1100. He stays at his friend's house for 1½ hours. He then cycles home, the return journey taking 2 hours.

(*a*) At what time does John leave his friend's house to return home?

(*b*) At what time does he arrive back at his own house?

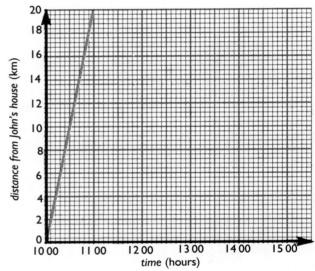

Figure 13

(*c*) Copy figure 13 and complete the graph of John's journey.

(*d*) Work out John's average speed on his return journey.

LEAG May 1988, Paper 2

12 The total playing time of a video tape is 4 hours. The length of the tape is 336 metres.

(*a*) What is the speed of the tape past the playing head in metres per minute?

(*b*) What is this speed, in centimetres per second, correct to two decimal places?

MEG June 1987, Paper 4

13 (a) Dave's journey starts from home on A roads. He travels a distance of 28 km at an average speed of 56 km per hour. How long does this part of the journey take?

(b) He then drives along the motorway to a service area, a distance of 140 km, at an average speed of 112 km per hour. How long does this part of the journey take?

(c) Dave leaves home at quarter past six. At what time does he arrive at the service area?

14 A train travels 186 km in 1½ hours. Find its average speed in km per hour.

15 A girl ran 400 metres in a minute. What average speed is this in

(a) metres per second?

(b) metres per hour?

(c) kilometres per hour?

16 Figure 14 illustrates how Matthew runs home for his P.E. kit. He then realises he has forgotten his key and so runs to his Grandmother's house for the spare key. He then runs home again, finds his P.E. kit and walks back to school.

(a) How far away from school is Matthew's Grandmother's house?

(b) How long did Matthew take finding his P.E. kit, once he got home?

(c) At what speed (in kilometres per hour) did he walk back to school?

NEA Syllabus A, May 1988, Paper 3

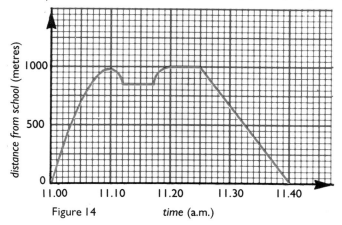

Figure 14　　time (a.m.)

17 During the week it takes Kuldip 45 minutes to drive to work at an average speed of about 30 m.p.h.

When Kuldip goes to work on Sundays he can drive at an average speed of about 40 m.p.h.

How long (to the nearest five minutes) does it take Kuldip to drive to work on Sundays?

18 The Patel family went by car from Birmingham to London to visit relatives. They travelled at an average speed of 90 km/h. On the return journey it was misty so they had to reduce their average speed in the ratio 2:3.

(a) What was their average speed on the return journey?

(b) The took 2 hours 12 minutes to travel to London. How long, in hours and minutes, did the journey take back?

MEG SMP Mode 2, June 1988, Paper 3

19 Jane decided to cycle 8 km to watch an air display. She set out at 2 p.m. and cycled at a steady speed of 18 km/h for 20 minutes.

She then stopped to chat with Peter for 10 minutes, after which time she persuaded him to accompany her to the air show. They walked to the show together at a speed of 6 km/h.

(a) Using a scale of 2 cm to represent 10 minutes on a horizontal axis and 2 cm to represent 2 km on a vertical axis, draw a distance–time graph for Jane's journey.

(b) At what time did Peter and Jane arrive at the air show?

(c) What was Jane's average speed on her way to the air show (including the stop)?

20 Because of bad weather, my journey from Norwich to Nottingham took 5½ hours instead of the usual 3½ hours.

(a) Calculate the percentage increase in my travel time, correct to one decimal place.

(b) Calculate the approximate percentage decrease in my average speed.

LEAG SMP, June 1988, Paper 4

21 Two girls decided to walk up a mountain. Figure 15 on the next page shows their journey from the start of their walk to when they reached the top of the mountain. They stopped for lunch on their way up.

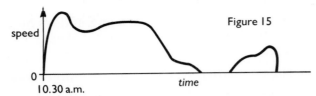

Figure 15

(a) The girls walked for about 2 hours before they stopped for lunch. Estimate

(i) the time they took to climb the mountain (including the lunch stop),
(ii) the length of the lunch stop.

(b) About how long after the start of the walk were the girls walking fastest?

22 Mr. Gould regularly takes his dog out for exercise, keeping it on a lead at all times. The distance–time graph in figure 16 shows the first ten minutes of a recent outing.

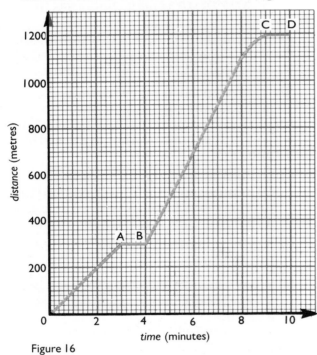

Figure 16

(a) Describe this outing as fully as you can.

(b) Sketch a speed–time graph for the first ten minutes of this outing.

MEG November 1987, Paper 6

23 A train runs between two stations, Marble Arch and Bond Street.

The journey takes 2 minutes. Figure 17 is the speed–time graph for the train during the journey.

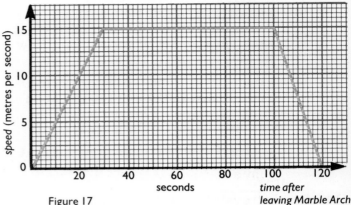

Figure 17

Use the graph to find

(a) the greatest speed of the train,

(b) the acceleration during the first 30 seconds,

(c) the length of time for which the train is slowing down.

(d) the distance the train moved at its greatest speed,

(e) the distance between the two stations.

LEAG SMP, June 1988, Paper 3

24 Figure 18 shows Debbie Brown's performance in a track race.

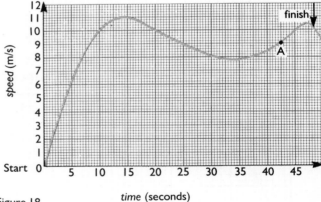

Figure 18

(a) What was her fastest speed during the race?

(b) How long did it take her to reach this speed?

(c) What was Debbie's average acceleration during this period of the race?

(d) Use your ruler to help estimate Debbie's approximate acceleration at the point A.

(e) What were Debbie's speeds at the moments when her acceleration was zero?

(f) By estimating the area under the graph find the length of the race.

25 The speed, v metres per second, of a car t seconds after the brakes are applied is given by the formula

$$v = 32 - t^2$$

(a) (i) Copy and complete the table below.

t	0	1	2	3	4	5
v	32			23		

(ii) Calculate, correct to 1 decimal place, the value of t when $v = 0$.
(iii) Using graph paper, draw a graph to show how the speed of the car varies with time. On the horizontal axis use a scale of 2 cm to represent 1 second and mark values of t from 0 to 6. Use a scale of 2 cm to represent 5 m/s on the vertical axis.

(b) Using your graph, find
(i) v when $t = 4.5$,
(ii) for how long the brakes have been applied when the speed is 21 m/s,

(b) By estimating the area between your graph and the t-axis, find the distance, in metres, travelled by the car before it stops.

MEG November 1987, Paper 6

26 A pebble is thrown upwards from the edge of a seaside cliff and eventually falls into the sea. The height of the pebble above the sea after t seconds is h metres. The table shows the values of h for given values of t.

t	0	1	2	3	4	5	6
h	24	30	32	30	24	14	0

(a) Using a scale of 2 cm for 5 m on the h-axis and 2 cm for 1 second on the t-axis, draw a graph of h against t for $0 \leqslant t \leqslant 6$.

(b) Find
(i) the height of the cliff,
(ii) how high the pebble rises above the level of the cliff top,
(iii) after how many seconds the pebble lands in the sea,

(iv) by drawing a suitable line, an estimate for the speed of the pebble after 5 seconds.

LEAG B, June 1988, Paper 4

27 The following table is based on the performance figures for a car as it accelerates from rest.

Time (t) seconds	0	2	4	6	8	10
Velocity (v) metres per second	0	10	18	23.5	27.5	31

(a) Draw the graph of v against t.

(b) By drawing the tangent to the curve at (4, 18), estimate the gradient of the curve at this point.

State the significance of this value.

(c) Estimate the area of the region bounded by the curve, the t-axis and the line $t = 10$ by approximating this area to a triangle and four trapezia.

State the significance of this value.

NEA Syllabus C, May 1988, Paper 4

28 Using a graph of 2 cm to represent 1 unit on each axis, plot the points whose coordinates are given in the table.
(Do *not* at this stage join the plotted points.)

x	0	0.5	1	1.5	2	2.5	3	4
y	0	1.9	2.7	3.0	3.5	3.7	3.9	4.0

The points are supposed to lie on a smooth curve, but for one point, A, the value of y has been calculated incorrectly.

(a) Mark the point A on your graph.

(b) Draw a smooth curve through the other points and use your curve to estimate the correct value of y which should have been given for A.

(c) By drawing a suitable straight line, estimate the gradient of the curve at the point where $x = 0.5$.

(d) Using three trapezia of equal widths, obtain an estimate for the area of the region bounded by the curve, the x-axis and the lines $x = 1$ and $x = 4$.

LEAG June 1986, Paper 4

EXERCISE 21 Pythagoras' theorem and trigonometry

1 A rectangular field is 100 m long and 105 m wide.

How far is it from one corner to the opposite corner?

2 A pupil constructed a rectangular frame measuring 48 cm by 14 cm using four pieces of metal similar to the piece shown in fig. 19(a). He cut two pieces of length 48 cm and two pieces of length 14 cm, joining them together as in fig 19(b).

Figure 19

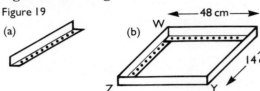

Before fixing them tightly, he checked that the frame was rectangular by measuring the diagonal *WY*. Use Pythagoras' theorem to calculate the correct length of *WY*.

SEG A Summer 1988, Paper 3

3 The Royal Mail 'Data Post' International parcel service accepts parcels up to the maximum sizes indicated in figure 20.

$a + b + c = 900$ mm maximum.
None of a, b, c to exceed 600 mm.

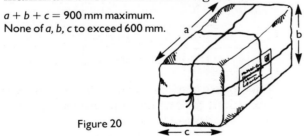

Figure 20

(*a*) Would the following parcels be accepted? (Answer 'yes' or 'no' and give a reason when your answer is 'no'.)

(i) A parcel with $a = 600$ mm, $b = 170$ mm and $c = 150$ mm.
(ii) A parcel with $a = 500$ mm, $b = 350$ mm and $c = 150$ mm.
(iii) A parcel with $a = 650$ mm, $b = 100$ mm and $c = 150$ mm.

(*b*) A picture in a rectangular frame 610 mm by 180 mm is placed diagonally in a rectangular box as shown in figure 21. The base of the box has dimensions 600 mm by 180 mm.

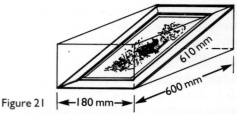

Figure 21

(i) Use Pythagoras' theorem to calculate the depth of the box.
(ii) Would this box be accepted for the 'Data Post' International parcel service? Give a reason for your answer.

MEG November 1986, Paper III

4 Four sticks are joined together to make a rectangle which is to be part of a model. Another stick is added as the diagonal to make the rectangle rigid. The stick for the diagonal is 25 cm long.

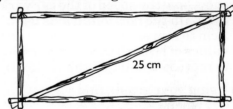

25 cm

(*a*) If the sticks for the shorter side of the rectangle are 7 cm long how long are the sticks for the longer side?

(*b*) In another part of the model a rectangle of a different shape needs to be made. By chance the strengthening diagonal is again 25 cm long.

All the sticks of this second rectangle are a whole number of centimetres long. What are their lengths?

5 The trapezium shown in figure 22 is isosceles (the opposite sides which are not parallel are the same length).

The lengths of the parallel sides are 5 cm and 17 cm. The perimeter of the trapezium is 42 cm.

(*a*) Find the distance between the parallel sides of the trapezium.

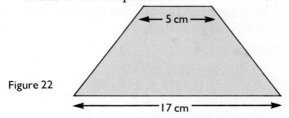

Figure 22

(*b*) Find the area of the trapezium.

(c) Is the area of the trapezium greater or less than the area of the rectangle of the same perimeter if the length of the rectangle is equal to

(i) the length of the shorter of the parallel sides of the trapezium?
(ii) the length of the longer of the parallel sides of the trapezium?
(iii) the average of the lengths of the parallel sides of the trapezium?

6 The graph of the line whose equation is $8x + 15y = 120$ cuts the x-axis at P and the y-axis at Q.

(a) Find the coordinates of P and Q.

(b) Find the length of the line between P and Q.

7 The footpath marked on Kirsty's map cuts diagonally across a field as shown in figure 23.

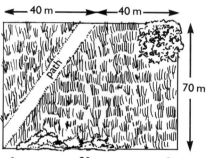

Figure 23

(a) Because the field is planted with crops and no path is visible Kirsty and Jasbir decide to walk round the edge of the field instead of across it. How much extra distance do they have to walk?

(b) Kirsty and Jasbir are in the middle of what they planned as an 8 km walk. If they have repeatedly to make additions to their journey of this magnitude estimate the length of the walk they actually do.

8 The lengths of the diagonals of the rhombus are 16 cm and 30 cm.

(a) Find the area of the rhombus.

(b) Find the perimeter of the rhombus.

(c) A rectangle has the same area and perimeter as the rhombus. Find the lengths of its sides.

(d) Is the total length of the diagonals of the rhombus more or less than the total length of the diagonals of the rectangle?

Section E of chapter 10 explained how to find the angle of tilt of a square.

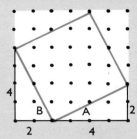

To find the angle A you divide 2 by 4 and then press

inv   tan   or   tan^{-1} .

To find the angle B you divide 4 by 2 before pressing

inv   tan   or   tan^{-1} .

You always divide the side *opposite* the angle by the side *next to* the angle.

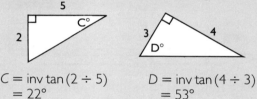

$C = \text{inv tan}\,(2 \div 5)$ $D = \text{inv tan}\,(4 \div 3)$
$\quad = 22°$ $\quad = 53°$

If you know the length of one of the sides next to the right-angle and want to know
the length of the other side, you use the method explained on page 000.

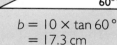

$a = 6 \times \tan 28°$ $b = 10 \times \tan 60°$
$\quad = 3.2$ cm $\quad = 17.3$ cm

When you use this method the side you are trying to find must always be *opposite* the angle. So to find c you do *not* use the angle 42°.
You calculate the *other* angle which is 48°.

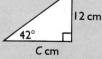

$c = 12 \times \tan 48°$
$\quad = 13.3$ cm

You can remind yourself about how to use sines and cosines by referring to Exercise 14 on page 136.

9 Which of the following gives the value of x?

(a) $12 \sin 25°$

(b) $12 \cos 25°$

(c) $12 \tan 25°$

(d) $12 \sin 65°$

(e) $12 \cos 65°$

(f) $12 \tan 65°$

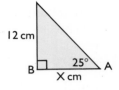

10 To find the height of a tower someone stands 80 m from the foot of the tower and measures the angle of elevation, correct to the nearest degree. This is 27°.

Find the height of the tower to a sensible degree of accuracy.

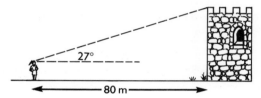

11 The length of the shorter sides of a rectangle is 8 cm and the length of the longer sides is 10 cm.

(a) Find the length of a diagonal of the rectangle, correct to the nearest mm.

(b) Find the larger of the angles between the two diagonals of the rectangle.

12 The triangle ABC in figure 24 is isosceles.
Find

Figure 24

(a) the length of BD,

(b) the length of AD,

(c) the area of the triangle.

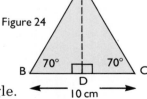

13 A window cleaner uses a ladder 8.5 m long. The ladder leans against the vertical wall of a house with the foot of the ladder 2.0 m from the wall on horizontal ground.

(a) Calculate the size of the angle which the ladder makes with the ground.

(b) Calculate the height of the top of the ladder above the ground.

Figure 25

(c) The window cleaner climbs 6.0 m up the ladder (see figure 25). How far is his lower foot from the wall?

MEG May 1988, Paper 5

To calculate b when you know the length a you multiply a by $\sin 40°$

$$b = a \times \sin 40°$$

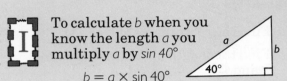

So, to calculate a when you know the length b you divide b by $\sin 40°$

$$a = b \div \sin 40°$$

So y is found like this

$$y = 8 \div \sin 57°$$
$$= 9.5 \text{ cm}$$

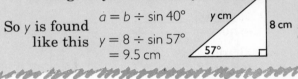

14 The ramp shown in figure 26 is to allow wheelchair access.

Figure 26

The planners decide that, to make the ramp safe, the maximum angle to be allowed between the ramp and the ground is 8°.

(a) The height of the steps is 0.84 m.

What is the minimum length for the ramp?

(b) The angle of the flight of steps is 30°.

If the minimum length of ramp is used how far is the bottom of the ramp from the bottom of the steps?

15 A walker comes to a closed farm gate in a bad state of repair. The gate is 2 m wide and drags on the ground as it is opened.

The walker can squeeze through a gap of not less than 0.4 m.

What is the minimum angle which the walker must open the gate in order to squeeze through?

16 In figure 27, ST represents a ramp, 3.50 m long, used when goods are moved from a warehouse on to a lorry. The end T rests on the lorry and is 1.35 m above the horizontal ground. The end S is 0.60 m inside the warehouse and is on the horizontal floor of the warehouse, 0.55 m above ground level.

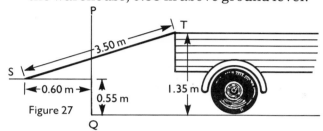

Figure 27

(a) Write down the vertical distance between S and T.

(b) Calculate the angle which ST makes with the horizontal.

(c) Calculate the horizontal distance between T and the vertical wall PQ of the warehouse.

MEG May 1988, Paper 6

17 Figure 28 shows the end ABCD of a fish tank which is tilted so that BC makes an angle of 50° with the horizontal ground XY.

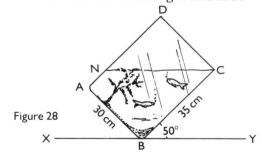

Figure 28

ABCD is a rectangle, AB = DC = 30 cm and BC = AD = 35 cm.

(a) Calculate, correct to 2 significant figures,

(i) the height of C above the ground,
(ii) the height of A above the ground.

(b) The tank is filled with water to the level of C. The point N is where the surface of the water meets AD.

(i) State the size of angle DCN.
(ii) Calculate, correct to 2 significant figures, the length of ND.

(iii) Calculate, correct to 2 significant figures, the area of the trapezium ABCN.

(c) The corner A is lowered until AB is horizontal. Calculate the depth of the water in the tank in this position.

MEG June 1987, Paper 5

18 A coastguard (C) is at the top of a vertical cliff (BC). The top of the cliff is 40 m above sea level. The coastguard sees a swimmer, Sarah, in the sea at an angle of depression of 8°.

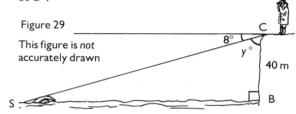

Figure 29

This figure is *not* accurately drawn

(a) Write down the value of *y* in figure 29.

(b) Using trigonometry, calculate the distance, to the nearest m, that Sarah is from the bottom of the cliff.

Sarah can swim at an average speed of 0.4 m/s.

(c) How long will Sarah take to reach the bottom of the cliff if she swims straight towards it? Give your answer correct to the nearest minute.

LEAG Specimen 1991, Paper 3

19 (a) A survey is being made for an overhead electricity power line. Two pylons are to be placed at A and B and a third pylon at either P or Q. A, P and B are in a straight line. The measurements that have been made are shown in figure 30. Calculate

(i) the length AP,
(ii) the length QP,
(iii) the value of θ,
(iv) the length of QB.

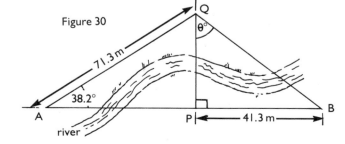

Figure 30

(b) Erecting each pylon costs £2450 and the cable costs £25 per metre. Crossing the river between A and P costs £1520 and crossing the river between Q and B costs £945.

Calculate the cost of erecting the power line along each of the two alternative routes.

NEA Syllabus B, May 1988, Paper 3

20 A regular hexagonal badge is cut from a cardboard circular disc of radius 6 cm.

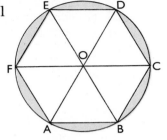

(a) Find the length of the perpendicular from O to AB.

(b) Find the area of triangle ABO.

(c) Find the area of the circle, to a sensible degree of accuracy.

(d) What percentage of the cardboard disc is thrown away to make the hexagonal badge?

21 (a) The image of an aeroplane is spotted on a radar screen at a point A on a bearing of 036° and distant 30 miles. Five minutes later its position is at B on a bearing of 300°, as shown in figure 31.

Calculate the x and y coordinates of A and B.

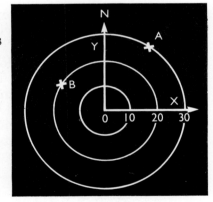

Figure 31

(Give your answers correct to two decimal places.)

(b) Calculate the distance AB in miles.

(Give your answer correct to two decimal places.)

(c) Calculate the speed of the aeroplane, assuming that it is flying at constant speed and in a horizontal straight line.

NEA Syllabus B, May 1988, Paper 4

22 (a) When a ladder is held vertically against a wall it reaches 1 ft higher up the wall than when it is placed with its base 5 f from the base of the wall.
(i) If the length of the ladder is x ft, use Pythagoras' theorem to write down an equation involving x.
(ii) Find the length of the ladder.

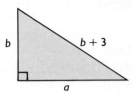

(b) (i) Find the value of b when $a = 9$ cm.
(ii) Find the value of b when $a = 10$ cm.
(iii) What types of number a produce an integer value for b?

23 Jasmine is asked to calculate the height of a tower.

From a point A she finds the angle of elevation of the top of the tower C to be 40°.

She walks 50 metres towards the tower and finds the new angle of elevation of the top of the tower to be 60°.

Her results are illustrated in figure 32.

(a) Express, in terms of x and h,

(i) tan 60
(ii) tan 40

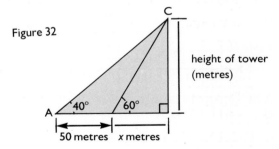

Figure 32

(b) Using the two equations in part (a), show that

$$x(\tan 60 - \tan 40) = 50 \tan 40$$

(c) Use Jasmine's results to find the height of the tower, in metres, to 3 significant figures.

SEG A Summer 1988, Paper 4

EXERCISE 22 Vectors

1 A lifeboat sailed from Tenby 3 km east and 1 km south to rescue a boy from a dinghy. This is shown on the grid in figure 33 as a vector $\begin{pmatrix} 3 \\ -1 \end{pmatrix}$.

The lifeboat then continued 2 km east and 6 km north to deliver the boy to Pennully where an ambulance was waiting.

(a) Copy figure 33, and on it draw the vector representing this part of the rescue.

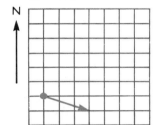

Figure 33

(b) State the vector representing the direct return journey from Pennully to Tenby.

NEA Syllabus A, May 1988, Paper 3

2 Figure 34 shows the screen for a game of computer hockey. The 'passes' and 'shots' can be described using vectors. For example the pass from B to A is $\begin{pmatrix} -3 \\ 8 \end{pmatrix}$ Figure 34

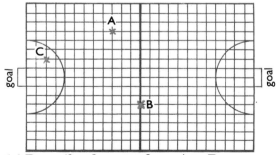

(a) Describe the pass from A to B.

(b) Describe the pass from B to C.

(c) C scores a goal. Give the vector of a direct shot which would score.

MEG SMP 11-16, June 1988, Paper 3

3 Calculate the length of the vectors

(a) $\begin{pmatrix} 8 \\ 15 \end{pmatrix}$ (b) $\begin{pmatrix} -20 \\ 21 \end{pmatrix}$

4 Figure 35 shows the positions of five factories B, C, D, E, F and the Managing Director's home H.

Figure 35
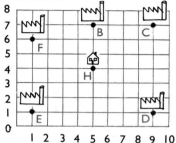

(a) (i) On Monday his journey is represented by $\begin{pmatrix} 4 \\ 3 \end{pmatrix}$ followed by $\begin{pmatrix} 0 \\ -6 \end{pmatrix}$.

Which two factories did he visit?
(ii) Write down a vector which gives his journey home from the second factory visited.

(b) On Tuesday he visited three factories and his journey was represented by $\begin{pmatrix} -4 \\ 2 \end{pmatrix}$ followed by $\begin{pmatrix} 0 \\ -5 \end{pmatrix}$ followed by $\begin{pmatrix} 8 \\ 0 \end{pmatrix}$.

When he is at the third factory how far from home is he?

(c) On Wednesday, his journey is represented by $\begin{pmatrix} 0 \\ 3 \end{pmatrix}$ followed by $\begin{pmatrix} 4 \\ 0 \end{pmatrix}$ followed by $\begin{pmatrix} 0 \\ -6 \end{pmatrix}$ followed by $\begin{pmatrix} -4 \\ 3 \end{pmatrix}$.

Find the total length of his journey.

MEG SMP Specimen 1987, Paper 1

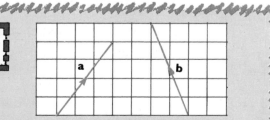

Sometimes small letters are used to represent vectors.

In the diagram above the vector **a** is $\begin{pmatrix} 3 \\ 4 \end{pmatrix}$ and **b** is $\begin{pmatrix} -2 \\ 5 \end{pmatrix}$

So $2\mathbf{a} = \begin{pmatrix} 6 \\ 8 \end{pmatrix}$, $-3\mathbf{b} = \begin{pmatrix} 6 \\ -15 \end{pmatrix}$ $2\mathbf{a} + 3\mathbf{b} = \begin{pmatrix} 0 \\ 23 \end{pmatrix}$

5 If **a** and **b** are defined as in the box above, what are the following?

  (a) 2**b**

  (b) − 4**a**

  (c) 3**b** − 2**a**

  (d) − 3(**b** + **a**)

6 If $\mathbf{c} = \begin{pmatrix} 4 \\ -3 \end{pmatrix}$ and $\mathbf{c} - 3\mathbf{d} = \begin{pmatrix} -2 \\ 9 \end{pmatrix}$ what is **d**?

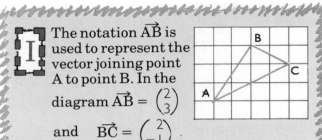

The notation $\overrightarrow{AB}$ is used to represent the vector joining point A to point B. In the diagram $\overrightarrow{AB} = \begin{pmatrix} 2 \\ 3 \end{pmatrix}$

and $\overrightarrow{BC} = \begin{pmatrix} 2 \\ -1 \end{pmatrix}$.

7 A is the point (1,4), B is the point (5,2) and $\overrightarrow{AD} = \begin{pmatrix} 7 \\ 3 \end{pmatrix}$.

  (a) Write down the coordinates of the point D.

  (b) ABCD is a parallelogram. Find $\overrightarrow{AC}$.

          MEG June 1986, Paper 3

8 A is the point (2,3), and C is the (10,7).

  (a) Find $\overrightarrow{AC}$.

  (b) Write down the coordinates of the midpoint of AC.

  (c) B is the point (4,1). If ABCD is a rectangle, find the coordinates of the point D.

          MEG June 1987, Paper 3

9 If $\overrightarrow{PQ} = \begin{pmatrix} 4 \\ 1 \end{pmatrix}$ and $\overrightarrow{PR} = \begin{pmatrix} 3 \\ 2 \end{pmatrix}$ what is $\overrightarrow{QR}$?

10 If $\overrightarrow{AB} = \begin{pmatrix} -3 \\ 2 \end{pmatrix}$ and $\overrightarrow{CB} = \begin{pmatrix} 2 \\ -3 \end{pmatrix}$ what is $\overrightarrow{AC}$?

EXERCISE 23 Maps and bearings

1 Figure 36 shows the relative positions of Carmarthen and Builth Wells.

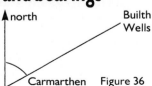

Figure 36

  (a) Use your protractor to find the size of the marked angle.

  (b) What is the bearing of Builth Wells from Carmarthen?

2 Get the resource sheet called *'Distance map of England'*.

  (a) Which town marked on the map is approximately due south of London.

  (b) Which of the towns marked is the closest to due west of Liverpool?

  (c) Which town is on a bearing of 300° from Oxford?

  (d) What is the bearing of Penrith from Berwick-upon-Tweed?

  (e) What is the bearing of Berwick-upon-Tweed from Penrith?

  (f) Comment on your answers to (d) and (e).

3 Rachel walks 600 m south west from a point A to a point B. She then walks 750 m due east to a point C.

  (a) Using a scale 1 cm to represent 100 m, draw a diagram to represent Rachel's journey.

  (b) What is the direct distance from point A to point C?

4 The scale of a map is such that a distance of 5 cm on the map represents an actual distance of 2 km.

  (a) What distance on the map represents 10 km?

  (b) What distance on the map represents 5 km?

  (c) The distance between two places on the map is 8 cm. What is the actual distance between them?

5 The scale of a map is 1:25 000.

  (a) On the map the distance from the pub in one village to the church in the next village is 15 cm. What is the actual distance between the pub and the church in kilometres?

  (b) The actual length of a lake is 3 km. This lake is shown on the map. How long is the lake on the map?

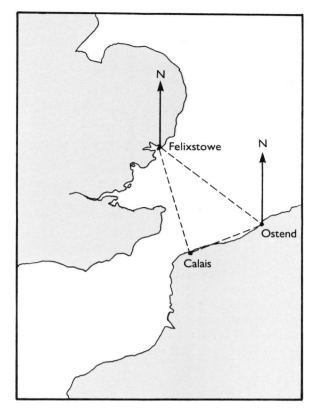

6 (*a*) The distance between Felixstowe and Calais is 120 km. What is the scale of the map?

(*b*) A ship sails straight from Felixstowe to Ostend, then straight from Ostend to Calais, and then straight from Calais to Felixstowe.

(i) Use your protractor to find the bearing of the first leg of the journey.
(ii) What is the bearing of the second leg of the journey?
(iii) What is the total distance in km travelled on all three legs of the journey?

7 Figure 37 represents a coast guard station C and a lifeboat station L which is 10 km due north of C.
A ship S in distress is due east of C and on a bearing of 130° from L

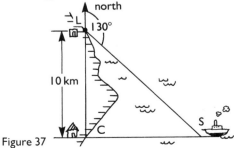

Figure 37

(*a*) Using a scale of 1 cm to represent 1 km, draw an accurate diagram showing C, L and S.

(*b*) Use your diagram to find the distance of the ship from the lifeboat station.

(*c*) A lifeboat leaves L and travels to S at a speed of 18 km/h. How many minutes will it take to reach S? Give your answer to the nearest whole number.

(*d*) Find the bearing of L from S.

MEG May 1989, Paper 4

8 Figure 38 shows two radar stations A and B which are 50 km apart.

A plane is at P when it is 'picked up' by the radars.

BP = 50 km and angle PBA = 70°.

(*a*) What type of triangle is ABP?

(*b*) Calculate angle PAB.

(*c*) Work out the bearing of
(i) P from B
(ii) P from A

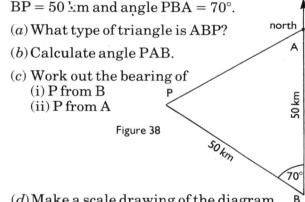

Figure 38

(*d*) Make a scale drawing of the diagram using a scale of 1 cm to 5 km.

(*e*) The plane flies due north from P for 30 km to a new position Q.

(i) Draw on your diagram the journey PQ.
(ii) How far is Q from the radar station A?

MEG SMP May 1988, Paper 2

9 A ship sails 40 km on a bearing of 110° from a point A to a point B. It then changes course and sails a distance of 32 km on a bearing of 067° to a point C.

(*a*) Using a scale of 1 cm to represent 4 km draw an accurate diagram of the course of the ship.

(*b*) On what bearing would the ship need to sail to return directly from C to A?

(*c*) How long would it take to make the return journey from C to A if the ship travelled at an average speed of 13.5 km/h?

10 The scale of a map is 1:380 160.

What distance (in miles) is represented on the map by 2 inches?

(There are 5280 feet in a mile.)

11 Beckthorpe House (B) is 25 km from Appletree Inn (A) on a bearing of 150°.

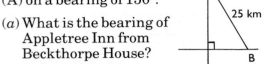

(a) What is the bearing of Appletree Inn from Beckthorpe House?

(b) Calculate how far, in km correct to three significant figures, Beckthorpe House is south of Appletree Inn.

LEAG SMP June 1988, Paper 3

12 At 11 a.m. a coastguard observes a ship 8 km away and due west of the coastguard station.

The ship sails at a steady speed on a fixed bearing, and at 11.40 a.m. is 6 km due south of the coastguard station.

(a) On what bearing is the ship sailing?

(b) What is the ship's speed?

(c) At what time does the ship reach the point where its path is nearest to the coastguard station?

13 Figure 39 shows the Isle of Man and part of England. The point B represents Barrow and the point C represents Castletown. Barrow is 90 km due east of Castletown.

Figure 39

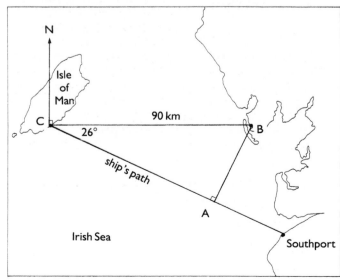

At 1400 hours, a ship left Castletown travelling at 15 km/h towards Southport. The point A represents the ship's position when it is nearest to Barrow. Angle BCA = 26°.

(a) Calculate the distance AB, giving your answer correct to two significant figures.

(b) Calculate the distance AC, giving your answer correct to two significant figures.

(c) Find the time at which the ship reaches A.

(d) Calculate the bearing of

  (i) Southport from Castletown,
  (ii) the point A from Barrow.

MEG November 1986, Paper III

14 Figure 40 shows two navigation lights A and B with A due north of B. From a ship S, the bearing of A is 310° and the bearing of B is 220°.

Figure 40

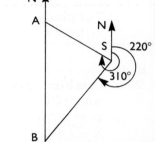

(a) Calculate

  (i) the angle ASB,
  (ii) the angle ABS.

(b) The distance AB is 2000 m; calculate the distance SA and SB.

SEG A Summer 1988, Paper 3

15 Figure 41 shows the route taken by a boat on a fishing trip. The boat starts from a port A and sails 16 km on a bearing of 042° to its first stop at the point B. In the figure, N is the point which is due north of A and due west of B.

(a) Calculate, to the nearest 0.01 km,
  (i) the distance AN,
  (ii) the distance BN.

The boat then sails 12 km due east to its second stop at the point C.

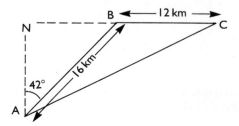

Figure 41

(b) Calculate
  (i) the distance AC, in km, to the nearest 0.01 km,
  (ii) the bearing of C from A, to the nearest degree.

(c) What is the bearing of A from C?

The boat travels at 6.4 km/h.

(d) Find the time it takes to return directly to A from C.

LEAG B June 1988, Paper 3

EXERCISE 24 Types of number 2

1 The Dead Sea is 385 m below normal sea level. A plane is flying at 65 m above normal sea level when over the Dead Sea.

  (a) Find the actual height of the plane above the Dead Sea.

  (b) The plane reduces height by 240 m. What is its new height above the Dead Sea?

MEG May 1988, Paper 1

2 (a) One February morning the temperature was −7°C at 4 a.m. and −2°C at 7 a.m. How much had it risen between 4 a.m. and 7 a.m.?

  (b) Between 7 a.m. and 10 a.m. the temperature rose 9 degrees. What was the temperature by 10 a.m?

  (c) How much had the temperature risen between 4 a.m. and 10 a.m?

3 The daytime temperature in a settlement in Canada one Winter's day was −12°C. At night the temperature dropped 7 degrees. What was the night-time temperature?

4 Look at figure 42.

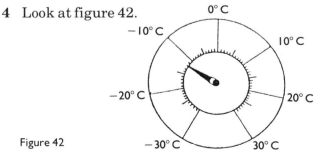

Figure 42

  (a) Write down the temperature marked by the pointer.

(b) At 5 p.m. the temperature was 10°C. By midnight the temperature had fallen 14°C. What was the temperature at midnight?

(c) The temperature at 6 a.m. was −10°C. At 9 a.m. it had risen 8°C. Write down the temperature at 9 a.m.

MEG SMP Specimen, Paper 2

5 The noon temperatures in eight cities on 2 March 1988 are shown below.

City	Temperature
Copenhagen	1°C
Gibraltar	11°C
Helsinki	−3°C
New York	5°C
Montreal	−14°C
Prague	−2°C
Stockholm	−5°C
Singapore	29°C

(a) How many degrees difference is there between the highest and the lowest of these temperatures?

(b) Which of the other cities had a temperature nearest to that of Prague?

MEG May 1989, Paper 1

6 Use the information contained in the newspaper extract to obtain an estimate of the total world population in billions.

Great Wall stormed by Queen

From Alan Hamilton Peking

The man and the woman who can jointly claim to hold 'titular sway over one half the world's population met yesterday and discussed whether you could see England from the top of the Eiffel Tower.

The Queen, who as head of the Commonwealth chalks up the round billion or so, lunched with Mr. Deng Xiaoping, the chain-smoking, expectorating, 82-year-old Sichuan peasant who, although only second in his hierarchy, is the strong man and *eminence grise* who rules 1.2 billion Chinese.

The Times

NEA Syllabus C, May 1988, Paper 1

7 What is the value of
  (a) $4^3 + 3^4$?
  (b) $2^4 − 4^2$?
  (c) $3^0 + 3^1 + 3^2$?

8 By how much is $(13 + 17)^2$ bigger than $13^2 + 17^2$?

9 Add three quarters of a million to three hundred and twenty eight thousand, giving your answer in standard form.

10 The total thickness of the pages of a dictionary is 5 cm. The last page is numbered 1792.

Find, in metres, the thickness of one page. Write your answer in standard form to a sensible degree of accuracy.

11 The sun burns 5 million tonnes of hydrogen a second.

How many tonnes of hydrogen does it burn in a year? Write your answer in standard form.

12 The diameter of a molecule of oil is about 2×10^{-9} m.

Approximately how many layers of molecules of oil are there in an oil tank if the depth of oil in the tank is 3.5 m? Give your answer in standard form.

13 The table below gives some information about some of the planets in our solar system.

Planet	Radius km	Mass kg	Distance from the sun km
Mercury	2.43×10^3	2.30×10^{23}	5.97×10^7
Earth	6.38×10^3	5.98×10^{24}	1.50×10^8
Saturn	6.04×10^4	5.69×10^{26}	1.43×10^9
Jupiter	7.14×10^4	1.90×10^{27}	7.78×10^8

Using the table, write down the name of

(a) the planet with the greatest mass,

(b) the planet with the smallest radius,

(c) the planet which is just over 5 times as far away from the Sun as the Earth.

NEA Syllabus A, May 1988, Paper 3

14 Refer to the table shown in question 13.

There are occasions when the Sun, Mercury and Jupiter are all in a straight line with Mercury in the middle.

What is the distance from Mercury to Jupiter on these occasions?

15 Refer to the table shown in question 13.

Suppose a scale model were made of the solar system, in which the Earth was represented by a ball of radius 5 cm.

(a) What size ball should be used to represent Saturn?

(b) If the model were to show a moment in the solar system when the Earth was as far as possible from Saturn (on opposite sides of the Sun), how far would the Earth need to be from Saturn on the scale model?

16 Refer to the table shown in question 13.

What is the ratio of the mass of Jupiter to the mass of Mercury? Give your answer in standard form.

> **By John Hooper,**
>
> *Energy Correspondent*
>
> More oil was supplied to the non-Communist world last year than in any year since 1980, according to figures compiled by the International Energy Agency, Opec, whose production shot up by 12 per cent as the organisation battled to regain its share of world markets, accounted for almost all of the increase.
>
> The statistics also show that the collapse in prices brought about by Opec's campaign spurred consumption to its highest level for five years. In 1986, the non-Communist world used up an average 46.6 million barrels a day – 2.5 per cent more than the previous year, or 2.7 per cent more after compensating for the effects of the miners' strike in Britain which boosted the use of oil power by power stations in 1985.

Source: The Guardian

17 The above article on world oil consumption is taken from *The Guardian* (13.1.87).

The answers to both parts of this question should be given in standard form.

(a) Estimate the total oil consumption, in barrels, by the non-Communist world in 1986.

(b) Assuming that this consumption will continue to increase at 2.5% per annum, estimate the total consumption in barrels in 1987.

NEA Syllabus C, May 1988, Paper 3

18 (a) Write down a rational number between 1 and 2.

(b) Write down an irrational number between 1 and 2.

(c) Which of the two numbers you have written down is the larger?

SEG B Summer 1988, Paper 3

19 In attempting to beat the land speed record of 600 m.p.h., a racing car covered a measured mile at an average speed of 625 m.p.h.

(a) Express, in standard form, to three significant figures, the time it took in hours.

(b) The car then covered the same distance in the opposite direction at an average speed of 575 m.p.h. For record purposes, the average speed of the car was calculated to be 'the average speed over the two miles (there and back)'. Did the car equal, break, or not break the land speed record? (Work to four significant figures.)

NEA Syllabus B, May 1988, Paper 4

20 According to Faraday's law of electrolysis, the mass in kilograms, M, of copper deposited during electrolysis is given by the formula
$$M = kIt$$
where k is the constant 3.3×10^{-7}, I is the current in amps and t is the time in seconds.

How long (in hours and minutes, to the nearest minute) will it take to deposit 30 g of copper using a current of 2 amps?

21 The time, T minutes, taken by the Moon to eclipse the Sun totally is given by the formula
$$T = \frac{1}{v}\left(\frac{rD}{R} - d\right)$$
d and D are the diameters, in kilometres, of the Moon and Sun, respectively;

r and R are the distances, in kilometres, of the Moon and Sun, respectively from the Earth;

v is the speed of the Moon in kilometres per minute.

Given that
$d = 3.48 \times 10^3$, $R = 1.48 \times 10^8$,
$D = 1.41 \times 10^6$, $v = 59.5$,
$r = 3.82 \times 10^5$,
calculate the time taken for a total eclipse, giving your answer in minutes, correct to 2 significant figures.

MEG, May 1988, Paper 3

EXERCISE 25 Equations I

I You will find your calculator useful for most of the questions in this exercise. Many equations can be solved, either by spotting the answer, or by using trial and improvement methods.

It is always worthwhile to check the answer to an equation. A calculator makes this easy to do.

1 Copy the statements below, but replace each box by a number which makes the statement true.

(a) $\square + 4 = 51$ (b) $100 - \square = 37$

(c) $9 \times \square = 153$ (d) $\square \div 13 = 16$

(e) $\square + 17 < 23$ (f) $\square^2 = 81$

2 Nelista started with a number, x. She doubled it and then added 7. Her answer was 23.

(a) Write down an equation involving x.

(b) What number did Nelista start with?

3 Solve the following equations.

(a) $7x = 56$

(b) $3y - 5 = 22$

(c) $25z = 300$

(d) $\frac{W}{4} = 25$

4 (a) Find, in terms of x, the perimeter of the quadrilateral shown in figure 43.

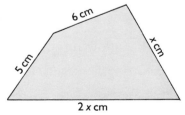

Figure 43

6 cm

5 cm

x cm

2 x cm

(b) The perimeter is 35 cm. Write down an equation involving x.

(c) Find the value of x.

(d) What are the lengths of the longest and shortest sides of the quadrilateral?

5 Deborah is Sharon's daughter. Sharon is six times as old as Deborah.

By the time Deborah is old enough to vote Sharon will be eight times as old as Deborah is now.

How old is Sharon?

6 Darren asked his gran how old she was. She replied 'In 7 years time I shall be three times as old as I was when I got married.'

Darren's gran then told him she had been married for 41 years.

(a) Taking her age now to be y years, write down an equation involving y.

(b) How old is Darren's gran?

7 A group of students on a Business Studies course are making 'Solitaire' games which they are selling for £1 each. Apart from a loan of £20 which has to be repaid, all the income is profit.

(a) Write down an expression for the total profit after n games have been sold.

(b) How many games have to be sold to give an average profit of 75 p on each game?

NEA Syllabus C, May 1988, Paper 4

8 Look at figure 44.

The length of AE is twice the length of AB.

The length of DE is 12 cm.

(a) Write down the length of AD.

The perimeter of the rectangle ABCD is 17 cm.

(b) Find the value of x.

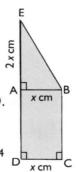
Figure 44

LEAG Specimen 1991, Paper 3

9 Solve the following equations.

(a) $3(x-2) = 18$

(b) $4(y+3) = 48$

(c) $3z + 7 = 5z - 13$

(d) $\dfrac{W}{2} + \dfrac{W-1}{4} = 8$

10 Solve the following equations.

(a) $2x = -6$

(b) $3(y +4) = -24$

(c) $3.4z + 2.8 = 16.4$

(d) $5(w + 3) = 12 - w$

11 Given that

8 bolts and 6 nuts weigh 138 grams
and 3 bolts and 5 nuts weigh 71 grams

work out the weight of the following:

(a) 4 bolts and 3 nuts

(b) 11 bolts and 11 nuts

(c) 3 bolts and 3 nuts

(d) 1 bolt

(e) 1 nut

NEA Syllabus A, May 1988, Paper 4

12 Solve the simultaneous equations

$3x + 2y = 18$
$5x + 4y = 32$

13 Solve the simultaneous equations

$5x - 4y = 18$
$6x - 7y = 4$

14 Solve the simultaneous equations

$2x + 3y = 4$
$5x + 6y = 7$

15 Julie and Mike were on a walking holiday. Each day they went to the same bread shop to buy rolls for their lunch.

On Monday they bought two ham rolls and three cheese rolls and paid £2.20.

Because they liked the ham rolls so much, on Tuesday they bought four ham rolls and one cheese roll and paid £2.30.

Mike wondered whether there was much difference between the prices of ham rolls and cheese rolls.

(a) What is the difference in price between a ham roll and a cheese roll?

(b) On Wednesday they decided to have one cheese roll and one ham roll each. What did they pay?

16 (a) When $x + y = 5$ and $3x - 2y = 4$ find the values of x and y.

(b) The organisers of a charity concert sold 500 tickets. There were two prices: £3 for adults and £2 for children. The money received from the sale of adult tickets was £400 more than the money received from the sale of children's tickets. How many adult tickets were sold?

SEG A Summer 1988, Paper 4

17 Find the coordinates for the point of intersection of the lines $7x + y = 1$ and $y = x - 3$.

18 The cost, $£C$, of making n articles is given by the formula

$$C = a + bn$$

where a and b are constants.

The cost of making 4 articles is £20 and the cost of making 7 articles is £29.

Write down two equations in a and b.

Solve these equations to find the values of a and b.

LEAG B June 1988, Paper 4

19 The curve $y = a + bx - x^2$ passes through the points $P(1, 12)$ and $Q(2, 12)$.

(a) Show that $a + b = 13$ and write down another equation involving a and b. Find the value of a and the value of b, and hence write down the equation of the curve.

(b) Find the coordinates of the points at which the curve crosses the x and y axes.

MEG June 1987, Paper 6

20 The product of two consecutive odd numbers is 3363. What are the numbers?

21 The length of a cuboid is 1 cm more than the width and the height of the cuboid is 1 cm less than the width.

The volume of the cuboid is 50 cm³.

Find the width correct to 1 decimal place.

22 (a) Work through the flow diagram seen in figure 45, writing down the values of x, y and z in a table, as shown, recording only the first three decimal places of your answers.

x	y	z
2	1.333	

(b) Cube the last value of x and comment on the result.

(c) Give the last value of x correct to two decimal places.

MEG SMP, June 1988, Paper 3

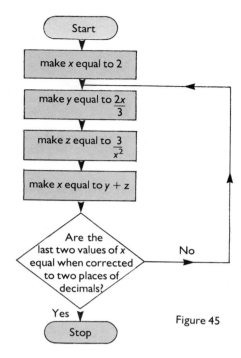

Figure 45

23 $y = x^2 - 5x + 1$

(a) Copy and complete the following table.

x	4	4.5	5
y			

(b) What do your results show about the solutions of the equation $x^2 - 5x + 1 = 0$?

(c) Find, by trial, a solution of $x^2 - 5x + 1 = 0$, correct to one place of decimals.

MEG SMP Specimen 1987, Paper 3

24 A sequence is defined by $u_1 = 1$,

$$u_{n+1} = \frac{1}{1 + u_n}$$

(a) Calculate u_2

(b) Calculate u_4

MEG SMP, June 1988, Paper 4

25 The nth term of a sequence is given by the formula

$$u_n = \frac{1}{1 + u_{n-1}} \text{ and } u_4 = 3$$

(a) Calculate the value of u_5

(b) Calculate the value of u_3

NEA Syllabus B, May 1988, Paper 4

26 A sequence of numbers $x_1, x_2, x_3, \ldots$ is related by the iterative formula

$$x_{n+1} = \frac{1}{2}\left(x_n + \frac{5}{x_n}\right)$$

For example, when $x_1 = 2$

$$x_2 = \frac{1}{2}\left(2 + \frac{5}{2}\right) = 2.25$$

(a) Use this value of x_2 to calculate the value of x_3.

(b) This formula is used to find the square root of a number. Which number?

(c) Use this formula to find this square root correct to four places of decimals.

(d) How did you use the formula to make sure that your answer was correct to four places of decimals?

(e) Write down an iterative formula which could be used to find $\sqrt{11}$.

NEA Syllabus C, May 1988, Paper 4

27 The iteration formula for a sequence is

$$u_{n+1} = \frac{17}{11 - u_n}$$

(a) Start with $u_1 = 0$ and find u_2, u_3, u_4, u_5, u_6.

(b) What does the limit of the sequence appear to be, to three significant figures?

(c) Write x for both u_{n+1} and u_n in the formula. Show that the equation for the fixed point can be written

$$x^2 - 11x + 17 = 0$$

(d) Figure 46 shows the graph of $y = \dfrac{17}{11 - x}$.

Use this graph to help you solve

$$x^2 - 11x + 17 = 0$$

Write down the solutions to this equation, giving as many significant figures as you are certain of in each case.

(e) Now write the equation in the form $x^2 =$

Hence find another iteration formula.

Using this new formula with a suitable starting value, find the other solution of the quadratic equation to four significant figures.

Show all your working.

MEG SMP 11-16, June 1988, Paper 4

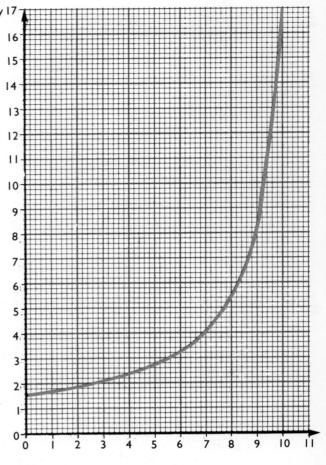

Figure 46

28 (a) Show that the equation $2x^2 - 2x - 1 = 0$ can be written as

$$x = \frac{2x + 1}{2x}$$

(b) Define a sequence by

$$u_{n+1} = \frac{2u_n + 1}{2u_n}$$

If $u_1 = 1$ write down $u_2, u_3, u_4, \ldots, u_9$.

(c) Hence give one root of the equation $2x^2 - 2x - 1 = 0$, correct to three decimal places.

(d) Repeat (b), but with $u_1 = -1$. What happens?

(e) Use a graphical calculator, a graph plotter or graph paper to obtain a sketch of the graph of $y = 2x^2 - 2x + 1$.

From your graph write down the two roots of $2x^2 - 2x - 1 = 0$, correct to one decimal place.

29 Figure 47 shows part of the graph of $f: x \rightarrow x^3 - 2x - 1$ and the solution $x = w$ of the equation $x^3 - 2x - 1 = 0$.

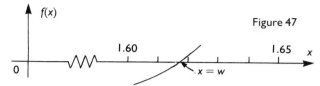

Figure 47

(a) From this diagram, estimate the value of w correct to *two* decimal places.

(b) Show that $x^3 - 2x - 1 = 0$ may be written as

$$x = \sqrt{2 + \frac{1}{x}}$$

(c) Using

$$x_{n+1} = \sqrt{2 + \frac{1}{x_n}}$$

and taking x_1 to be the value you obtained as your estimate for w in part (a), calculate x_2, x_3, and x_4.

In each case, write down all the digits shown on your calculator.

(d) Continue this iteration until you can give the value of w correct to five decimal places.

Write down this value of w.
LEAG SMP June 1988, Paper 4

30 (a) Figure 48 shows the straight lines $5x + 3y = 30$ and $2x + 5y = 14$. The lines cross at the point P and the line $2x + 5y = 14$ meets the axis $x = 0$ at Q.

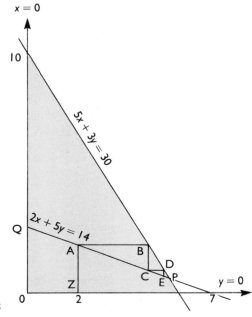

Figure 48

Calculate the coordinates of Q.

(b) Z is the point $(2, 0)$.

Lines ZA, AB, BC, CD, DE, . . . are drawn parallel to the axes, meeting the two given straight lines at A, B, C, D, E, . . . as shown in figure 48.

Calculate

(i) y_A (the y coordinate of the point A)
(ii) x_B (the x coordinate of the point B)
(iii) y_C
(iv) x_D

(c) By continuing the process, calculate the coordinates of the point P where the two lines meet.
(Give each coordinate correct to two decimal places.)

NEA Syllabus B, May 1988, Paper 4

EXERCISE 26 Length, area and volume 2

When answering questions in this exercise you might need to refer to the formulae on pages 247, and 248.

 Wherever appropriate, give all your answers to a sensible degree of accuracy.

1 Figure 49 shows a shape drawn on a rectangular grid. Each square measures 1 cm by 1 cm.

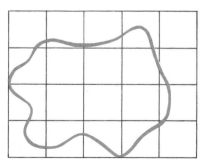

Figure 49

Estimate the area of the shape in cm².

NEA Syllabuses A and B, May 1988, Paper 2

2 A pint of water is poured into each of the vases shown in figure 50. Which vase has the greatest height of water?

LEAG June 1986, Paper 1

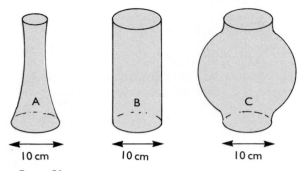

Figure 50

3 Figure 51 shows a cylindrical water tank.

There are six marks on the tank which are equally spaced from the bottom. Mark 6 is at the top of the tank.

Figure 51

(*a*) When the water level is at mark 4, fifteen litres are poured in. The water level rises to mark 5.

(i) How much water was there in the tank?
(ii) How much water is there now in the tank?
(iii) How much water does the tank hold when it is full?

(*b*) When the water level is at mark 5, water is drawn off until the level falls to exactly half way between mark 1 and mark 2.

How much water is drawn off?

MEG SMP Specimen 1987, Paper 1

4 All the triangles in figure 52 are equilateral and the shaded triangle has an area of 5 cm². What is the area, in cm², of the whole figure?

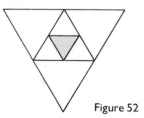

Figure 52

LEAG June 1987, Paper 2

5 The perimeter of a circle is usually called the circumference.

(*a*) Find the perimeter of each of the following shapes

(i) an equilateral triangle with sides each 9 cm long

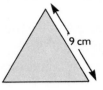

(ii) a square with sides each 6 cm long

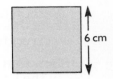

(iii) a circle with radius 4 cm

(iv) a semicircle with radius 5 cm

(*b*) List the shapes in the order of their perimeters, with the shortest perimeter first.

6 (*a*) A circle has a radius of 9 cm. Work out, to the nearest centimetre, the circumference of the circle.

(*b*) An equilateral triangle is drawn with the same perimeter as the circle. Work out the length, to the nearest centimetre, of one of the sides of the triangle.

LEAG SMP May 1988, Paper 2

7 Each of the wheels of Sarah's bike has a diameter of 400 mm.

(*a*) What is the circumference of each wheel?

(*b*) Sarah goes for a 2 km bike ride. How many complete turns does each wheel make during the bike ride?

8 A metal frame, shown in figure 53, is made for a window. The lower part consists of two rectangles, each 90 cm by 35 cm, and the upper part is a semi-circle with radius 35 cm.

Calculate the length of metal used in making

(*a*) the straight pieces

(b) the curved piece. (Take π to be 3.14 or use the π button on your calculator. Give your answer correct to the nearest whole number).

Figure 53

(c) the total frame.

SEG A Summer 1988, Paper 2

9 When the label shown in figure 54 is fitted round a cylindrical container, it has an overlap of 11 mm.

Figure 54

(a) Measure the length of the label in cm.

(b) Hence find the diameter of the container in cm.

NEA Syllabus C, May 1988, Paper 3

10 The base of a baking tin is a circle of metal which can be removed from the rest of the tin.

The radius of the base is 8 cm. What is the area of the base?

11 A Christmas decoration is made by cutting a piece of card into the shape shown in figure 55.

The perimeter of the shape is four quarter circles. The radius of each quarter circle is 10 cm.

Calculate the area of one side of the decoration.

Figure 55

12 Figure 56 shows an athletics track, consisting of straight sections and semi-circular ends.

The total length of the inside lane of the track is 400 m. The straight sections are 70 m long.

What is the radius of the bends on the inside lane of the track?

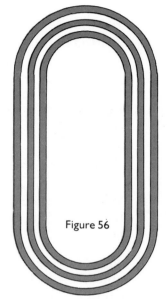

Figure 56

13 A baked bean can has a height of 10.5 cm and a radius of 7.5 cm.
(a) Calculate the volume of the can.
(b) Calculate the can's surface area.

14 A piece of metal is in the shape of a block. The uniform cross section of the block is a square of side 200 mm.

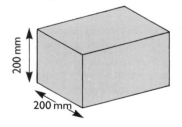
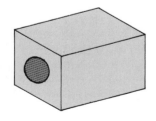

A component is manufactured by cutting a circular hole of radius 80 mm through the block.
(a) Find the area of the square end of the block after the circular hole has been made.
(b) Before removing the circular hole the block weighs 2 kg. What does it weigh after the hole has been removed?

241

15 A shed is in the shape of a prism whose cross section PQRS is a trapezium (see figure 57).

Figure 57

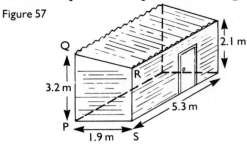

(a) Find the area of the trapezium PQRS.
(b) Find the volume of the shed.

Figure 58

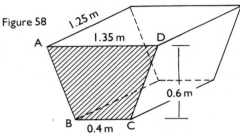

16 Figure 58 above shows a container used at a lime kiln. It is in the shape of an open-top prism. Its cross section ABCD (shown shaded in the diagram) is a trapezium. The edges BC and AD are horizontal. BC = 0.4 m and AD = 1.35 m. The vertical height of the container is 0.6 m and its length is 1.25 m. Find

(a) the area, in square metres, of the cross section ABCD,

(b) the capacity, in cubic metres, of the container, if it is filled level with the top of the sides. Give your answer correct to 2 decimal places.

MEG May 1989, Paper 2

17 (a) A firm sells 500 g packs of butter in the form of a circular cylinder with radius 3.9 cm and length 10.5 cm. Calculate the volume of the cylinder.

(b) The firm also sells 500 g packs of butter in the form of a rectangular block with a square cross section of side 6.5 cm. Calculate the length of the rectangular block.

(c) The firm decides to sell 250 g packs of butter in the form of a circular cylinder.

(i) If the radius of the (250 g) cylinder is 3.9 cm, find the length of the cylinder.
(ii) If the length of the (250 g) cylinder is 10.5 cm, calculate the radius of the cylinder.

MEG May 1988, Paper 5

18 Figure 59 shows the design of a sand pit to be dug in a children's playground.

Figure 59

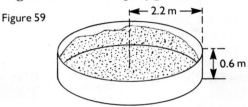

It is in the shape of a circular cylinder with radius 2.2 m and depth 0.6 m.

The wall of the sand pit is to be lined with firm plastic sheets.

The sheets to be used are 1.5 m long and 0.6 m wide.

(a) Find

(i) the circumference, in metres, to the nearest 0.1 m, of the sand pit,
(ii) the number of sheets of plastic which must be bought.

The pit is to be filled completely with sand (to a depth of 0.6 m).

(b) Calculate the volume, in m³, to the nearest 0.01 m³, of sand required

The mass of 1 m³ of the sand is approximately 1.2 tonnes.

(c) Find the mass, in tonnes, to the nearest tonne, of sand required.

It is decided to order the plastic sheets and the sand, to the nearest tonne, from a local builder's yard. The charges at this yard are:

Loose sand	£11.50 per tonne
Plastic sheets (1.5 m × 0.6 m)	£2.58 each
Delivery charge	£5 (fixed rate)
(ALL prices include VAT)	

(d) Find the total cost of the materials, including the delivery charge.

LEAG B June 1988, Paper 3

19 Angharad decides to lay a concrete path round her semicircular flower bed.

The path is to be 1.5 m wide and the thickness of the concrete is to be 80 mm.

Calculate the volume of concrete required.

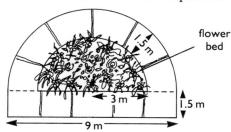

flower bed

20 Phiz is sold in cylindrical cans of radius 3 cm.

large

standard

(a) A standard can contains 350 cm³. Find its height. (use 3.14 as the value of π or use the π button on your calculator.)

(b) A large can has the same radius, but has height 22 cm. Small cans cost 20 p each. If large cans are to be better value for money, calculate the maximum cost for a large can.

SEG B Summer 1988, Paper 4

21 Gillian is making 25 simple skirts for a pantomime. Each skirt is made from a sector of material as illustrated in figure 60. Small silver buttons each 0.5 cm diameter are put around the bottom on a piece of ribbon 1 cm wide.

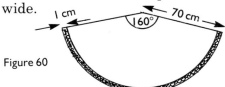

Figure 60

(a) Calculate the approximate length of ribbon needed on each dress. (Give your answer to two significant figures.)

(b) Use your answer to part (a) to estimate how many small silver buttons will be needed on each dress, if the buttons are sewn in a straight line just touching each other.

NEA Syllabus A, May 1988, Paper 3

22 It is suggested that a new thirty-pence coin is to be introduced. It would be based on an equilateral triangle ABC of side 1.50 cm. Arcs of circles of radius 1.50 cm are centred at A, B and C. This is shown in figure 61(a).

Figure 61

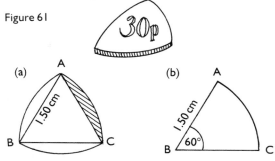

(a) What fraction of the area of the complete circle is the area shown in figure 61(b)?

In figure 61(a) you may assume that the area of triangle ABC is 0.974 cm².

(b) Calculate the shaded area correct to 3 significant figures.

(c) Calculate the area of the top face of the coin correct to 3 significant figures.

MEG SMP June 1988, Paper 4

23 (a) The Earth is approximately a sphere of radius 6400 km.

Find the approximate area of the Earth's surface.

(b) The radius of the Moon is approximately one quarter of the radius of the Earth.

Find the approximate area of the Moon's surface.

24 A witch's hat in the shape of a cone is to be made by cutting and bending a circle of paper.

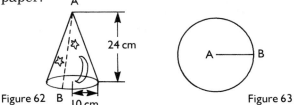

Figure 62   Figure 63

The radius of the hat is to be 10 cm and the height is to be 24 cm (see figure 62).

(a) Calculate the circumference of the hat.

(b) Calculate the slant height of the hat.

Figure 63 shows the circle of paper the hat is to be made from.

The circle is cut along AB and then bent so that some of the circumference is doubled under. The position of AB on the final hat is shown in figure 62.

(c) What is the radius of the circle required to make the hat?

(d) What is the circumference of this circle?

(e) What length of circumference has to be doubled under to make the hat?

(f) What is the surface area of the finished hat?

(g) What percentage of the surface area of the finished hat is double thickness?

25 Figure 64 shows the windscreen of a car, the shape of which is a trapezium.

AP = 22 cm
AB = 45 cm

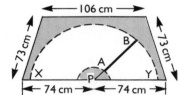

Figure 64

The windscreen's wiper blade rotates backwards and forwards about the point P. The tip of the blade B rotates between the point X and the point Y.

The wiper on the blade is that portion of the blade between A and B. The portion of the blade between P and A does not wipe.

(a) Find the area of the windscreen which is wiped by the wiper blade.

(b) What percentage of the area of the windscreen is wiped by the blade?

26 Figure 65 shows the dimensions of a barn. ATB is an arc of a circle, centre O and radius r metres.
(Note: the centre O is not shown on the diagram.) T is the highest point of one end of the barn and is 1 metre vertically above M, the midpoint of AB.

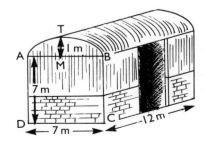

Figure 65

Draw a sketch of the end of the barn (include O on your sketch) and put the lengths of AM, MT and OA on your sketch.

(a) (i) Write down the length of OM in terms of r.
(ii) Form an equation in r.

(b) Solve this equation to show that r = 6.625.

(c) Using this value of r, calculate

(i) the size of angle AOB,
(ii) the length of the arc ATB,
(iii) the area of the roof surface.

LEAG June 1986, Paper 4

27 Tennis balls have a radius of 4 cm.

A box (which has a lid) is just big enough to contain six tennis balls. The arrangement of the balls in the box is shown in figure 66.

(a) Find the volume of the box.

(b) Find the volume of empty space in the box when the six balls are inside it.

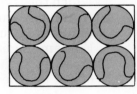

Figure 66

(c) Find the percentage of the volume of the box which is empty when the six balls are in the box.

(d) Calculate the surface area of the box and the lid.

A cylindrical tube (which has a lid) is just big enough to contain three tennis balls.

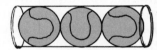

(e) Find the volume of the tube.

(f) Find the percentage of the volume of the tube which is empty when the three balls are inside.

(g) Find the total surface area of two tubes, each of which holds three tennis balls.

(h) Comment on the advantages and disadvantages of tubes and boxes for storing tennis balls.

28 (a) The ice cream in a 'Conetti' is in the shape of a circular cone with base radius 3.6 cm and vertical height 11.4 cm. The curved surface is completely covered with wafer of negligible thickness.

(i) Calculate the volume of the ice cream.

(ii) Calculate the area of the wafer.

(b) The 'Conettis' are packed in a rectangular box with their curved surfaces in contact with the base of the box. A vertical cross section through the axis of one Conetti is shown in figure 67.

Calculate the least possible height of the box.

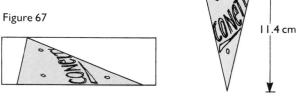

Figure 67

(c) The ice cream is also sold in containers in which the ice cream has the shape of a circular cylinder of height 3.6 cm. The volume of ice cream in each container is the same as in one Conetti.

Calculate the radius of the cylinder.

MEG May 1988, Paper 6

29 A flat metal component is to be made in the shape shown in figure 68. The curves AB and DC are both arcs of circles with centre O. The radius of the arc AB is r, the radius of the arc DC is R. The angle AOB = 60°.

(a)(i) Write down a formula for the area of sector ODC in terms of R.

(ii) Show that the area of the shaded region ABCD is

$$\frac{1}{6}\pi(R^2 - r^2)$$

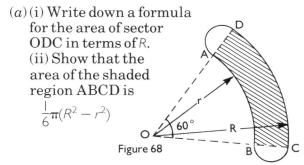

Figure 68

The unshaded ends of the shape are both semicircles.

(b)(i) Write down the length of the diameter BC in terms of R and r.

(ii) Find the total area of the two semicircles in terms of R and r.

(c) Find the area, in mm², to the nearest mm², of metal sheet required to make the component when OD = 39 mm and OA = 27 mm.

(d) The metal sheet is 1.4 mm thick. Find the volume, in mm³, to the nearest mm³, of the component.

LEAG B June 1988, Paper 4

30 (a) Calculate the volume of a sphere of radius 2.5 cm, giving your answer correct to the nearest cubic centimetre.

(b) An apple, which may be considered as a sphere of radius 2.5 cm, has its core removed. This is done by boring a circular hole of radius 0.7 cm through the centre of the apple. Figure 69(a) shows a cross section through the centre of the apple, with the core removed.

(a)

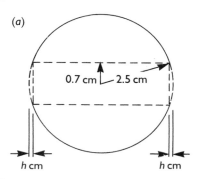

Figure 69

(b)

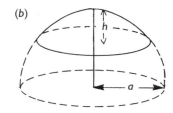

(i) Show that the height, h centimetres, of the spherical cap at each end of the core is 0.1 cm.

(ii) Given that the volume of a spherical cap of height h, removed from a sphere of radius a (shown in figure 69(b)), is given by

$$V_{cap} = \frac{\pi h^2(3a - h)}{3}$$

calculate the volume of core removed. Give your answer correct to the nearest cubic centimetre.

(c) Express the volume of apple removed as a percentage of the volume of the original apple.

MEG November 1987, Paper 6

INFORMATION

Units

Abbreviations

m   metre
km   kilometre
mm   millimetre
cm   centimetre

in   inch
ft   foot
yd   yard

l   litre
cl   centilitre
ml   millilitre

fl oz   fluid ounce

g   gram
kg   kilogram

oz   ounce
lb   pound

kj   kilojoule
kcal   kilocalorie
(also called calorie)

Equivalents of Units

1000 m = 1 km
1000 mm = 1 m
100 cm = 1 m
10 mm = 1 cm

12 in = 1 ft
3 ft = 1 yd

1 l = 1000 cm^3

20 fl oz = 1 pint
8 pints = 1 gallon

1 cubic centimetre
= 1 millilitre

16 oz = 1 lb

1000 g = 1 kg
1000 kg = 1 tonne

1 cubic centimetre
of water weighs
1 gram

Rough metric equivalents

1 m is approximately 1.09 yd
1 in is approximately 2.54 cm

1 kg is approximately 2.2 lb

1 l is approximately 1.75 pints
1 gallon is approximately 5 l

Triangles, quadrilaterals and circles

(a)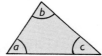

Angle sum of
triangle
$a + b + c = 180°$

Angle sum of
quadrilateral
$a + b + c + d = 360°$

(b)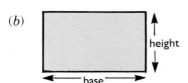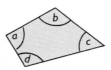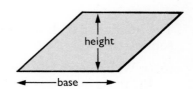

Rectangle:
four right angles;
diagonals are of equal length

Area of rectangle
= base × height

Square:
four right angles;
all sides of equal length;
diagonals of equal length
and meet at right angles;
diagonals bisect angles at
corners (bisect means cut in half)

Parallelogram:
opposite sides parallel
and of equal length

Area of parallelogram
= base × height

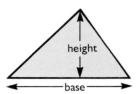
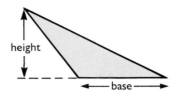

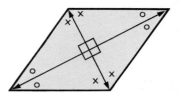

Triangle: Area of triangle = $\dfrac{\text{base} \times \text{height}}{2}$

Rhombus:
all sides of equal length;
diagonals meet at right-angles;
diagonals bisect angles at corners

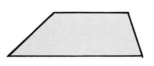
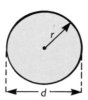

Kite:
two pairs of sides of
equal length

Trapezium:
one pair of sides parallel

Area of trapezium =
height × average of
parallel sides

Circle

Circumference of circle = π × diameter = πd

Area of circle = π × radius × radius = πr^2

(c)

Equilateral triangle:
three sides of equal length;
three angles equal

Isosceles triangle:
two sides of equal length;
two angles equal

Scalene triangle:
three sides of different
lengths

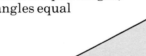

Acute-angled triangle:
all angles acute

Right-angled triangle:
one angle a right angle

Obtuse-angled triangle:
one angle obtuse

(d) **Pythagoras' theorem**

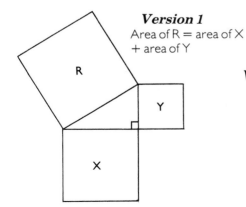

Version 1
Area of R = area of X
+ area of Y

Version 2

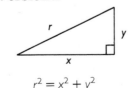

$r^2 = x^2 + y^2$

Version 3

This version is useful when calculating
areas of squares on dotty paper.

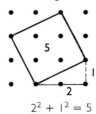

$2^2 + 1^2 = 5$

$2^2 + 2^2 = 8$

To find the area of
an $\binom{a}{b}$ square you
square a and square
b and add the answers.

247

(e) **Trigonometry**

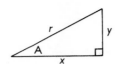

$x = r \cos A$ (Note that x is *next to* A)
$y = r \sin A$ (Note that y is *opposite* A)
$y = x \tan A$ (Note that y is *opposite* A)

$\sin A = \dfrac{y}{r}$

$\cos A = \dfrac{x}{r}$

$\tan A = \dfrac{y}{x}$

Three-dimensional shapes

Cuboid;
all faces rectangles

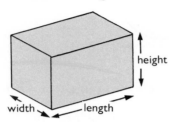

Volume of cuboid =
length × width × height

Prism:
constant cross-section

Volume of prism =
cross section × length

Examples:

Volume of *triangular prism* =
area of triangle × length

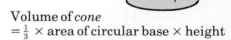

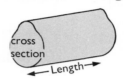

Volume of
cylinder =
area of
circular
end × length

Area of
curved
surface
of cylinder =
circumference of
circular end × length

Pyramid

Volume of pyramid =
$\frac{1}{3}$ × area of base × height

Examples:

Volume of *tetrahedron* =

$\frac{1}{3}$ × area of triangular base × height

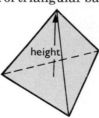

Volume of *cone*
= $\frac{1}{3}$ × area of circular base × height

Area of
curved
surface of
cone = $\pi r l$ where $l^2 = r^2 + h^2$

Sphere

Volume of
sphere = $\frac{4}{3} \pi r^3$

Surface area
of sphere = $4 \pi r^2$

Approximating

After doing a calculation involving measurements you should not normally give the answer more accurately than the *least* accurate measurement that was given.

For example, if you are finding the volume of a box with edges of length 2.4 m, 3.15 m and 4.3 m you multiply the numbers together on a calculator. The answer the calculator gives is 32.508. But two of the measurements given have *only 2 figures* in the number. So the answer you give should have *only 2 figures* in the number. So the answer you give is 33 m. (The 32 was rounded up to 33 because the next figure was 5 or more).

If the number is a large number you should not count the zeros at the end when working out the length of the number. The number 3400 has only 2 figures that count, not 4. The calculator gives the answer to 3400 × 3.27 as 11118, but a sensible approximation is 11000 (leave only 2 non-zero figures).

If the number is very small do not count the number of zeros at the beginning when working out how many figures are in the number. The number 0.00453 has 3 figures that count.

If the last figure is zero and is after the decimal point then you have to count it as one of the figures. 6.30 has 3 figures. The zero has been put on the end to show that the measurement is accurate to the nearest hundredth.

When giving sensible approximations you should also use your common sense. If you are working out how much someone should pay *don't* give the answer as £3.4527. Give it as £3.45. If you are giving the length of a rectangular field don't give it as 112.4 m. It would not have been measured that accurately and, in any case, fields are *not* exact rectangles. This length should probably be given as 110 m.

Sometimes you have to use your common sense and give an answer more accurately than the rule above implies. For example, if the question talks about a ladder 4 m long you should perhaps assume that it is 4.0 m long and give two figures in your answer.

If you are told that the area of a square is 5 cm^2 and are asked to find its length, you do this by finding the square root of 5. You might think it more appropriate to give your answer as 2.24 cm rather than as 2 cm. What you should not do is give your answer as 2.236067977 cm.